Inter-America Series

Edited by Duncan Earle and John Peterson

In the new "Inter-American" epoch to come, our borderland zones may expand well past the confines of geopolitical lines. Social knowledge of these dynamic interfaces offers rich insights into the pressing and complex issues that affect both the borderlands and beyond. The Inter-America Series comprises a wide interdisciplinary range of cutting-edge books that explicitly or implicitly enlist border issues to discuss larger concepts, perspectives, and theories from the "borderland" vantage and will be appropriate for the classroom, the library, and the wider reading public.

University of Texas Press AUSTIN

Crossing Borders

SOCIAL

CATEGORIES,

METAPHORS,

AND NARRATIVE

IDENTITIES

ON THE

U.S.–MEXICO

FRONTIER

REINFORCING BORDERS

PABLO VILA

First edition, 2000

Requests for permission to reproduce material from this work should be
sent to Permissions, University of Texas Press, Box 7819, Austin, TX
78713-7819.

⊗ The paper used in this book meets the minimum requirements of
ANSI/NISO Z39.48-1992 (R1997) (Permanence of Paper).

Library of Congress Cataloging-in-Publication Data

Vila, Pablo, date
    Crossing borders, reinforcing borders : social categories, metaphors,
and narrative identities on the U.S.-Mexico frontier / Pablo Vila. — 1st ed.
        p. cm. — (Inter-America series)
    Includes bibliographical references and index.
    ISBN 0-292-78739-1 (hardcover : alk. paper) —
    ISBN 0-292-78740-5 (pbk. : alk. paper)
    1. Ciudad Juárez (Mexico) — Social conditions.   2. El Paso
(Texas) — Social conditions.   3. Mexican-American Border Region —
Social conditions.   4. Group identity — Mexico — Ciudad Juárez.
5. Group identity — Texas — El Paso.   6. Group identity — Mexican-
American Border Region.   I. Title.   II. Series.
HN120.C48.V54   2000
306'.0972'16 — dc21
                                                              99-046270

CONTENTS

PHOTOGRAPHS

This volume is the first book-length product of research conducted over the course of more than six years in the El Paso–Ciudad Juárez area beginning in the early 1990s. Because it is difficult to summarize in only one publication the findings of more than two hundred group interviews, I decided to present the material in two different volumes that position the analysis in distinct but closely tied discursive domains. Therefore, this book has to be read taking into account that I must begin with the discussion of topics brought to incisive attention by the dynamics of the border itself: the discourses of national identity and with it, region, ethnicity, and social constructions of race. By these means I explore how people express what, in absence of a better concept, we can address as "pure state" notions of themselves and others without further qualification in terms of other possible subject positions people also occupy on the border, such as class, gender, and religious affiliation, among others. For these, a second volume is forthcoming.

This second book (provisionally entitled *Border Identities: Narratives of Class, Gender, and Religion on the U.S.–Mexico Border*), will address the complex overlap of the different regional, national, and ethnic systems of classification, metaphors, and narratives people use to identify themselves and "others" (the object of analysis of the present volume), with some subject positions that have appeared frequently in my fieldwork in the region. These include class, gender, and religion—topics with tremendous relevance to the issues dealt with first in this volume regarding national identity and its complex ramifications. As Avtar Brah points out regarding the specific case of women:

> Within . . . structures of social relations we do not exist simply as women but as differentiated categories such as *working-class* women, *peasant* women, *migrant* women. Each description references a specificity of social condition. And real lives are forged out of a complex articulation of these dimensions . . . in different womanhoods the noun is only meaningful—indeed only exists—with reference to a fusion of adjectives which symbolize particular historical trajectories, material circumstances and cultural experiences. (Brah 1992, p. 131)

This situation also obtains in the case of the border identities I discuss in this book, starting with the interplay of national, regional, and ethnic/racial identities. In this sense the real lives of Juarenses and El Pasoans are forged out of the complex articulation of racial, ethnic, regional, national, religious, gender, age, and class identity categories (among others). Consequently, while the present volume takes the reader to the natural starting point of border identity research, the second volume will more fully elaborate the ties these narratively constructed identities have with religion, gender, and class than I can do here. The complexity of border identity construction is reflected in the point made by Wilson and Donnan (1998, p. 13):

> Because of their liminal and frequently contested nature, borders tend to be characterised by identities which are shifting and multiple, in ways which are framed by the specific state configurations which encompass them and within which people must attribute meaning to their experience of border life . . . this is true not only of national identity, but also of other identities such as ethnicity, class, gender and sexuality, identities often constructed at borders in ways which are different from, and shed light on, how these identities are constructed elsewhere in the state.

I totally agree with these authors, and the testimony of one of my Mexican immigrant interviewees can shed some light to the complexities Wilson and Donnan refer to:

Nora: It's just that over there [in Mexico] they teach women to be submissive. From the beginning they teach us that the man can do whatever . . . that he is more liberal. If he *anda* [strays], has other relationships, then we as women must accept it. And that is not the case here [the United States]. Here they start telling you that no, that the woman has the same value as a man, that if she sees an injustice she has the right to react, even if she loves her husband. If you see that the marriage isn't going anywhere, your children's happiness and your own come first. That is what I like about living here. I like that.
Pablo: In Mexico you would probably be more submissive?
Nora: Yes, over there you have to put up with it, *aguanta, aguanta, y aguanta* [over and over again]. You're stuck carrying the load. What is the saying? "It's your cross to bear." So bear your cross! But, come on, no!
Pablo: Let them crucify someone else! [laughs]

As we can see, Nora regrets that Mexican culture supposedly teaches submissiveness to females, allowing only males to be "liberals." Nora is equating "liberalism" with the unrestricted exercise of heterosexual sexuality, something that males are allowed in Mexico, but not females. In the United States, according to Nora, females can be as liberated as males. They can also be as "modern" as their male counterparts, where modernity is equated with sexual liberation, as we saw above, but also with the equal value of males and females. According to Nora, in the United States each person has his/her own value, and no one has to put aside his/her happiness in order to maintain a marriage that is not fulfilling. And the metaphor of the cross is not introduced by chance; what this interviewee is rejecting is part of the Catholic tradition (which on the border is very much intertwined with the idea of Mexicanness) that, Nora believes, oppresses women.

In this complex overlapping of subject positions that is the process of identity construction on the border, what Nora is expressing is how profoundly her life in the United States has changed her narrative identity, how profound is her process of, at least in religious and gender terms, becoming Mexican American. First, she has changed her gender identity; the gendered "other" is not only the American or Americanized male (and the more macho Mexican type male), but also the submissive Mexican female (herself in the past). Second, she has changed her religious identity; at least she does not accept any longer what traditional Catholicism predicates about woman's position in society. We encounter here a very interesting overlapping between gender, religion, and nationality (with "Mexican" understood as a nationality, not as an ethnicity, in Nora's use), elements of identity that are processed in a comparison between her own past, present, and possible future—that is, processed as a narrative.

It is precisely the complexity of the process of identity construction of most of my interviewees on both sides of the border that required (to be fully respectful to their multifarious accounts of who they believe they are) the organization of the entire research project in two separate volumes. In this way I can analyze in depth in the present volume how very different "others" are constructed when region and nationality are used, as in Juárez (the Southern Mexican immigrants, the Northerners, the Juarenses, the Fronterizos, the Chilangos, the Mexican immigrants, the Mexican Americans, the Pochos, the Chicanos, the Americans, the Anglos, etc.), as opposed to when region, nationality, ethnicity, and race are used, as in El Paso (the Juarenses, the Juareños, the Mexicans, the Northern Mexicans, the Mexican immigrants, the Mexican Americans, the Chicanos, the Americans, the Anglos, the African Americans, the Jews, the Asian Americans, the Tiguas, and the like). In the construction of such "others," several narrative plots are crucial. On the

Mexican side of the border, we find narratives like "All Juárez's social problems are due to the immigration of people from Southern Mexico," "Americans are slaves of their consumer attitude," "Mexican immigrants living in the United States constantly brag about their economic success," "Mexican Americans many times want to humiliate Mexican nationals," and so on. On the American side, we find narratives like "All poverty is Mexican," "Mexican immigrants are behind most of El Paso's social problems," "Chicanos do not want to grow," "The real Mexicans are those of the past," "The problems are not the Mexicans but Mexico," "The real problematic people in El Paso are the Mexican Americans who live on welfare, not the Mexican immigrants who cannot receive welfare," and so on. Such identity construction is the starting place for unraveling my field research.

I leave to the second volume a more robust investigation of the complex intertwining of narratives about region, nation, ethnicity, and race with those about religion, gender, and class discourses. In this way, narratives such as "Juarenses are less Catholic than Southern Mexicans" and "Mexican Americans are less Catholic than Mexican nationals" function on the border as narrative plots around which many border inhabitants construct their "coherent" regional, national, ethnic, and race identities. At the same time, very developed narratives about "the libertine Fronterizo" or "the bossy American woman" also serve many of my interviewees to buttress their social identities as border actors. Likewise I must wait until the second book to show how the general absence of class discourses in the region is linked to a metaphorical displacement through which to go up in the social scale is equated by many of my interviewees with moving from one country (Mexico) to the other (the United States). In such metaphorical displacement, one of the most important narratives I discuss in this book, "All poverty is Mexican," occupies a very prominent position.

This book has been made possible by the help of numerous people. First of all I want to thank the interviewees who participated in the group discussions with the photographs. Without their willingness to share with me their daily joys and sorrows, as well as their narratives about themselves, none of this endeavor would have been possible. I would also like to thank the agencies that supported, in different stages, my research: the Social Science Research Council, the Population Research Center of the University of Texas at Austin, the Institute of Latin American Studies of the University of Texas at Austin, the Center for Inter American and Border Studies of the University of Texas at El Paso, the University Research Institute and the Liberal Arts Faculty Development Grant of the University of Texas at El Paso, the sociology and anthropology departments of the University of Texas at El Paso, the Division of Social and Policy Sciences at the University of Texas–San Antonio, the Seminario de Estudios de la Cultura in Mexico City, and especially, El Colegio de la Frontera Norte.

Several persons have played a particularly important role in the process of writing this book. Very special thanks go to Angela Escajeda and Pablo Luna for their outstanding assistance during the initial fieldwork and after that for their critical reading of my drafts; to Yvonne Montejano, Theresa Hughes, Berta Hall, Zulma Méndez, Araceli Arceo, Joel González, and Sylvia Richards for their help in the process of reinterviewing people; and to Sherry Jewel for her incredible help with the translation of most of the testimonies from Spanish to English. Also important were other students that kindly helped me with other translations: Bibiano Maldonado, Eduardo Acosta, Karina Gerdau-Radonic, Damariz Macías, Adrianna Sáenz, Ivan Cervantes, and Mark Alvarado.

Howard Campbell deserves a very special place in my acknowledgments: Where do you find a fine anthropologist, with more than twenty years of experience working in Mexico, the author of two highly acclaimed books about Mexican culture, who is willing to read the thousands of different drafts you give him and return them with their English polished, plenty of very thoughtful criticisms . . . two days later!? Thank you very much, Manny! My advisors in Austin (Bryan Roberts, Henry Selby, and Harley Browning) also deserve a

ACKNOWLEDGMENTS

very special acknowledgment, because they also were kind enough to go through the different versions of this book and always provided very good advice. I cannot thank them enough for their time, energy, care, kindness . . . and the list goes on. Duncan Earle and an anonymous reviewer advanced very important points that, I am sure, improved very much the final product of my research. And Duncan was particularly encouraging and helpful in the final process of editing the volume, when I thought it couldn't be done.

The book was also improved by my participation in a two-year long seminar about the border, organized by Victor Zúñiga, whose participants were Norma Alarcón, Jorge Arditti, Victoria Novelo, Laura Velazco, Olivia Ruiz, and Luis García. To all of you, thank you so much for your comments and criticisms.

Other people have read and criticized different chapters of this book: John Peterson, Cheryl Howard, Debbie Nathan, Melissa Wright, Sarah Hill, Leslie Salzinger, José Manuel Valenzuela, Néstor García Canclini, Elea Aguirre, Patricia Fernández de Castro, David Mariscal, Eduardo Archetti, Elizabeth Mahan, Jan Fairley, Jorge González, Samuel Schmidt, Susan Kern, Antonio Alfau, Eduardo Barrera, Elizabeth Jelín, Kathy Staudt, and Dennis Bixler-Márquez. All of them made insightful comments that I really appreciate.

Theresa May and Mandy Woods, at the University of Texas Press, were very helpful in all the process that led to the finishing of this book. And Sue Carter, the editor of the manuscript, performed miracles with my particular version of the English language.

I am a social scientist, but I also have several other identities that overlap with my professional one. I want to thank those people who, due to their relationship with me in my other subject positions, also made this book possible. First of all, I have to mention my children, Juanchi and Paloma, who filled me with joy and truly understood the importance of their father's research. Second, my parents, Becky and Daniel, from whom I learned the importance of critical thinking. Then, my friends Oscar Riccardi, Nora Agostini, Enrique Figueroa, Mónica Maselli, Fernando Nachón, Juan Silva, Tito Palermo, and my aunt Fanny Szmidt for many phone sessions connecting El Paso with Argentina that kept me alive. My aunt, Zulema Vila, was a very important actor in this drama, supporting me many times, helping me with the French translations of several books and articles. Alexandra and Tony Alfau are my family when I am in Austin. That says enough about their importance in my life. The kindness, encouragement, and help of Abigaíl García were also invaluable in finishing this book.

CROSSING BORDERS, REINFORCING BORDERS

On the eve of the enactment of the North American Free Trade Agreement (NAFTA)—which was supposed to improve relations between the United States and Mexico—the U.S. Border Patrol in El Paso implemented a new strategy to deter the influx of undocumented immigrants. The tactic, called "Operation Blockade,"[1] strung agents at close intervals, in highly visible positions directly along the international boundary. Conceived of by Silvestre Reyes, a Mexican American who grew up in Canutillo, twenty miles from El Paso, the operation won nearly unanimous support from both Anglo and Mexican American El Pasoans. Various polls indicated an impressive 80 to 90 percent rate of community support for the blockade (78 percent among the Hispanic population of the city).[2]

Some people were surprised that the border patrol garnered so much support from Mexican American El Pasoans, assuming that Mexican Americans, many of whom are also immigrants, would support Mexican immigration out of ethnic loyalty.[3] We have to remember, though, that the relationship between El Paso and Juárez has long been portrayed as an example of peaceful border coexistence. This portrayal seems accurate when the El Paso–Juárez border is compared to the Tijuana–San Diego border, where the border patrol is given wide support by a well-organized civilian force that wants, at any price, to stop any further illegal northbound immigration. However, as I will try to show throughout the book, below the facade of a smooth relationship, there is an ongoing tension that surfaces here and there, involving many Anglos, Mexican Americans, African Americans, and Mexican nationals.

Events in recent years shed some light on the phenomenon. At first there was the euphoria triggered by the local border patrol's Operation Blockade (analyzed in depth in Chapter 5). That milestone was quickly followed by a heated discussion in the pages of the *El Paso Times* among interested observers about whether a Mexican flag had been placed correctly on a mural (below, above, to the right or the left of the American flag). A couple of months later, a mariachi group greeted a football team at the airport, and many people complained, "We do not live in Mexico!" And then a city representative got some flak (or approval, depending on whom you talk to) because he asked a citizen to speak English at a city council meeting instead of Spanish. Thus, we are confronted from time to time with the fact that Juárez and El Paso are not really "sister cities"—or at least not sisters of a family without internal conflict.

The point I want to stress here is that not only was Operation Blockade very popular in El Paso, but it also provoked open displays of resentment between many Mexican Americans and Mexican nationals. In fact, it was not uncommon to hear many El Pasoans denounce the latter as the cause of El Paso's most telling social problems: crime, drugs, unemployment, welfare scams, and the like.

The outstanding support received by Operation Blockade does not seem to be an isolated case: a poll conducted by the *El Paso Times* showed that 62 percent of El Pasoans would support a law similar to California's Proposition 187 (*El Paso Times*, April 29, 1995). Moreover, when every other city in the United States with a significant Mexican population was protesting against the beatings of two undocumented immigrants in Riverside in April 1996, El Paso not only did not have any major rally, but that same week elected the mastermind of Operation Blockade, Silvestre Reyes, as the Democratic candidate for Congress. Reyes beat his opponent José Luis Sánchez by more than 15 percent in the first round, and beat him again in the second, even though Sánchez was the candidate of the Democratic establishment. Reyes based his campaign on his status as the city's "hero," because, supposedly, he was the one who "finally" stopped illegal immigration from Mexico.

In this book I will attempt to unveil the complicated process of identity construction that underlies how many Mexicans, Mexican Americans, African Americans, and Anglos perceive each other in the Ciudad Juárez–El Paso area. I will present and discuss throughout the book some discursive devices people use to make sense of the "other" and, in the same process, of themselves. I will concentrate on how border residents use social categories, metaphors, and narratives in such construction.

The analysis is based on an extensive series of small group interviews distributed across class, gender, age, nationality, ethnicity, and time of migration. The fieldwork extended from September 1991 to June 1997, and so far I have conducted 254 group meetings, interviewing 932 individuals on both sides of the border. Because I wanted to map differences in the process of identity construction, I interviewed both men and women of different ages, nationality, class backgrounds, ethnicity, and migration experiences. I started interviewing groups using the "classic" sociological categories described above, trying to get at least three or four groups in each country where each of those categories was represented. When the analysis of the material showed that those categories were not adequate for illuminating the process of identity construction, I added new categories to the research project and expanded the sample in that direction. This was what happened, for instance, with religion, a category not present at the beginning of the project that "asked" not only to be included, but also to have a prominent place in the investigation.[4]

The analyzed material flowed from discussions about various sets of photographs which were taken in the border area and which portray various everyday activities in Juárez and El Paso (public interactions, family life, religion, leisure, work, etc.). The interviews were structured as follows: people were first asked to look at the package of photographs to be discussed, then to select those photographs they wanted to talk about with the group. After the entire group had looked at the photos and chosen the shots they felt deserved comment, the first participant was asked to tell the group why he/she decided to select a particular photograph. When the interviewee had finished speaking, the others were asked if they had additional comments and if they agreed or disagreed with their companion. Usually, a discussion followed in which almost all participants expressed opinions about the photo or the issue it addressed. In those discussions people presented verbalized images (categorical ones) triggered by the photographs shown during the interviews. In addition, they told us stories to support the identity claims they were expressing in their categorical ascriptions. Following a well-established tradition in anthropology and sociology, I have changed all the names and altered many personal circumstances to protect the privacy of my interviewees.

Like Mishler (1986), I feel that whatever else the stories my interviewees told me were about, they were also a form of self-presentation in which my interviewees were claiming a particular kind of self-identity. At the same time, I also think that what is said in such stories functions to express, confirm, and validate that particular claimed identity (Mishler 1986, p. 243). The interviews were taped and then transcribed to analyze their content. I think that much of the usefulness of photo-interviewing stems from the fact that people believe photography depicts reality.[5] In commonsense discourse, photography is seen as the model of veracity and objectivity: people "read" a photograph, believing they are "objectively" describing reality (Bourdieu 1990b), while in fact they are projecting their particular understanding of reality onto the scene described. They do this because photography is the locus of two different biases that operate simultaneously. On the one hand, the photographic image is caught in the hegemonic way we have seen reality since the fifteenth century: perspective. On the other hand, individuals "read" that reality through their own prisms, which are totally attached to their understanding of the world that surrounds each of them — to their narrative identities and categorical systems. Because we are almost totally blind to the first bias and automatically equate photography with reality, the second bias also passes unperceived, allowing us to see a particular photograph as *the* unbiased perception of the referent portrayed by the shot. In this sense, the "quantum of truth" of a particular photograph (Berger 1980) depends heavily on the general categories that are already in the spectator's mind. This is photo-interviewing's *noeme* (Barthes 1991): by definition, photography requires the interviewee to project his/her narrative identity and categorical systems onto the scene depicted in order to make sense of it within his/her horizon of understanding. If, as I maintained above, the perception of photographs is in some way linked to the narrative plots that guide our general perception of reality, it is no coincidence that my interviewees perceived the same photographs differently, given that those photos "adjusted" to their plots in different ways. As Jerome Bruner comments: ". . . eventually the culturally shaped cognitive and linguistic processes that guide the self-telling of life narratives achieve the power to structure perceptual experience" (1987, p. 15). Therefore, if the ways of telling and the ways of conceptualizing that go with them become so habitual that they finally become recipes for structuring experience itself (Bruner 1987, p. 31), I think that analyzing the different ways my interviewees perceived the same photographs is a good route toward disentangling the different plots that guided their narrative identities.

Throughout the book I will propose that from the point of view of the process of identity construction, it is not an easy thing to live on the U.S.–Mexico border. On the Mexican side of the border this is so because the American influence on Juárez' inhabitants is viewed negatively by many Mexicans from the interior, who claim Juarenses have become *agringados* [Americanized]. On the American side of the border, although living near Mexico allows many Mexican immigrants and Mexican Americans to be in touch with their heritage, the presence of Mexico around the corner is also a constant reminder of the poverty and corruption many people identify with that country. In this book I want to show how, under certain circumstances, the close proximity of Mexico — the origin of Mexican American identity — instead of being a positive foundation upon which to construct a valued social identity, can be a liability to many Mexican Americans, who construct their identities by portraying not only Anglos as the "others," but also Mexican nationals (Vila 1997b).

Thus far, I have been talking about Mexican nationals, Mexican Americans, Chicanos, African Americans, and Anglos. But I wish to put all these labels "under erasure" (to use Derrida's term) because I believe that they conceal broad differentiations in the identity construction process, differentiations that should make us question the usefulness of these terms if we aim to understand attitudes and behaviors on the border.

In questioning the labels, I hope to avoid a common trap in sociology and anthropology: to ascribe directly a particular set of interests to individuals insofar as they are seen as members of *social categories*, where "making sense of social action . . . becomes an exercise in identifying social categories, deriving putative interests from them, and then doing the empirical work of looking at variations on those interests" (Somers 1992, p. 607). Instead, I argue that identity construction is a response to queries that are perceived to have situational expectations or requirements. Consequently, in this book I will use those social categories only as a narrative device, to save the reader from the difficult task of reading a ten-word sentence to identify what particular kind of, for example, Mexican American I am talking about. As Rosenblum and Travis (1996, p. 3) point out: "We have sometimes had to rely on essentialist terms we ourselves find problematic. The irony of simultaneously questioning the idea of race, but still talking about 'blacks,' 'whites,' and 'Asians;' or of rejecting a dualistic approach to sexual identity, while still using the terms 'gay' and 'straight' has not escaped us."

At the same time a particular disclaimer has to be made about the category "Anglo" as it is used here. In Ciudad Juárez and El Paso (and many other parts of the Southwest), Anglo is a "residual" category. For many people anyone who is not from Mexican, African, or Asian origin is an "Anglo" or an "American." This usage, of course, homogenizes a population of very heterogeneous origin, as is demonstrated, for instance, by the existence of an important Jewish community in El Paso. Hence, many of the "Anglo" interviewees I will present throughout the book are Irish Americans, German Americans, Jewish, and the like. However, not only the "others" referred to them as "Anglos," but most of the time they used that category themselves during the interview process. Therefore, for narrative reasons and also to be faithful to the common sense of the region, I will refer to this very heterogeneous people as "Anglos," and in the quotations that follow, they (regardless of their different ethnic origin) will be referred as "Anglos." A more detailed analysis of how the Jewish Americans, Irish Americans, German Americans, and the like construct themselves and the "others" will be the aim of a future research project.

My approach differs from that of those Mexican scholars who have claimed that the main process of identity construction on the Mexican side of the border is the constitution of the Anglos as the "others" (Bustamante 1983; Lozano 1990). I understand the border as a multiple mirror situation where Juarenses construct not only Anglos as the "others," but in many circumstances they portray Southern Mexicans, Mexican Americans, Asian Americans, and African Americans as "others" as well.[6]

This research also differs in many ways from that of those authors who have described the U.S.–Mexico border using the metaphor of "border crossing," "hybrids," and the like (R. Rosaldo 1989; Anzaldúa 1987; García Canclini 1990). When I decided to do my dissertation on the construction of identity on the U.S.–Mexico border, I was highly influenced by the "border studies" approach. As a matter of fact I was a close witness and a minor participant in its recent developments, because in 1989 I took a seminar at the University of Texas at Austin with Néstor García Canclini, and the seminar was structured around discussion of the manuscript that later became his very influential book, *Culturas híbridas* (García Canclini 1990). In that seminar I also read Gloria Anzaldúa (1987) and Renato Rosaldo's (1989) pathbreaking books, which not only provided me with important insights about border issues, but also changed completely the way I understood the relationship between culture and identity.

For that reason, I arrived in El Paso in 1991 with the "mission" of validating with an ethnographic work the ideas of García Canclini, Anzaldúa, and Rosaldo (hybridity, border crossing, third country, and the like), ideas that mostly were developed within a literary criticism framework, not an ethnographic one. Yet, as soon as I launched my fieldwork I discovered that these ideas were only partially addressing the much more complex process of identity construction in the area. First, because those authors tend to homogenize the border, as if there were only one border identity, border culture, or process of hybridization. On the contrary, I think that on the U.S.–Mexico frontier we have several borders, each of them the possible anchor of a particular process of identity construction. In this sense, I could easily identify at least four different border environments: Tijuana–San Diego–Los Angeles, the Sonora–Arizona border (extensively analyzed by Vélez-Ibáñez 1996),

Juárez–El Paso, and the Lower Rio Grande Valley–Tamaulipas border. Each is the locus of very different processes of internal and international migration, ethnic composition, and political identities on both sides of the border. Those differences are related in complex ways to different processes of identity construction; therefore I will write about Ciudad Juárez–El Paso, and not about the U.S.–Mexico border "in general."[7]

In fact, Renato Rosaldo (1994, p. 215), in a recent article, seems to be departing from his previous writings when he points out:

> In considering the dynamics of race from both dominant and subordinate positions I have found enlightening a 1990 work called *Migrant Souls* by the late Chicano novelist Arturo Islas, who died of AIDS on February 15, 1991. Set in Del Sapo, Texas (Del Sapo, "from the toad," is a playful anagram of El Paso), the novel breaks a taboo and addresses matters we, as Chicanos, all know but don't talk about. It speaks of the dynamics of racial differentiation within the Chicano community as well as the categorical divide separating Chicanos and Anglos . . . in the absence of other data, the novel can serve as a source of evidence for thinking conceptually about how race works among certain Chicanos.

One of the aims of this book is precisely to talk about matters "Chicanos . . . know but don't talk about," in the same location where the novel takes place, El Paso, providing the "other data" (ethnographic material) Rosaldo claims is missing.

Second, I believe that the process of globalization and hybridization is here to stay (Vila 1997b). Money, people, and culture constantly move, allowing people to anchor their identities in the new entities this process creates. Those new identities can range widely. Mixtecos can call themselves a binational indigenous community (and bury their dead *also* in California); people can be named after an old region whose name acquires a new meaning (Fronterizos is a good example here); "European" takes on a new meaning within the emerging European bloc (Nafteño may be an identity of the future). However, many people feel threatened by the idea of abandoning the kinds of national, racial, and ethnic names (and the culture those names involve) that have identified them for generations: Americans, Mexicans, and the like. Accordingly, some Mexicans are worried because McDonald's is displacing some *taquerías* (Mexican fast-food restaurants) in Juárez, and Americans are worried because salsa has displaced ketchup in some states — and on some of its missions, the shuttle crew brought tortillas rather than bread (because tortillas do not produce crumbs, a very important consideration in outer space). The problem is that both processes are occurring simultaneously, and different actors in the same region, for different reasons, react differently.

This way of approaching the issue of identity construction explains, for example, why it is no accident that a Fronterizo (i.e., border dweller) identity is used extensively on the Mexican side of the border, but not many people on the American side use that label to identify themselves. Such an identity flourishes in Juárez for two reasons. First, some Juarenses use their proximity to the United States to "upgrade" their Mexican social identity, claiming that it is advantageous to live near a First World country with easy access to its job opportunities, lifestyle, and consumer goods. This discourse is more common among middle-class Juarenses. Not by chance, they are the ones who make the most ostentatious use of the label "Fronterizos," and of the "sister cities" trope that I will discuss below. Middle-class Juarenses do this because they are more able than their lower class counterparts to claim an "American" lifestyle, in a milieu where being middle class is frequently equated with being Americanized.

Second, Juarenses are more likely to identify themselves as Fronterizos because they make extensive use of a regional system of classification to "explain" attitudes and behaviors. This way of understanding action allows them to anchor an identity label to a particular region such as the border. The combination of factors behind the Fronterizo label is present on the northern Mexican border, but not on the southern one. Ergo, it is rare to hear someone calling her-/himself Fronterizo on the Mexico–Guatemala border (Vila 1997b).

Things are different on the U.S. side of the border. There, few people (Mexican Americans included) perceive any "upgrading" of identity in claiming proximity to a Third World country. Moreover, Americans tend to use an ethnic classification system rather than a regional one; this distinguishes them from Mexicans, who tend to use region as a way to anchor identity. Not coincidentally, then, it is very rare to hear an El Pasoan call her-/himself a Fronteriza/o or its virtually unheard-of English equivalent, a "borderite." Of course, many Mexican Americans call themselves "Mexicans," but the polysemous (and contradictory) use of this reference is so extended that it is precisely one of the issues examined in this book. Therefore, I understand Proposition 187, Operation Blockade, the English Only movement, and the like as desperate attempts to separate "us" from "them," when "they" live among "us" (or very close to us) due to the globalization process. And not by chance, at least in El Paso, many Mexican Americans seem as threatened as Anglos by that process (Vila 1997b).

For that reason I suggest that authors who use "crossing borders" metaphors alone do not portray the entire picture. As Wilson and Donnan (1998, p. 6) comment: "Only the idea of the border as an image for cultural juxtaposition has entered wider anthropological discourse." I think that we need to complement these metaphors with another one referring to "reinforcing borders," or something similar, because many people do not want to cross those borders, or to live "on borders and in margins, keeping intact one's shifting and multiple identity and integrity" (Anzaldúa 1987, p. i). On the contrary, many people want to reinforce borders. Looking for a multiple reading of the border situation, I found the different narratives I discuss in this book. Some of them employ the "hybrid" model proposed by Anzaldúa (a model more attuned to Derrida's logic of the supplement, of *differance*, rather than of identity; a logic of both/and), but other identity narratives reinforce the bold limits—the strict categorical distinctions (the "islands of meaning" [Zerubavel 1991]), the Western logic of identity, the logic of either/or—that are the antipodes of a "hybrid" or "mestiza" way of thinking. Consequently, I understand Anzaldúa's beautiful text as representing the utopia we have to appreciate and struggle for on the border, a utopia that because identity is a strange sedimentation of past, present, and future is already present in some border actors (Vila 1997b).

The book is structured as follows. Chapters 1 to 4 discuss important organizers of common sense in the region—that is, those discourses of region, race, ethnicity, and nation that "order" the very complicated border reality. The border offers a unique opportunity to look at the complex process of identity construction and its constant use of arbitrary classification systems to make sense of people's social identities. In Chapters 1 and 2 I discuss the process of identity construction on the Mexican side of the border, where discourses of region and nation predominate and those of race and ethnicity are either secondary or complexly intertwined with the former. I start, in Chapter 1, by addressing the highly developed regional system of classification that many Juarenses use to make sense of their own attitudes and behaviors and those of the "others." In that system, categories like Fronterizos, Juarenses, and Norteños are used to make sense of "us," those who live in Juárez, and categories like Sureños and Chilangos are used to make sense of "them," those who live elsewhere in Mexico. As is the case in many systems of classification, the regional one used in Juárez implies a hierarchical ordering of its different categories. That is why the remainder of the chapter is used to examine the highly stigmatized way in which many Juarenses portray "those who come from the South," where in the account of many interviewees who are native of Juárez, all Juárez' social problems seem to be caused by the despised Sureños. In this regional system of classification, the inhabitants of Mexico City, the Chilangos, occupy center stage, and many of my interviewees are not very kind in their portrayal.

In Chapter 2 I move from regional to national commonsense discourses and address the way in which many Juarenses construct the "Americans" as the "others." Hence if in the first chapter I showed how some Fronterizos construct their identities *in relation to other Mexicans* using the United States as a point of reference, in this chapter I show how they define their profile *in relation to the Americans*, drawing heavily on their Mexicanness. In the process of marking their differences from the Americans, many Juarenses point to some features they believe belong to the "others," among the most important being the rampant consumerism that seems to characterize American culture.

Interestingly enough, if all those living on the other side of the border are points of reference in the construction of some Fronterizo and Juarense identities, then Anglos are not the only important mirror to look at in constructing one's identity. In this chapter I show how, for some interviewees, Anglos are less important than other border actors in the Ciudad Juárez–El Paso area, because nearly 70 percent of El Paso's inhabitants are of Mexican origin. Accordingly, in the particular case of Juárez, the Mexican Americans living in El Paso are a constant point of reference in the construction of identity. As in the case of Anglos, for many of my interviewees, the construction of a Juarense identity also requires the simultaneous establishment of closeness and distance in relation to the Mexican Americans. For that reason in Chapter 2 I also analyze the metaphor of the "sister cities" (heavily used in Juárez) to show how the idea of closeness is constructed. At the same time I show how differences are forged to characterize the Mexican American as the "other" in my analysis of how the term *"pocho"* is used.

In Chapters 3 and 4 I cross the border and take a look at some processes of ethnic, racial, and national identity construction in El Paso. A peculiar characteristic of the U.S.–Mexico border is that people changing countries are not only crossing from one country to another, they are also moving from one national system of classification to another — both systems in which they have a place.

Therefore, in Chapter 3 I show how in El Paso, as in other areas of the country, the discourse of race and ethnicity is pervasive. Nevertheless, here it combines with a discourse of nationality in a volatile mixture that, for many people, marks almost anything that is stigmatized as Mexican. A lot of people on the American side of the border constitute their identities against this backdrop. Needless to say, in this context, the constitution of a valued identity is relatively straightforward for middle-class Anglos and relatively difficult for many people of Mexican descent, regardless of class. Thus, the bulk of the chapter describes the different ways in which those interviewees attuned to the hegemonic discourse of the region construct the "Mexican" as the stigmatized "other." The first part of the chapter explores what I call the "all poverty and social problems are Mexican" thematic plot, and how many of my Anglo, African American, and Mexican American interviewees tend to blur the difference between Mexican ethnics and Mexican nationals to construct a stigmatized "Mexican" other.

I also explore in Chapter 3 other possibilities used by many interviewees in the construction of the "Mexican" other, for instance, the attempt made by some people to build the "Chicanos" as those Mexicans to whom the "all poverty is Mexican" should apply; or the effort made by some of those who call themselves Chicanos to redefine the "all poverty is Mexican" thematic plot, moving its cause from laziness to discrimination; or the construction of the Mexican national as the stigmatized other by many Mexican Americans in an attempt to open a gap inside the Mexican ethnic category, addressing the differences that supposedly separate Mexican Americans from Mexican nationals. In the construction of the Mexican nationals as the "others," tropes of difference are essential; that is why I also analyze the "Third World country versus First World country" trope in this chapter.

In Chapter 4 I show how some poor people of Mexican descent relate to the "all poverty is Mexican" narrative plot. I first discuss the problematic situation of some Mexican immigrants in El Paso. If they are poor they have by necessity to follow a quite distinct path in the constitution of a valued social identity, because they confront an ethnic and racial classification system that denigrates them without the escape hatch of economic success used by many middle-class Mexican Americans to detach themselves from immigrants (the topic of Chapter 3). At the same time, if these interviewees currently maintain family ties with Mexico, they have to make sense of contemporary Mexican poverty without portraying Mexican nationals as the "others."

Some of the most interesting narratives I have found among many Mexican immigrants in El Paso claim that the Mexicans of the "all poverty is Mexican" thematic plot are the Mexican Americans who live off welfare. Other immigrant interviewees claim that the Mexican Americans who discriminate against Mexican immigrants are the real "others." At the same time, because many of these immigrants still use Mexican and/or Fronterizo categories, metaphors, and narratives to construct the "other," mixing frames of reference (sometimes in a single portrayal of the "other") to make sense of their identities, it is not a coincidence that some of the narratives I have found in Juárez repeat themselves on the American side of the border. Among the most prominent of them is the construction of the "American" as the other. Finally, in this chapter I also show how many middle-class Mexican immigrants take advantage of the "all poverty is Mexican" thematic plot to construct a valued identity of immigrants with dignity (those who have "made it") living in the United States.[8]

In Chapter 5 I connect my own research, which can be broadly defined as discursive analysis, with some events experienced by Juarenses and Paseños that show the degree to which the discourses I discovered in my fieldwork are ingrained in attitudes and behaviors. The opportunity to make that connection came when the border patrol launched Operation Blockade in September 1993. The staggering amount of mutual resentment this operation unleashed between many Juarenses and El Pasoans was a surprise not only for local people, but also for border scholars in general. What happened? I think that the nationwide anti-immigrant wave was responsible for part of the support the operation received. But I attribute a great part of the overwhelming support obtained by the border patrol to the fact that the agency was doing physically what many El Pasoans (both Anglo and Mexican Americans) had been doing symbolically before — separating themselves from Mexican nationals in order to construct a narrative identity as people living *in* the United States.

In this chapter I follow, step by step, the different (and usually positive) reactions Operation Blockade unleashed in El Paso, as well as the more ambiguous reactions in Juárez. Many El Pasoans reacted with what was described by some journalists as "euphoria" because the blockade would supposedly solve all the social problems of the city — because behind those problems, of course, many people saw the shadow of the "illegal aliens." The reaction in Juárez was more ambiguous. On the one hand many Juarenses either discovered for the first time or confirmed what they already knew — that many El Pasoans despise Mexicans. But, on the other hand, because many Juarenses believed that the blockade was not against them (the highly Americanized Mexicans who eagerly support El Paso's commerce), but against the despised Southern Mexicans, who, supposedly, were the only "aliens" trying desperately to cross the border by "illegal" means, they did not take the negative comments as directed toward them.

I also show in this chapter how the more-than-dubious results of the blockade did not change the "euphoric" climate of El Paso about the border patrol strategy. The problem, I think, is that data showing that very few things changed after the blockade are not going to change the narrative identities of people who are totally impermeable to facts. Some individuals, while not acknowledging the narrative character of their own identities, "accuse" facts of having a narrative structure — that is, of being discursively malleable. For these people, facts can be manipulated, but the basic plot behind their own narrative identities cannot. The relationship between "facts" and narratives is a very complex one, and the possibility of accommodating "new," "unexpected," or "contradictory" facts to one's narrative identity seems to depend more on how flexible one's plot is than on how forceful the facts are. In this sense, if people's negative images about the "others" can be changed at all, it will not be by opposing their narrative identities with "facts," but rather by confronting them with the "narrative character-ness" of their identities. That was precisely what I did in a pilot dialogical social science experiment I conducted in the region between 1995 and 1996. The analysis of that exercise is the topic of Chapter 6.

In that chapter I show how I attempted to dialogically engage my interviewees in a discussion of how their own narratives functioned as cultural artifacts that influenced their visions about themselves and the "others." Using a dialogic methodology, I asked people to consider the narrative character of their identities. In this way I introduced them to the idea that, if we are all storytellers, we are also characters in the stories of others. We may usually be the "good guys" in our own scripts, but we frequently end up as "bad guys" in other people's stories. Of course, people usually believe (myself included) they have excellent "reasons" and "data" for describing themselves and other characters the way they do, and for constructing identities accordingly. For this reason, I hoped my interviewees could entertain the possibility that they were playing similar games as everybody else, where Anglos, Mexicans, African Americans, Mexican Americans, and Chicanos seem to weigh themselves and the "others" on a moral basis to prove who is better. My hope was that by engaging people in negotiating scripts about themselves and "others," their need to portray the "other" so negatively might be diminished. Chapter 6 is the description and the analysis of this more than provisional dialogical endeavor, and shows how most of my interviewees were able to examine and reflect on the themes they were using to organize their lives, and to interpret their own actions and the actions of others. That is, I show how my interviewees were able to make their stories "better," in Rosenwald's (1992) sense: (1) a story that is more comprehensive than the previous one; (2) a story in which one's relation to the world and relationships with others and oneself are recognized as being ambivalent and contradictory; (3) a story that helps to comprehend the earlier, "defective" ones; (4) a story that is structurally more complex, more varied, and contrastive in the events and accompanying feelings portrayed — more interesting and three-dimensional. My bet is that through those "better" stories (but of course not *only* through those stories), people have more possibilities to construct fuller lives for themselves and the "others."

Finally, the Appendix addresses the theoretical basis of my analysis. I start from the theoretical assumption that identity is not a "thing" that an individual "has" once and forever, but rather, a construct, which undergoes constant negotiation with "others" as its contours are defined and redefined over time. As Bhavnani and Phoenix (1994, p. 9) comment, "[E]ach individual is both located in, and opts for a number of differing, and at times, conflictual, identities, depending on the social, political, economic and ideological aspects of their situation." That is, identities are contextually constructed.

I also note in the Appendix that social identity may not be an "essential inner state," yet neither is it produced solely by the power of external discourses, à la Althusser (1971). Instead, it derives from a complex interplay of categories, metaphors, and narrative identities about ourselves and "others" over time. Thus, while I believe that identities are constructed within a culturally specific system of classification (where the different subject positions that converge to form what appears as a unified and unique self are cultural constructions created by discourses), and that metaphors help to understand who we are, I also believe that people develop a sense of themselves as subjects *in part* by imagining themselves as protagonists in stories — hence, my interest in the narrative identities of border residents.

What are the implications of all this for the U.S.–Mexico border? Mexicans and Americans belong to national societies that share some aspects of their respective classification systems — both in terms of positions and their attributes. However, they differ greatly in other aspects that also impinge on the everyday attitudes and behaviors of their inhabitants. On the border, these similarities and differences meet, and the result is an unusually complex common sense, in which people are forced to move from one classification system to another, sometimes on a daily basis. Not only do people move from one system to another, but the proliferation of classification systems within which a single person can be placed means that people constantly mix different systems of classification to make sense of the perceived "others."

At the same time, border residents make continuous use of tropes (metaphors, metonymies, etc.) to make sense of themselves and others. The importance of tropes in any process of identity construction is that they help in the meaningful organization of experience. Many times tropes frame narratives and bind the beginning of the narrative inextricably to its conclusion. In this way tropes lend structural coherence to the narrative and suggest how they are bounded, that is, where they begin and end (Riessman 1993, p. 44). But in other circumstances particular narrative plots "ask" for some tropes instead of others.

Finally, I try to prove in the Appendix that narratives about oneself and "others" are crucial to processes of identity construction. My hypothesis is that social occurrences are constructed as "experience" not only in relation to discourses that give them meaning in general but also within plots that organize them coherently. Therefore, it is precisely the plot of my narrative identity that guides the process of selectivity toward the "real" that is part of every identity construction. In this selection of the "real" is also included the relationship that we have established between our own plot and the multiple interpellations and tropes that culture in general (and the classificatory systems in the case of interpellations in particular) offers us for identification. If this is so, the narratives on either side of the border function as themes around which many border residents construct their "coherent" identities. In Juárez, central narratives are that "All social problems are related to Southern Mexicans," "Juarenses have become Americanized," "Fronterizos are losing their Catholic traditions," "Mexican Americans have become Americanized," "Americans are slaves to consumerism," "American women boss their husbands," among other thematic plots. On the American side, pervasive narratives are that "All poverty is Mexican," "Catholic practices are very traditional in Mexico," "All criminality is coming from Juárez," "Mexican males are very macho," and many other scripts. Because of the primacy of these narrative plots, they determine how occurrences are processed and what criteria will be used to prioritize and render meaning to events.

But narratives, in one way or another, have to deal with "structural" conditions (ignoring them, negating them, partially taking them into account, negotiating with them, trying to modify them, etc.). For that reason, I think that knowing some very basic data about the region is important. Ciudad Juárez and El Paso were until 1848 one city, and when the Guadalupe Hidalgo treaty divided it, the treaty did not divide the economic and social relationships between both cities in the same way. This was so because, among other things, the area is isolated; almost nothing can be found for several hundred miles.

The strong relationship between the two cities strengthened during the first part of this century, and the years of Prohibition in the United States not only started the growing tourist industry in Juárez (Martínez 1994, p. 21), but also allowed the formation of a new bourgeoisie that grew due to its relationships with "the other side." The smuggling of alcoholic beverages from factories installed on the Mexican side of the border favored the "original accumulation" of some Mexicans who, over the years, became major political and economic actors (Lau 1986, p. 11). At the same time, not only has the bourgeoisie established a strong economic relationship with the United States in general and with El Paso in particular, but also almost the entire city is, in some way or another, closely linked to "*el otro lado*." As Oscar Martínez (1986, p. 148) points out:

> . . . much of the personal income earned by residents in Juárez is generated directly or indirectly by the presence of the American economy . . . according to the El Paso Chamber of Commerce *Area Fact Book* for 1981–82, considerably more than half of the earnings of the Juárez labor force originate in El Paso and in the tourist and maquiladora sectors on the Juárez side.

It is obvious that at the hub of the region is El Paso, a city of 515,342 inhabitants in 1990 (Lorey 1993, p. 49) whose economic output accounts for more than half the entire economy of the region ($8.6 billion). Also, this economy is highly influenced by the boom of the maquila industry in Northern Mexico, and functions as the area's service center. Due to the strong interrelationships that link this city with Juárez, it is not surprising to find that retailing is one of the most important activities in El Paso, and that up to 40 percent of the trade can be attributed to Mexican shoppers.

"If El Paso is the hub of the Paso del Norte trade area, Juárez is the axle" (Institute of Manufacturing and Material Management 1991, p. 4), and the most important reason for the incredible growth in recent decades is, indisputably, the maquiladora industry. That becomes clear when we discover that Juárez has captured more than 15 percent of Mexico's maquila industry, with 290 firms which, at the beginning of the 1990s, employed more than 129,000 workers. For all these reasons, Ciudad Juárez, a city of 789,522 inhabitants according to the 1990 census, is a very especial case on the border.

First of all, Juárez' population is much more homogeneous than those of other major Mexican border cities. On the one hand, the migrant component is very different in Ciudad Juárez than in the other primary cities along the border: in Tijuana more than 58 percent of the population was born outside the state of Baja California, but in Ciudad Juárez the people born outside Chihuahua account for only 34 percent. Hence, the impact of outer migration is felt less in Juárez than in other cities of the border (Lorey 1993, p. 51). In addition, people outside Chihuahua who decide to migrate to Juárez are different from other people on the border. They come from the Northern states closer to Chihuahua: Durango, Zacatecas, and Coahuila. Those who were born in these Northern states accounted for 20 percent of Juárez' population in 1990. In this sense, if we put together Chihuahua and the other Northern states mentioned above, 86 percent of Juárez' population originally came from the North (Lorey 1993, p. 51). This is a very different picture from that offered by Tijuana, for instance, which attracts many migrants from Central and Southern Mexico: in 1990, 40 percent of Tijuana's population was born in Central and Southern Mexico (Lorey 1993, p. 51).

If this is the picture regarding internal migration, Ciudad Juárez stands as a different border city in other aspects, too. Ciudad Juárez–El Paso stands in sharp contrast to Tijuana–San Diego in terms of the type of Mexican immigrants who work on a regular basis on the American side of the border. First, the number of American nationals living in Juárez but working in El Paso is far greater than that in Tijuana–San Diego, with 39 percent and 11 percent, respectively, living on the Mexican side but working on the American side (Alegría Olazábal 1992, p. 132). This is so because many Juarenses have their children in El Paso so that those children will become American citizens. Consequently, they are actually Mexicans who have lived all their lives in Juárez, but legally they are U.S. citizens. According to Teschner (1995, pp. 100–101), the main reasons behind this practice are (1) the possibility of the entire family becoming, over time, American citizens due to the "unification of families" provisions of the various immigration and naturalization acts; and (2) the prospect of American-born children attending El Paso schools.

But even more important is the fact that the migration that crosses from Juárez (legal and illegal) to El Paso is basically a local one; that is, people cross to work nearby, either in El Paso itself, or in Western Texas or Southern New Mexico. On the whole they do not migrate to work in other places in the United States that are far from Ciudad Juárez. Nonetheless, the fact that many Mexicans cross the border daily to work in El Paso does not mean that the city offers them very good salaries. On the contrary, although El Paso salaries are much better than those Juarense workers earn, El Paso is still one of the poorest major cities in the United States. Thus, El Paso's per capita annual income at the beginning of the 1990s was only $10,778, which was relatively low compared to the state's average of $16,702. Thus El Paso, like other border communities, has not shared the economic robustness of the state's economy:

> In fact, as a percentage of state per capita income, the per capita income for El Paso declined from 72.7 percent to 68.6 percent during the years 1978 to 1988 . . . poverty in El Paso is high. While 11.8 percent of Texas families fall below the poverty level, 18.6 percent of families in El Paso are living in poverty. Within the El Paso Hispanic community, 28.6 percent of all households fall below the poverty level. (Institute of Manufacturing and Material Management 1991, p. 39)

And this characteristic of El Paso is not new; during the 1970s, with its $4,733 per capita income, the city was placed 260th among the 266 most important Standard Metropolitan Statistical Areas (SMSAs), and it was the poorest city with a population over 100,000 in the nation. At the same time, El Paso was ranked 307th among the 313 SMSAs in 1985 (Stoddard and Hedderson 1989, p. 14).

This is the general picture of the city, but in the poor neighborhoods of El Paso, the situation is even worse. Furthermore, the poor neighborhoods are the more "Mexican" ones. A study carried out by the Bureau of Business and Economic Research at the University of Texas at El Paso (1992) showed that 43 percent of the population living in the poorest neighborhoods of El Paso were born in Mexico. Among these foreign-born respondents, 42 percent arrived in the United States in 1975 or later, 29 percent in 1980 or later, and 15 percent in 1985 or later. At the same time, the level of poverty of these neighborhoods is such that their inhabitants depend heavily on government support, and 47 percent of them receive some kind of income transfer. Particularly important here are food stamps, which are received by 20 percent of the sample.

Another measure that shows the problems of El Paso's economy is unemployment, which in the mid-1970s ranged from 14 percent to 20 percent, placing El Paso at the top of all United States cities with a population over 100,000 (Stoddard and Hedderson 1989, p. 15). In the early 1990s the rate was around 11 percent.

As we can see, these "structural" conditions are related in complex ways to some of the main narratives that I discovered in the region and that I will analyze throughout the book. One of the main narratives on the American side asserts that "all poverty is Mexican national." It is true that Ciudad Juárez is a poor city, but it has a very prosperous bourgeoisie and its middle class supports a big part of El Paso's commerce. Another narrative asserts that "most of Juárez' social problems are due to the humongous migration from Southern Mexico." Yet only 14 percent of Juárez' population comes "from the South." In the book, we will have the opportunity to see how in the "symbolic struggle" between data and narratives, many times the latter win over the former.

So much for the organization of the book and some basic data about the area; what follows is my acknowledgment of the shortcomings of my endeavor. First of all, I am fully aware that absent from this book is my own narrative, or, in other words, the basic plot from which I ordered the complex reality offered by my interviewees in their testimonies (Vila 1997b). Following Riessman (1993), I have basically created a "metastory about what happened by telling what the interview narratives signify, editing and reshaping what was told, and turning it into a hybrid story" (p. 13). Ergo, I present the material as if I were writing a "realistic text." However, the "realistic" tone of the book is a well-thought-out strategy linked to the "afterlife" I expect for the book and the current academic/political project I am involved with, not my intention to speak, finally and with ultimate authority, for others — an impossible goal due to the problems involved in "representation" (Baudrillard 1983; Probyn 1993; Said 1979; Spivak 1988). I still consider myself part of the recent trend in sociology and anthropology in which many social ethnographers have backed away from totalized truth telling, instead relativizing their partial truths in the distorting glass of biography and partisan, polemical, and suspect authority.[9]

I decided to write a "realistic text" and commit all the mistakes narrative theoreticians ask us to avoid because the story I tell targets particular people; it might have taken a different form if someone else were the listener.[10] As I noted earlier, using a dialogic methodology, I asked some of my interviewees to think about how their identities have a narrative character precisely because I had such serious doubts about the relationship between narratives and facts, that is, the always present possibility of "tailoring" facts to fit a particular narrative. For this reason, I wanted to explore with my interviewees how the ways in which Mexican immigrants, Mexican Americans, Anglos, and African Americans understand their identities on the border are (among other things) well-developed narratives, not "true" descriptions of reality (Vila 1997b). If in this book I emphasize how narratives, categories, and metaphors work in the process of identity construction, it is not because I believe that those are the only devices people use to develop a sense of identity.[11] My emphasis on narratives and the idea of reporting the complex data I am working with as realistic accounts in this research project is "strategic," and derives from my hope that by engaging people in negotiating scripts about themselves and "others," their need to portray the "other" so negatively may be diminished.

Introduction

As I mentioned in the Introduction (and develop at length in the Appendix), I think that people on the border use extensively social categories and interpellations to understand who they are and who the "others" are.

Regarding the use of social categories, we have to remember that Mexicans and Americans belong to national societies that share some aspects of each other's classification systems — both in terms of positions and their attributes. However, they differ greatly in other aspects that also impinge on the everyday attitudes and behaviors of their inhabitants. On the border, these similarities and differences meet, and the result is an unusually complex common sense, in which people are forced to move from one classification system to another, sometimes on a daily basis. Not only do people move from one system to another, but the proliferation of classification systems within which a single person can be placed means that people constantly mix different systems of classification to make sense of the perceived "other." On the Mexican side of the border the main classificatory system relies on *region*, while the American system stresses *race and ethnicity*. Consequently, on the one hand it is very difficult to separate the different identities that continually overlap in the accounts of Juarenses and El Pasoans, where gender, class, religion, age, race and ethnicity, and region endlessly intersect with each other. On the other hand a regional logic on the Mexican side and a racial and ethnic one on the American side somehow overdetermine the ways in which the complex mix of the different identities are accounted for by the inhabitants of the region.

The border offers a unique opportunity to look at the complex process of identity construction and its constant use of arbitrary classification systems to make sense of people's social identities. In the present chapter I will discuss the highly developed regional system of classification that many Fronterizos use to make sense of their own attitudes and behaviors and those of the "others."

In the Juárez interviews, two discourses are predominantly used to make sense of "us" and "them": one referring to regional and the other to national identity. The oft-repeated phrases "*nosotros, los de la*

Chapter 1

THE MEXICAN SIDE
DISCOURSES OF REGION

frontera" [we, the people of the border] and "*nosotros, los de Juárez*" [we, the people from Juárez] (or even more affectionately, "*nosotros, los de Juaritos*"[1] [we, the people from dear Juárez]), as well as the labels Juarenses, Norteños [Northerners], and Fronterizos [frontiersmen or borderites], are used to explain attitudes and behaviors Juarenses consider a particular feature of their region.[2] In this classification system, Mexicans are divided by city, state, and region and characterized accordingly. Yet "region" in this context does not coincide with a fixed geographical area. Instead, it marks a symbolically understood space that can be as large or as small as the speaker requires. Hence, for some of our interviewees, "the South" starts only fifteen miles from Juárez, and a Chilango is anyone who lives from that point southward![3] Employing this geographic differentiating mechanism, Juárez residents contrast Norteños and Sureños [Southerners] mainly to distinguish themselves from the Chilangos of Mexico City and from the inhabitants of Central and Southern Mexico (they do this because Sureños supposedly have more Indian ancestry than Norteños). Secondarily, Juárez residents distinguish between Fronterizo and non-Fronterizo Norteños, in part to differentiate themselves from the people who live in Chihuahua City (the capital of the state).

It is important to point out that different actors use the above labels in different ways. On the one hand the self-reference "*nosotros, los de Juárez*" was more prominent than "Juarenses" among most of the interviewees from poorer neighborhoods; and they always used "*nosotros, los de la frontera*" instead of "Fronterizos." In contrast, middle-class people in Juárez used all the above labels alternatively. Regardless of class, age, gender, or religion, though, the interviewees all preferred the reference to the city instead of the region. "Fronterizo" was used almost exclusively by middle-class people.

When it comes to labels, most interviewees, regardless of social class, preferred the "*de* . . ." Spanish construction instead of the regional adjectives "Juarense," "Norteño," and the like to identify the "others." It was thus much more common for interviewees to talk about "*ellos, los de Tamaulipas*," "*de Monterrey*," "*de Chiapas*" [they, the people from Tamaulipas, Monterrey, Chiapas], than for them to use the corresponding regional adjectives "Tamaulipecos," "Regiomontanos," or "Chiapanecos." In a typical interview, one could hear how people alternated "we from Juárez" with "Juarenses," while at the same time virtually always referring to the "others" as "those from . . ."

I believe that these ways of addressing themselves and the "others" are very important, and that they are inextricably linked to the strong regional system of classification that seems pervasive in Juárez. From a grammatical point of view, using the expression "*de . . . (Juárez, el sur, Chihuahua, Torreón, el norte, la frontera*, etc.)" implies something completely different from saying "Juarense," "Sureño," "Chihuahuense," and so forth. This is so because agency is put on the place of origin and not on the person. Therefore, if someone did something because "*¡tenía que ser del sur!*" [he/she must have been from the South!] (a very common expression in Juárez), and not because "he/she was a Sureño," this means that the most basic cause of the behavior is place of origin, and not the person her-/himself. It is as though the real motivator of attitudes and behaviors is region, which exerts an irresistible social pressure that is almost impossible to avoid.

The fact that middle-class people mix both forms of appellation is significant: compared to poorer people, middle-class individuals are less willing to think of their personal destiny as totally attached to something impossible to modify—something as immutable as one's place of origin. Middle-class use of expressions like "Juarense," "Norteño," and the like is, again, a way of attributing agency to people instead of to regions. Here we must remember that the "*de . . .*" expression in Spanish denotes possession, as if a region somehow inescapably possesses its natives. Such a construction does not exist in English, where the "from . . ." does not denote possession.

At the same time, the fact that interviewees used more regional adjectives in their self-identification than when they were addressing "others" further reinforces my argument: while they believe that the region "marks" people generally, they also feel that it marks the "others" much more than themselves. Accordingly, many Juarenses (in this case through the symbolic use of the regional adjective) believe they have a freedom of action that they deny to "others," because those "from . . ." are slaves of what their native region instills in their identities.

The only exceptions to this rule seem to be Chilangos; almost all my interviewees referred to people from Mexico City as "Chilangos" and did not use the "*de . . .*" expression. This is not a true exception, however, because "Chilangos" is not a real regional reference. Chilango is not a regional adjective corresponding to the inhabitants of Mexico City or the Distrito Federal (such a term would be "Mexicano"—which coincides with the name of the inhabitants of the country in general—or "Defeño"), but an insulting nickname that alludes to a small, slippery fish. To use the label Chilango, then, is not to use an adjective corresponding to a region, but instead to refer metaphorically to the supposed characteristics of Mexico City's inhabitants—characteristics they have *because* they live in the nation's political center, Mexico City. And what many Juarenses seem to do is establish a close parallelism between the centralized politics of the Mexican state and the attitudes and behaviors of the inhabitants of the capital. Some Juarenses appear to believe that Chilangos use this political centralism to their personal advantage, regardless of their class, gender, age, or power position.

Chihuahua's Historical Autonomy and Juárez' "city of vice" Stigma and Regional Classificatory Systems

Why do many Juarenses[4] use such a refined regional system of classification? I think they do so because of a combination of different historical developments. Some are shared between Juarenses and Chihuahuenses in general. But others correspond to the peculiarities of Juárez and other border cities. Among the first, Juarenses share with Chihuahuenses the idea that their region is very different from Central and Southern Mexico:

> The "peculiarities" that distinguish the North and Northerners from the Center and its inhabitants are . . . generally attributed to the region's frontier past. For Chihuahuans these "peculiarities" are metonyms of an irreducible difference, one that makes the North "another country" (*otro país*) and Northerners a distinct people. Constantly contrasted with the "brownness" of Southerners, the "whiteness" of *norteños* is the visible index of what is viewed as a distinct, northern "nature." Relative to other Mexicans, *norteños* were and are considered to be brave, independent, rebellious, self-sufficient, and hardworking. Northern society was and is more democratic, egalitarian, and open to individual achievement. (Alonso 1995, pp. 15–16)

In this sense, in both scholarly and folk discourses it is argued that the struggle against the Apache shaped Northern society in fundamental ways, producing a distinct regional identity. We have to remember here that from the seventeenth century through 1886, the Apache continued to raid Chihuahuan settlements and haciendas for livestock and captives (Alonso 1995, p. 22).

> Relations between dominant and subordinate groups and classes, and between subjects and the state, were substantially modified by the social distribution of the means of force . . . peasants [and] hacienda workers . . . benefited from their military role and were able to achieve a better class situation and status position than the peons of the Center and South . . . The

distribution of control over organized violence also had an important impact on center-periphery relations . . . After independence the central government was weak and the national treasury was poor. Control over frontier warfare passed to provincial governments, fostering a resentment of the Center, which had left the frontier in a state of "orphanhood" . . . Provincial control of warfare also fostered the development of a regional imagination of community, of a consciousness of being Chihuahuans first and Mexicans second . . . In addition, the organization of warfare itself fostered a parochial consciousness . . . since their primary military responsibility was the defense of the local community. (Alonso 1995, pp. 48–49)

Consequently, the "imagined community" (Anderson 1983) Chihuahuenses have developed for themselves not only differentiates the supposedly "white" North from the "brown" South, but also creates a profound sense of parochialism that stresses the more democratic characteristics of the North when compared to the more authoritarian government of Southern and Central Mexico.

These are the features that many Chihuahuenses have used historically to delineate their identity in relation to the South. Yet one peculiarity that Juárez does not share with the rest of Chihuahua (but which it does have in common with other border towns) is the "city of vice" stigma. This is the most prominent peculiarity, and, I believe, is the one that has led to the strong regionalism found in the city nowadays. The "city of vice" stigma, which has clung to the city since the turn of the century, has influenced the creation of a "border city identity." Juárez residents have always struggled to turn that pejorative label on its head— by highlighting what Juarenses have by virtue of living on the border, and which other Mexicans do not have: easy access to the United States, to its culture and consumables and work possibilities. Here it is important to recall not only that Juárez has a very bad reputation throughout Mexico, but that other Mexican border cities, especially Tijuana, have terrible reputations as well. Different discourses, ranging from movies or popular songs to academic accounts, almost invariably portray the border as a site of violence, drugs, and prostitution.

But if the border in general has this bad reputation, Juárez' and Tijuana's images are still worse. Over many years, the presence in San Diego and El Paso of major U.S. military facilities transformed Tijuana and Juárez into providers of "leisure" (alcohol and prostitution) for the predominantly single, male population of those military bases. This commonsense image was well captured in Rubén Vizcaíno's ironic (and sexist) observation that although Mexico did not participate directly in World War II, it actually did help the American soldiers through the "leisure" provided by Mexican prostitutes.[5]

Considering the above-mentioned situation, it should not be surprising that many Juarenses have developed an especially strong regional identity. It is an identity so idealized in everyday discourse that, not coincidentally, everything valued is located in Juárez, and everything not valued lies either south of Juárez (i.e., in the rest of Mexico) or across the border.

But, who are the "others" who appear more prominently in the commonsense discourse of the interviewees? One group is, of course, "those from the South." This phrase has two different meanings. On the one hand it refers to everyone but Norteños, or even more stringently, to everyone except Juarenses. On the other hand, though, some interviewees used that expression to refer to migrants coming to Juárez from the more "Indian" states of Central and Southern Mexico. In this last usage, "those from Southern Mexico" is a euphemism that replaces a discourse of ethnicity that has been erased from discussion by the official (Central) rhetorical celebration of Aztec, Mayan, and various other Indian roots of Mexican culture. Thus, the discourse is reintroduced into Fronterizos' narratives through a metaphor of region that speaks about "that which cannot be said." Hence, when some interviewees talk about people from Southern Mexico, they refer to anyone who is not from Chihuahua or Juárez ("Southerner" used in strictly geographical terms), but other people refer to Indians and depict them in very negative ways: as being backward, without fighting spirit, and more prone to leisure than to work. Here it is important to remember the presence of a powerful regional hegemonic discourse that claims that the North was almost untouched by *mestizaje*, and that Northern Mexico tends to be "white," whereas Central and Southern Mexico tends to be "Indian" (or at least mestizo), that is, dark-skinned. As I mentioned above, this history of origins is often related to the history of war against the Apaches, where conditions on the frontier tended to erase differences between whites and mixed bloods. In this sense, the differences between Spaniards and the castes became blurred and a process of "whitening" took place due to the peculiar war conditions. Ana Alonso states:

> A "whitened" history of origins accompanied and naturalized the "bleaching" of the population. According to this invented tradition, the conquest and settlement of the frontier had been carried out by Spaniards, that is, whites, and miscegenation with Indians had been negligible, and with Blacks,

impossible. On the frontier Indians became radically the other; they were an enemy to be exterminated or segregated in enclaves rather than incorporated in colonial society . . . Chihuahuans today boast of their collective "whiteness" . . . As ethnic affiliation became redefined in Chihuahua and in the North as a whole, whiteness became central to the creation of a regional sense of community and personhood. This invented tradition of origins is very much alive today and is regularly invoked in the construction of a distinct norteño identity, opposed to that of the Mexicans of the Center, who are subjectively apprehended as "less white" and disparagingly referred to as Chilangos. (Alonso 1995, p. 68)

This history of origin differs sharply not only from a similar history espoused by Central and Southern Mexicans, but also from the Chicano myth of Aztlan. Consequently, it is not rare for many Juarenses to clearly detach themselves from the Indian heritage that Chicanos claim. As one student in the Universidad Autónoma de Ciudad Juárez (UACJ) interviews I discuss below observed as he told us of his encounter with Chicano students in El Paso:

Juan: . . . and I tell them: "Well, *you* are *la raza*, you are Cuauhtémoc, not me! I'm almost an American! . . . I feel very content in this double vision, because I'm not from Central Mexico (because really we don't have the same way of thinking), nor am I from the United States. Rather . . . I am from Juárez and I am a Mexican . . .

Juan — a very dark skinned native of Delicias with six years of residence in Juárez, but who likes to call himself a Juarense — is happy with his Fronterizo identity and culture, where being from Juárez comes first and being from Mexico second; and the joke he makes is a very important remark about the particular sequence in which he understands his identity: "Well, *you* are *la raza*, you are Cuauhtémoc, not me! I'm almost an American!"

Therefore, the Chicanos' search for their Indian heritage is totally at odds with Fronterizos' (and Norteños') search for their heritage. Many Fronterizos and Norteños pride themselves on being "whites," and on lacking Indian blood. The "cult" of the "*güero*" child (a child with white skin and/or blond hair) in some Mexican families is well-known all over Mexico. Accordingly, Juan's joke represents a very important stance in relation to his Fronterizo identity. It is an identity that, at least in the case of Juan and other Norteños and Juarenses who heavily use "Sureños, like Indians" as the "other," attempts to detach itself not only from how Chicanos construct their Mexicanness, but also from similar efforts made by other Mexicans to recover their Indian heritage. It is not surprising then that Juan stated the Fronterizo "task" this way:

Juan: . . . but we are performing a different task . . . what is it? It is to make them [the Americans] understand that we don't go around wearing Indian shoes and to make them understand that they are not Superman . . .

In this sense, if region seems to be the primary way to construct identity on the Mexican side of the border, color markers of identity are not absent in Chihuahua generally or Juárez in particular. However, those color markers do not work in isolation as they do on the American side of the border, where being a Black is a datum in itself. Instead, those markers are resignified in terms of region, a move that provides other identity markers that "compensate" (or not) for skin color: "Many of the *no indios* [in colonial classification] had Indian and Black ancestors, but they were classified as gente de razón because they upheld a 'civilized' style of life" (Alonso 1995, p. 65). Thus, those scholars who claim that skin color (by itself) is the most important identity marker in Ciudad Juárez are completely missing the point. It is totally wrong to claim that, for instance, those who do not have "*buena presentación*" or are not "*gente atractiva*" — meaning blond or at least white-skinned — sometimes are literally told at the door of the most important Juárez discotheques not to go in. The experience of my interviewees in those popular discos is quite different: if you are dark-skinned but you talk with a Norteño accent or you are tall and have other "European" features (all of them very important identity markers of being a Fronterizo), you can enter without any problem. And, if you are white, have European features, but you also have some traits that easily identify yourself as a "*güero de rancho*" [a blonde coming from the countryside], then you have more difficulty entering those discos. Hence, skin color is overdetermined by a very entrenched regional system that not only mechanically equates South and Central Mexico with Indians, who are short and dark-skinned, and Northern Mexico with Europeans, who are white and tall, but also equates people from the countryside with backwardness, regardless of color of their skin. If we do not grasp how regional categories overdetermine color on the border, it is impossible to understand why it is not uncommon to hear extremely negative discourses about Indians in general, but especially about Southern Indians (Mazahuas, Mixtecos), whereas Northern Indians like Tarahumaras ("our Indians") are portrayed in a much more positive way.

Another social actor that many Juarenses want to differentiate themselves from is the Chilango. Here again the term "Chilango" has several meanings. On the one hand many of my interviewees saw Southern Mexicans and Chilangos as the same, as if any Southerner or Indian were like a Chilango. That was the case, for instance, when one of my interviewees described Chilangos as *"chaparros, prietos, y mamones"* [something like "shrimps, niggers, and assholes"]. In a more restrictive sense many of my interviewees referred to Chilangos as the inhabitants of Mexico City. In this second use, the negative reference to Chilangos is again a metaphor for something else. The interviewees seemed to almost mechanically equate Mexico's policy of centralism vis à vis the border with the behavior of Mexico's capital city inhabitants, as if all those inhabitants were taking personal advantage of Mexican centralism, regardless of their social class, gender, age, power status, and so on. Ergo, the Chilango is usually depicted as someone to be avoided, someone who is constantly trying to take advantage of the Juarense, while the latter is usually described as someone with a big heart who is always exposed to the malevolence of others.

At the same time that many Juarenses establish a regional identity that distinguishes them from other Mexicans, they also differentiate themselves from the Americans on the other side of the border. This is not a contradiction in relation to their valued Fronterizo identity, because although they frame their access to the United States as a valuable resource, this does not mean that they necessarily want to live in the United States or become Mexican American. To buttress their position, these interviewees usually emphasize the advantages of a Mexican "lifestyle" over the frenetic, money-driven culture of U.S. residents. Consequently, in constituting a Juarense identity, Juárez residents symbolically defend a way of being and living that, while acknowledging American influence, highly values its *"mexicanidad"* (Mexicanness).

Next I will provide some examples that illustrate how the regional system of classification works in Juárez. An important disclaimer seems appropriate here: due to the enormous variety of identity discourses I have encountered in my fieldwork, what follows is only an illustration of possible discourses, without any intention of being exhaustive in mapping *all* Fronterizo discourses. Therefore, the next section shows how many of Juárez' inhabitants use interpellations, narratives, and metaphors anchored in regional criteria to construct their social identities.

Regionalism and Identification Hierarchies

The regional classification system used in Juárez is so strong that, facing a problem of identity definition, some interviewees relied first on the system they are most familiar with; only if this attempt failed did they bring another one into play. That is what happened with Margarita and Robustiano[6] as they tried to make sense of a picture showing the "Centro Chicano" of El Paso (shown in Chapter 3).

> **Pablo:** What does the word Chicano mean to you?
> **Robustiano:** Chicano? . . . I think Chicano means . . .
> **Feliciano:** *Cholo* . . .
> **Margarita:** *No* . . . from another *state*.
> **Robustiano:** No . . . Chicano comes . . . from . . . let's say from Mexican and American people . . . Because people *arreglada* [with American immigration papers], can't be Chicano . . . they are, let's say only a repatriate . . . The Chicana, Chicanos are from, let's say the child of a *gabacha* or a *gabacho*[7] . . . and a Mexican. I think that's what it must be.

The important thing to note in this conversation is how Margarita first attempted to make sense of "Chicano" — a word that has meaning only within the ethnic classificatory logic of the United States — by using the Mexican regional classification logic.

Regionalism is so strong that some interviewees refer to it with astonishment. This was what happened in one of the meetings we had with a group of doctors working in a poor colonia in Juárez. In that particular interview Alejandro expressed his shock at something he witnessed while attending college in Monterrey, where the students prefer to socialize with each other only if they hail from the same state:[8]

> **Alejandro:** You go to Monterrey . . . And people ask you: "Where are you from?" From Chihuahua, from Sinaloa . . . I was at the university in Monterrey . . . you have to search out the people from Chihuahua, from Torreón, from Veracruz, because we're not [looked upon] as Mexican, even though we're in Mexico!

In another interview with the doctors, the flow of conversation led us to ask what labels they preferred the "others" to use in addressing them. A very interesting discussion followed as some interviewees clearly addressed the issue of the situational character of identity and discussed how they preferred different labels applied to them in different situations.

> **Alejandro:** [In another country people surely would ask you] "Where are you from?" "I'm from Juárez." [If I went to the] United States: "I'm Mexican, I'm from Mexico." Then: "From what region?" "Well, from Juárez." But I'm Mexican . . . maybe I'd feel proud if they called me Hispanic . . .

I'm American, I'm Hispanic; or maybe if they'd ask me *specifically*, "Where are you from? . . . From Juárez." But I think that over there [in the U.S.] I would associate with other Hispanics . . . In the interior of the United States I'd be Hispanic, and then if someone asked me exactly [where I'm from]: "From Juárez," and as to the country: "Mexico," even if they said I'm a drunk and everything else.

Thus, although Alejandro acknowledges that his identity will change depending on the particular situation in which he is placed, his Juarense identity is nevertheless so intense that he completely skips any reference to the Mexican state he lives in, Chihuahua! For him the jump is from Mexico to Juárez, without any reference to the state Juárez is in, as if Chihuahua were without any relevance to his identity construction. Here again we confront a social construction of region, because there is no objective measure to define a region. Alejandro could call his region Northern Mexico, "*la frontera*," Chihuahua, and so on. Nevertheless he chooses Juárez, the city, as his definition of region. This localism was also stressed by the other native Juarenses present at that interview:

Angela: And you, miss?
Socorro: I would say I'm from Juárez.
Angela: In other words, for you, if you went to the United States or to El Paso, it would be the same . . .
Socorro: Yes, in all places . . . because I'm very proud, I love Juárez very much.

A similar situation occurred in a set of interviews we conducted in a trade union with a group of young people working at different maquiladora plants in Juárez.[9] The participants (all of them Catholics) were males and females from different regional backgrounds: Aurora had come from Veracruz four years previously; Secundino was from San Luís Potosí; Felipe and Jesús were native Juarenses. All of them had completed (but not finished) some secondary education. In one of those interviews, Felipe was trying to explain why he is so proud of being a Juarense in order to differentiate himself from both the other Mexicans and the Mexican Americans:

Felipe: People who go over there [to the United States] lose their identity, their nationalism . . . right!? I love being Mexican, being from Chihuahua and being in particular from Juárez and the "Chaveña" . . . I love that, and as he said, *¡de aquí para allá todo!* [If you are from Juárez, you can count on me. If you are not . . . I am sorry . . . !]

The hierarchy of his identifications is quite clear, showing again how regionalistic some Juarenses are. Accordingly, he mentions he is proud of being a Mexican in order to differentiate himself from those, the Mexican Americans, who supposedly are not proud of that national identity anymore. But when he refers to his identity *inside* Mexico, he points out that he is *particularly* proud of being a Juarense and from "la Chaveña," his neighborhood—a very traditional working-class enclave. Therefore, his loyalties and identifications are very strong, as he himself suggests when he stresses that *"∂e aquí para allá todo."* He again uses a spatial metaphor when he makes this claim.

The "all of Juárez's social problems and poverty are related to people from the South" Narrative

The Southern Mexicans as Lazy

If categories are very important in the process of identity construction, narratives are important as well (see Appendix). In this sense, in many of my interviews, Southern Mexicans and Chilangos were often portrayed as having very negative characteristics, in narratives whose theme usually stresses that "all of Juárez's social problems and poverty are related to people from the South." This discourse is pervasive in the city and does not recognize class, gender, age, religion, or ethnic differences, and I have encountered very negative narratives about Southerners among working-class young people, middle-class maquiladora managers, upper-middle-class professionals, Catholics, and Protestants.

That was what happened in an interview we conducted with some lower-middle-class students in their twenties who were studying at a vocational school (to pursue careers as typists or secretaries) and living in poor neighborhoods. They worked in different types of low-paid clerk positions. All had been born in Juárez of migrant parents who had come from other Northern states (Durango, Coahuila, etc.), and all professed the Catholic faith. In this interview the extreme desire to differentiate themselves from Southerners was pervasive from the beginning:

> **Abigaíl:** We are different. I think that the border here . . . *is different from the rest of the republic.*
> **Ernesto:** People from the border are . . . fighters, don't you think?
> **Jorge:** Yes . . . we people from the border are more . . . inclined to work.

In this testimony we have some of the most important claims many Fronterizos use in their narratives about Southerners. These interviewees are claiming that Fronterizos not only work harder than Southerners and they struggle more than the latter, but also that they are also more "advanced," more frugal and less leisure oriented.

> **Jorge:** . . . people here . . . who live in Juárez, you ask them: "Are you going on a trip or something?" "*No,*" they tell you, "because I have to stay and work, or I have some other things to do." On the other hand, there, in the center of the republic, you can ask someone: "Hey . . . what places have you been to?" And of course, the people over there know numerous states, various cities . . . We, on the contrary, are a little more . . . let's say *enslaved to our work.*
>
> **Ernesto:** More tied . . . more tied to work . . .

These interviewees' claim that they are more frugal, hard working, and less leisure oriented than Southerners leads them to portray the latter as basically lazy and absolutely responsible for their misfortune.

> **Jorge:** But these are some of the differences of the border! Its because people who come from the interior of Mexico to live here . . . they come to live in terrible conditions!
>
> **Ernesto:** But those people are . . . are people with a pathetic spirit! Because . . . ask a bricklayer . . . or even a maquiladora worker! Ask them . . . they work . . . from six in the morning to six in the afternoon to get a few extra hours and many of them make good wages, but just ask them, where do they go on Fridays? . . . typical . . .
>
> **Ramiro:** To dance . . .
>
> **Jorge:** To dance, get drunk!
>
> **Ernesto:** To get drunk . . . and what for? So that during the week they'll be asking for money for the bus . . .

In these statements border residents are differentiated from their Southerner non-border counterparts by their attitude toward work — as if the Protestant work ethic were a side effect of long-term contact with the United States. And it is precisely this work attitude that recently arrived maquila workers are described as lacking. As a result, many interviewees are totally convinced that all native Juarenses either live in better conditions in Juárez or have already "*arreglado*"[10] — that is, they are already living and working in the United States. Thus, the only truly poor people they recognize in Juárez are those from elsewhere in Mexico, and this leads them to explanations of poverty that focus on cultural or moral deficiencies imported from "the South." In this manner, a discussion about morals and values (a discussion about identity) is framed in regional terms in the narratives of many Juarenses who want to prove how different they are from Southerners. In these narratives there is a pervasive plot establishing that "all poverty and social problems are associated with Southerners":

Ernesto: Yes. Ask a bricklayer, "How much do you make?" He will tell you: "Well, you know . . . if I work all week, including *Monday* . . . ," because you know, Monday is the typical day . . . [when people do not go to work]

Jorge: Hangover . . .

Ernesto: Hangover, right? . . . "If I work all week including Monday, I'll bring home five thousand . . . six thousand pesos!" But just ask him, "Where do you go on Saturday?" (And he only works half a day!) . . . The rest of Saturday . . . on Sunday, and then he gets home very hung over in the morning, and without any money!! Why? Because they are people with a pathetic spirit!

Pablo: Would you say the same thing about people who work in maquiladoras, or is it just the people who work in construction?

Abigaíl: No, in general!!

Ernesto: No, everybody!!

Jorge: . . . they are people . . . that do not have enough desire to improve themselves!

Abigaíl: Even more because . . . because poverty . . . does not mean . . . [that] if a person is *clean* . . . he or she will continue to be clean.

Ernesto: Poverty . . . is not the same as being dirty.

Ramiro: Poverty is one thing, laziness is another . . .

The problem these types of testimonies identify is not low salaries, but the culture and the morals of the people themselves. The problem, in other words, is said to be "a particular kind of mentality." It is in this context that the term "*flojo*" [lazy] emerges to complete the image. As they address these issues, many Fronterizos depict themselves as people with more positive attributes than Southerners. Hence, a moral battle around the concept of *mexicanidad* is fought by many Juarenses in several different camps, one of which—the battle to establish that Southerners have less moral value than Juarenses—is crucial. Here, the Juarense or Fronterizo identity works as a symbolic frontier that distinguishes the dignified poor from those without dignity, and the rightful Mexican from the unrightful one. By ascribing extreme poverty to the "other"—to those newcomers to the city who work in the maquilas or construction and that supposedly all come from the South,[11] Fronterizos are by definition protected from falling into extreme poverty themselves.

At the same time that these interviewees assert their greater diligence compared with Mexicans from the interior, they invert one of the negative images their non-border compatriots hold about them: the *agringado* claim. Therefore, many of our interviewees raised the issue of the fevered consumption of American goods on the border, but did so only to claim that this disease afflicts not "true" Fronterizos, but Southerners who are new arrivals to the border:

> **Jorge:** That's what all people are doing . . . they come here to the border, all of them from the South . . . The *majority come from the South*! The only thing they do . . . because here it's cheaper . . . they buy boomboxes and televisions . . . they come here just to buy electronic things such as televisions and stuff! While you who live here in the city . . . you are used to all this stuff . . . the fad has passed and other *things* are calling your attention! In the meantime we see the people from the maquilas with *boomboxes*! . . . these things don't attract our attention anymore!

In this sense, my interviewees argue, it is recent migrants from Southern or Central Mexico who are easy prey to American consumerism. They, on the other hand — "the real Juarenses" — invest their money in a more responsible fashion on durable goods not dictated by mere faddishness. In other testimonies, the Juarense is described as having a more modern sensibility than the Southerner, a greater fighting spirit, a greater sense of solidarity, and a greater capacity to assume risks.

> **Ernesto:** . . . many times, people from the South tend to . . . just . . . conform themselves and enclose themselves in their world! Their spirit of hope tends to fade out! It's different here. Many times we help one another here and we try to get out of that situation . . . today I help you, tomorrow you help me, right?

But sometimes there is such a strong need to establish this differentiation from the "other," the Southerner, that the symbolic barrier acquires physical status, and some interviewees proposed deterring "undesirable" migration from the South just as Americans stop Mexicans trying to migrate to the United States. As one of the leaders of the trade union I referred to above said:

> **Felipe:** I get very mad . . . and I always . . . I don't know if all of those who live here, who were born here think . . . "If I were a ruler, I'd stop all the arrival of people [from the interior of Mexico] here" . . . I mean control it . . . do it in almost the same manner as the United States is doing it, make a kind of border . . . now, I don't think like that, but for a long time

I blamed all the people that were coming here because of what they generated, like all those houses made out of cardboard . . . and it gets me very
angry seeing so many people living without homes; I get angry seeing so
much trash in my town and my house, and I blamed the people coming
from other parts of Mexico, I would say, "If they would not come, they
would not dirty me . . ."

This kind of discourse does not recognize class barriers, and I also found
it in middle-class interviewees. That is what happened in the interviews
with the physicians, where Alejandro laid almost all blame for Juárez'
problems on the shoulders of those from elsewhere in Mexico:

Alejandro: . . . The Juárez citizen is very enterprising, noble of heart . . .
I want someone to tell me how many of the people who are inmates at
CERESO [the city's jail] are natives of Ciudad Juárez, what percent of them,
and if it's over ten percent . . . (really, they're all from Zacatecas!) [12] . . .

As noted, the discourse claiming that "all Juárez' problems come from
the South" is pervasive, and it unfolds in several directions. We already
have some clues about those directions, considering Felipe's *coraje*
[anger] because he believes that Juárez' overpopulation, poverty, and
dirtiness are directly related to Southern immigration. On the other
hand, Alejandro's comments suggest that crime in Juárez is Southern.

The Southern Mexicans as Criminals

I encountered very similar statements in many interviews—for instance, in one I conducted with a middle-class Seventh Day Adventist
family in Juárez. The Figueroa family is composed of Héctor, the father,
a retired officer in a law enforcement agency in Juárez; Verónica, his
wife; and Nancy, their daughter, an undergraduate student at the Universidad Autónoma de Chihuahua. Verónica completed her primary education and Héctor underwent some secondary education without com-
pleting it. In that interview Héctor also expressed the belief that public
insecurity in Juárez began when people from the South started to come
to Juárez in the mid-1980s to ameliorate their economic situation after
the big peso devaluation of 1982:

Héctor: It was from 1980 on when one began to see problems. The police
lost control and the delinquency surpassed them. Since then . . . when
you're downtown, well you have to be cautious, right?
Pablo: What events did happen in the 1980s that led to all this?

Héctor: Well, mainly the peso devaluation that López Portillo provoked when Echeverría left office. It killed the peso and again, another fall. Then people from the interior of the country came here to Juárez to look for fortunes and one of their goals was to cross to the United States, to the country of opportunity. But they discovered that many of them couldn't cross, whereas before they could cross with some freedom, they could cross and set themselves up, because people really do go over there to work! But those who can't make it, well they stay here and break the law, right? And then crime rises over the established order.

Pablo: From what zones of the interior of Mexico do you think all those people come from, from what states?

Héctor: Well mainly, the most wiped out states were Zacatecas, Durango, Torreón, Chiapas, Michoacán, Mexico City . . .

Like Alejandro, Héctor blames Southerners for Juárez' crime. Héctor also faults Southerners for certain behavioral changes he notices that Juarenses have undergone to deal with the high incidence of crime in their city following the "tremendous" influx of immigrants from the South.

Nancy: Well, mainly the majority of vandalism here is just . . .

Verónica: . . . people from the South.

Nancy: . . . just people from the South . . .

Héctor: . . . people from Juárez are considered very hospitable. Before, if a person asked for a glass of water, we would welcome them inside the house. Not anymore. Now you lock the door, you give them the glass of water but you don't welcome them in. Right? . . . That's how things changed completely. That's how people from Juárez were, very hospitable, and they still are, but now with many reservations.

Even in those interviews where this kind of negative image was not so blatant, the anti-Southerner stance was still apparent. It occurred in an interview I conducted with militants from a leftist party in Juárez. These interviewees work for the party full-time, are in their forties, and define themselves as Catholics. Javier has completed three years of high school and Julián has a master's degree in education.

Javier: Here is a maquiladora advertising for male and female *operadoras y operadores* [operators] [13] . . . it's the greatest thing the United States has brought to Mexico. But I ask myself, what is going to happen the day all these maquiladoras leave, what is going to happen to the people of Ciudad Juárez? It has mainly been a gold mine for the people of the interior of the country: "Come to work here, there is lot of work in Ciudad Juárez." But this has happened before in other countries, when the factories leave, it creates a social problem that . . . is going to be a social problem one hundred times worse than what we are suffering right now.

Pablo: What kind of people do you think work at maquiladoras? Are they people from Juárez or from other places?

Javier: Well I think 40 percent are from Juárez and 60 percent are from somewhere else. In high-level jobs, like engineering, the majority are from Ciudad Juárez, in low-level labor jobs, the majority come from the interior of the country.

Pablo: From what states, for example?

Javier: From Zacatecas, Durango, Coahuila, and Chihuahua.

Javier — a leftist militant — is also using the hegemonic narrative theme asserting that "all poverty is Southern." In this case, he recognizes that some Juarenses work in maquiladoras (something many of our interviewees denied). But he thinks they do it in managerial positions, whereas Southerners occupy only blue-collar jobs.

As we can see, the narrative theme that "all poverty and social problems are Southerners'" is pervasive in Juárez, and it is deployed through categories, narratives, and metaphors that establish that overpopulation, dirtiness, crime, delinquency, laziness, and the like, are not characteristics of Juarenses but of Southerners. I could quote other interviewees expressing very similar arguments, but I prefer to move on to other discourses which, instead of focusing on Southerners in general, focus on a particular kind, the Chilango.

PHOTO 1

A maquiladora's ad asking for workers.

Chilangos as Arrogant, Rude, and Ill-Tempered

When talking about Southerners, many interviewees equate them with Chilangos. This particular usage — all Southerners as Chilangos — means that many Juarenses believe all Southerners are *"mala gente"* [bad people], and that is the reason some Juarenses discriminate against them. This was the case in our interviews with a group of maquila managers in Juárez. Lily, Salvador, and Carolina are in their early thirties, hold professional degrees in administration, and work for a U.S.-owned maquila in Juárez. All of them are Catholics and were born in Northern Chihuahua.

> **Lily:** . . . for Southern people, coming here to a completely different environment . . . [is different from] people from Parral [Chihuahua] . . . who are sort of used to, or . . . have the idea that they are in their own territory, which is Chihuahua. But the people who come from other parts of Mexico, no! . . . it is a bigger shock for them, in addition to the idea many people [in Juárez] have that: "I'm from the South" . . . and everybody says, "From Juárez down, everybody is a Chilango . . . !" Right? [laughs]. Then he has to deal with that also, with the fear of being rejected by the people here.

There is no well-established geographical point to separate Chilangos (as Southerners) from non-Chilangos. People living in different regions want to separate themselves from Chilangos, using their own region as a point of departure to establish that "from here on, all the rest are Chilangos." As one of the students we interviewed at UACJ stressed:[14]

> **Esteban:** For example, many people say: "If you are from Delicias, everybody from Delicias [and all areas] south is a Chilango!" . . . "If you are from Camargo, everybody from Camargo south is a Chilango!" . . . "If you are from the Chihuahua capital, everybody from Avalos south is a Chilango! . . ."

Consequently, it is not by chance that the South, Southerners, and specifically Chilangos, start south of the interviewee's point of elocution.

As with the anti-Southerner stance, the anti-Chilango posture also pervades Juárez. In one of the interviews, Verónica told me a story about her niece's encounter with a Chilango months after Mexico City's earthquake:

> **Verónica:** I remember a niece that ran into a . . . what do you call them? Chilangos, the ones from Mexico City . . . and the earthquake incident had just happened. My niece stopped next to a sidewalk that was tilted, and as she opened the door it slipped, right?. She hit . . . someone from Mexico

City, she hit him in the hand. He turned around, very angry and insulted her, very disrespectful, he insulted her. Then my niece locked the doors, rolled down the window and told him, "Chilango, Chilango, go back to your land, where everything shakes . . ." [laughs]

In this brief narrative Verónica brings out the main elements of many Juarenses' resentment of Chilangos. Chilangos are supposedly rude and ill-tempered, and they think the street (and Mexico, by the way . . .) is theirs. We have to assume that Verónica's niece identified the Chilango by his accent and as soon as she noticed it, she "understood" why a person could react so violently to such a minor incident. The theme "it had to be a Chilango!!" connects the two events of the story (to hit someone on his hand and to receive an insult for doing it) in a meaningful way. Verónica's niece's reaction also confirms that many Juarenses dislike Chilangos, because she literally is asking him to leave Juárez and return to Mexico City. By telling us this story and laughing about it, the Figueroa family confirms the niece's position, making it theirs. The family's anti-Chilango stance is confirmed in another joke they told us.

Nancy: Chilangos *traen campo santo* [Chilangos bring with them all their dead] [laughs]
Pablo: Why?
Nancy: Because everywhere they go, you have pure *desmadre* [absolute chaos] . . .

Nancy's joke refers to the claim that when Chilangos migrate to other parts of Mexico they not only do so to stay, but in the process also bring all their family and friends. The reference to the cemetery has two possible explanations. For one, it could refer to the fact that when Chilangos migrate, they bring their dead as well. On the other hand, the meaning of the joke could be that when someone in the Chilango family dies in Juárez, the visitors coming to express their condolences take advantage of the situation and move to Juárez for good. Regardless of which meaning is the preferred one, its aim is to address the profound sensation of invasion (and chaos) many Juarenses feel in relation to Chilangos' migration to Juárez.

In another interview, this time with lower-middle-class retired schoolteachers, Alejandra expressed her anti-Chilango sentiments.[15] The teachers were joking about my Argentine identity (which has a very stereotyped character all over Mexico, but most prominently in Central Mexico: "Do you know what ego is? The little Argentine everyone has inside." "What is the easiest way to make money? To buy an Argentine for what it costs and to sell him for what he believes it costs").

> **Alejandra:** A friend says to the other, "I have a recipe for making a Chilango . . . but don't go over a milligram, because instead of a Chilango you'll get an Argentine" [laughs] . . . 100 grams of I don't know what . . . 100 grams of arrogance, but don't put too much of anything because instead of a Chilango, you'll get an Argentine . . .

Hence, a Chilango is a baser version of all the bad things that supposedly characterize Argentines, above all arrogance.

Besides arrogance, rudeness, and bad temper, many Juarenses' perception of Chilangos also includes the idea that Chilangos want to take advantage of everyone. This idea appeared prominently in an interview I conducted with a group of dental students in Juárez. In this interview, even the presence of Chilangos among the interviewees did not stop the other participants from expressing their negative opinions about them.[16]

> **Tomás:** This photograph caught my attention because of those three guys that you see here, they look like thugs, just there, waiting for the opportunity to hold up someone.
> **Rafa:** They are *gabachotes*.
> **Chela:** This is the typical useless kind, isn't it?
> **Rafa:** No, I see these guys more like the typical leeches, the kind who impregnate their wives, have three kids, their wives then say that their husband left them, they go and ask for money . . . whatever they send

PHOTO 2

A couple of men resting on a bench in El Paso's central plaza.

them while the leeches are there doing nothing and they receive money and live off of it, which is why they don't buy food, they don't pay rent, and I just don't know how they do it. Well, I guess a leech is the same as someone who is useless, right?, but these are the typical leeches . . . the typical, I don't know, . . . I was going to say Chilangos, but they don't have a Chilango face . . .

Lola: . . . ¡órale! [that's it, you did it!]

Chela: . . . thank you, friend!

Rafa: No, you gals are not Chilangas! You are now *fronteñas* [from the border]!

Lola: . . . yes, *fronteñas*, because Northerners, I don't think so . . .

We can see in this exchange about a photograph depicting two Anglos sitting on a bench the deployment of some of the most pervasive negative images regarding Chilangos: leeches, useless people, and the like. What is also interesting in this dialogue is Rafa's attempt to compound his aggressive joke, claiming that Chela and Lola (who were born and raised in Mexico City, but who have lived on the border for the past five years) are not Chilangas anymore, but Fronterizas, with all the positive connotations this label carries for a native Fronterizo like Rafa.[17]

As I mentioned, this anti-Chilango stance does not recognize class boundaries. Thus, it was also present in a set of interviews I conducted with a group of *cholos*[18] in a poor colonia on the west side of Juárez. All are teenagers and work in different maquiladoras. Some were born in Juárez; others came with their parents from different Northern states. All of them have completed their elementary education, but have not undergone any high school education. As some of them joked:

Chema: If you love Juaritos, kill someone from Mexico City . . .

Tito: . . . or the ones who live close by, the ones who live in Jalisco as well . . . those who think they are Jorge Negrete . . .

Here the interviewees are referring to Chilangos (and their neighbors living in Central Mexico)[19] as the "others" from whom they want to differentiate themselves in order to construct a Juarense identity. Chema's comment about being a patriot killing a Chilango refers to a very successful anti-Chilango campaign that appeared in Northern Mexico in the mid-1980s. Due to the 1985 earthquake and the government decentralization projects, many people from Mexico City moved from there to other parts of Mexico. Because Chilangos, as we already saw, are not very popular in Northern Mexico (or elsewhere in Mexico either, for that matter), many people in Juárez and other cities felt "invaded" by these unwelcome immigrants. An anti-Chilango stance appeared in the city, expressed by various attitudes and behaviors, and it was very common to see bumper stickers with the slogan: "If you are a patriot, kill a Chilango." Further, Tito's reference to Jorge Negrete is significant because this actor and singer for many years portrayed the role of the "*charro*," the Guadalajara rancher who somehow became the epitome of Mexican culture (and, at least for our Fronterizo interviewees, of centralism too). Therefore, Chema and Tito are constructing their Fronterizo identities by overlapping different aspects of their social identities. First, they organize their statements using the regional system of classification. Second, they stress a class issue by referring to Jorge Negrete as a representative of powerful Mexican *hacendados* who have the money and power they do not. And finally, by implication, they address their limited citizenship relative to that of Chilangos, who appear to enjoy a broader citizenship due to their use of Mexican centralism to their own advantage.[20]

The anti-Chilango stance is still prevalent among some Juarenses who have recently moved to El Paso. Humberto and Marta are among a group of recent Mexican immigrants living in a lower-middle-class neighborhood of El Paso. They migrated to El Paso from Juárez less than six years ago (Humberto was born in Sonora and Marta in Juárez), at first living in a public housing project. Both are in their early fifties and work as unskilled clerks in El Paso. They have some high school education. Talking about the betterment of their lives after moving to El Paso, these interviewees deploy a full-blown discourse which stresses that "all Juárez' problems are related to people coming from the South," and that also particularizes the Chilangos as the "others" from whom they want to separate themselves in order to construct a valued identity (in this case, one of Fronterizo migrants living in the United States).

> **Humberto:** We, people from the North, are more . . .
> **Marta:** . . . open.
> **Humberto:** The people from the South are *hypocrites*. They are very deceptive, the infamous *Chilangos*, they are very deceptive.
> **Marta:** They are full of themselves.
> **Humberto:** And to them, all that matters is *Mexico City*, outside of Mexico City there is nothing else, everything is useless . . . just them.

According to these interviewees, Chilangos are not only hypocritical, pretentious, and conceited, but are also ethnocentric, claiming that the only thing of value in the Mexican Republic is their city, Mexico City; everything else is worthless. No wonder many Juarenses have such a negative opinion of Chilangos. As with the anti-Southerner stance, I could mention many more anti-Chilango testimonies. Instead I want to end this chapter by describing various processes of negotiation that some of my interviewees enter into to delineate their identities in a city that, after all, is already inhabited by many people coming from the hated South.

Negotiating Meaning between Juarenses and Southern Mexicans

First, when people move from the interior of Chihuahua to Juárez, many of them undergo a process of identity change. In those cases, the move engenders a step-by-step change from a Northerner identity to a Fronterizo one. To illustrate this point, I will rely on the interview I conducted with the UACJ students mentioned above. During that session, I got some details about the process of abandoning a particular regional identity and acquiring a new one. Some of these students had come to Juárez from other cities in the state of Chihuahua only a few years before (Esteban was from Ciudad Chihuahua, Josefina and Ernestina from Camargo and Lisette, and Juan from Delicias. The other students were native Juarenses). They seemed to be in the process of abandoning their Norteño identity to fully acquire a Fronterizo one. Others seemed to be trading their Fronterizo identity for a Mexican one due to their interaction with people from around the world.

On the one hand, the move from a Norteño to a Fronterizo identity was happening even though the migrants had been discriminated against by Juarenses for coming from Chihuahua:

> **Pablo:** Since you came from Chihuahua, how have you felt about the quarrels between Juárez and Chihuahua?[21]
> **José:** They [Chihuahuenses] are full of themselves [laughs], they think they are superior to everyone.
> **Esteban:** Yes, it's true. When I arrived in Ciudad Juárez from Chihuahua, everyone was very unfriendly, but I did not know why.
> **Juan:** They were unfriendly?
> **Lisette:** We're unfriendly! [laughs]

Part of this process of changing identities seems to require, on the one hand, rejecting the criticisms people in Chihuahua make about Juárez. This rejection is also a rejection of their own "old" identity as Chihuahuenses, a "time–region" point from which they participated in those criticisms. On the other hand, changing from a Norteño to a Juarense or Fronterizo identity also requires valuing those characteristics that supposedly distinguish Juarenses from people elsewhere in Mexico: cosmopolitanism, liberalism, openness, and the like.

Esteban: A friend of mine once observed: "If you see people driving *muy estirada y con un dedo en la boca* [in a very snobby and arrogant way and they greet you like this . . .], they are from Ciudad Chihuahua, people here are more spontaneous, more open minded" . . . Yes, look, the mentalities of both are very different: the people of Chihuahua are more closed-minded, and way too traditional.

Josefina: It is a *rancho grande* [big town with the mentality of the country-side]. They close up shops during lunch, just like they do in a small town.

But, what is the axis of this identity change? As one of our interviewees put it:

Rosalía: Many of my friends have lived here all their lives and they feel they are from here, they are Northerners and everything, but they really are not from here, they were not born here. And suddenly, there is more allegiance in saying: "I'm from the North," right? . . . They came from the South but now they are from the North . . .

Pablo: When do people begin saying, "I am from the border," more than, "I am from the North?"

Rosalía: Well, maybe when they see everything as normal and when they can say more comfortably: "I am close to the United States," instead of saying, "I am far from Mexico City" or "far from those in the South." And now, especially, because of the situation you live in daily, always dividing your life between Juárez and El Paso, because part of your day is spent over there . . .

Thus, an entire shift of focus seems to be required to change a Norteño identity for a Fronterizo one. In such a change, the remoteness from Central and Southern Mexico suddenly becomes less important than closeness to the United States and daily interaction between cities in two different countries. Thus Norteño refers to an identity whose cleavage is the northern part of Mexico, while Fronterizo refers to an identity whose support seems to be the border with the United States. In this sense, the Norteño identity defines itself through its relationship with Southerners and with the, for many people, hated Chilangos of Mexico City, without mentioning, necessarily, its relationship with the United States and its inhabitants. If identity is basically a relationship, in the case of Fronterizo identity (an identity that is also constructed in relation to another country), the relationship is established twofold: vis à vis Central and Southern Mexico, and in relation to the United States, which is the subject of the next chapter.

In the very complicated identity construction process that some Juárez immigrants undergo, one possible route is the one taken by Esteban and Rosalía: that is, to trade their previous identities as Norteños or Chihuahuenses for a new one as Juarenses or Fronterizos. Another route is to stick to their own regional identity, and struggle to prove that Juarenses' stereotypes are wrong. Obviously, it seems easier for Norteños to take the first route than for Southerners to do so. After all, Northerners are closer to Juarenses (and farther from Chilangos) than are Southerners. Nevertheless, at least in theory, both possibilities are open to both groups, and different interviewees took different stances on the issue. What was common for all of them, however, was that the interviewees entered into a very intense process of identity negotiation with the native Juarenses they shared the interview with. In the trade union interviews, the participants were from different regional backgrounds: Aurora had come from Veracruz four years before; Secundino was from San Luís Potosí; Felipe and Jesús were native Juarenses. In those interviews, we could see how a process of "negotiation" took place between Juarenses and Southerners, a negotiation that, even so, never abandoned the regional system of classification that seems to be at the core of identity construction on the Mexican side of the border.

Accordingly, in the first interview the issue of many Juarenses' rejection of people from the South came up immediately, when Aurora said: "I don't know, here they treat those from over there [Veracruz] very badly . . . they always say to us: 'No, well, you're from Veracruz? Go back there! . . . What are you doing here?'" Not surprisingly, the native Juarenses tried to diminish the problem: few people overtly accept that they discriminate against other people. It is one thing to be in an interview where everybody is a native Juarense, but another thing to interact with the "other" in a common setting. Consequently, the first strategy some of our Fronterizo interviewees used was to try to "explain" the origin of that rejection, pointing out the fear many Juarenses feel about losing their jobs due to the constant flow of migrants from the South. As Jesús stressed: "Many people from here think that those people who come in are going to leave them without jobs." A second strategy was to deny that the *native* Juarenses were the most important detractors of the people from the South, displacing the blame onto people from other Mexican states!

Felipe: She said that the ones from here in Juárez do not like those from the South, but I don't think it is the ones from Juárez. For example in the maquila, there we all work together and there you can see there is a rejection of the "Jarochos" [people from Veracruz] . . . because they have been bad. But it's not the ones from Juárez, it is only the ones from the maquila, the majority of them are from Durango, from Torreón and from Zacatecas! So there, they are not Juarenses! The ones from Zacatecas don't like the ones from Veracruz! The ones from Durango who live in Juárez are the ones who don't like those from Veracruz! I, being from Juárez, accept them! I think if there was a survey done on who did not accept Veracruz people, I think that the majority of those who are not from Juárez, are the ones who don't accept them.

Hence, Felipe denies that native Juarenses are "anti-Veracruz," and in order to explain a conflict at the factory between Jarochos and other workers, he displaces the blame from Juarenses to people from other Mexican states, without any change to the regional system of social classification to make sense of workers' behavior at the maquila where he works. Felipe also addresses another well-entrenched narrative theme among Juarenses—"Juarenses do not work at maquiladoras, only immigrants do"—when he talks about the struggle at the factory and identifies the "anti-Veracruz" people: "But it's not the ones from Juárez, only the ones from the maquila . . ."

As the discussion developed, Aurora felt uncomfortable with the bad worker image that Felipe used to depict Veracruzanos. She thus tried to justify why Jarochos had problems with the other workers at the factory:

Aurora: I once knew a personnel supervisor, and through talking, we concluded that what happens is that the Veracruzano is used to hard work while being poorly paid, and when he comes over here and sees the work is well paid and easy, well what does he do?
Angela: Is maquila work easy for you?
Aurora: Yes, in comparison to how it is done over there and the type of schedule kept, yes, it is easy. What we do then . . . we stay overtime. "Do this," they tell us, and we work overtime because we see it as easy work. Really! Look at it this way: here, the majority of the supervisors like the Veracruzanos because they are good workers . . . which then bothers the people from here, because they will tell us, do this and . . . well, we do it quickly. Then people from over here tell us: "You people come over here . . . and take away our jobs."

Aurora's account illustrates the overlap between a regional identity and a work identity that also includes an implicit moral stance. According to Aurora, people from Veracruz are harder workers than people from Juárez, because they are used to worse conditions and they consider maquila work very easy. Compared with the work they have left behind, maquila labor seems very light. Therefore, Aurora tries to explain the rejection some Veracruzanos find in Juárez by stressing the different work attitude she notices between Juarenses and Veracruzanos. Thus she is making the same argument that some Juarenses use to differentiate themselves from "people from the South," but in the opposite direction — praising Southerners for their work ethic and blaming Juarenses for being *flojos*. Thus, the different regional identities here are embodied in different "workers' identities," which also touches on a particular way of understanding morals and values. This example again shows us how the construction of the regional "other" takes place in a constant overlapping with other aspects of identity: oneself as a worker, as a parent, as a husband, as a moral and faithful person, and so on. Those overlapping aspects of identity will be addressed in my forthcoming book, *Border Identities*.

Of course Felipe, the native Juarense, did not like the way Aurora described Juarenses' work attitude, so he argued that the "lazy workers" Aurora was referring to were not Juarenses, but people from other Mexican states. In this way he also combines regional identity with work and moral attitudes: "But we would also have to define: who is a Juarense? Right? . . . But what also happens, for example in Durango, what I have noticed about them is that they're quite lazy."

As we can see, when Juarenses and Southerners meet at the same interviews and engage in a process of identity negotiation, the regional system of classification does not disappear. On the contrary, it seems to reinforce itself, and some of the interviewees displace blame from the people at the table (and from their respective states) to Mexicans who were born in other states! Of course this discourse, while widespread, is not monolithic, and some other interviewees (very few, as a matter of fact) called for a rejection of the regional system of classification, arguing that the state one was born in does not account for the differences among people:

Secundino: I would like to summarize, right? . . . To conclude with the extensive commentaries, right? And accept, right? . . . That in every state of Mexico . . . there are all kinds of people: good, bad, hardworking, lazy . . .

Regrettably, Secundino's voice was only a marginal one at those interviews. The other participants paid little attention to his ideas.

The main point here is how important the regional system of classification is in the process of identity construction of many of Juárez' residents. Region works in Juárez to anchor different social identities (in terms of gender, class, race, ethnicity, religion, etc.) in terms of the supposedly invariant characteristics a particular part of the country inscribes in its inhabitants. In this sense, a geographical determinism is as deterministic as a racial one, but the origin of the "inevitable" is anchored in space instead of in biology, and time does not seem to modify what space supposedly determines. Of course this geographical logic is complexly related to other possible identities, above all racial ones, as the overlapping between Southern Mexicans and "Indians" demonstrates. But racial and/or ethnic identities are not the only identities that intricately mix with region on the Mexican side of the border, because national identities, religious, class, and gender ones are mixed, in complex ways, with region as well.

The American as the "other"

Introduction

Many people living in Juárez distinguish themselves not only from other Mexican nationals, but also from those living on the other side of the border. It is here where national references start playing an important role in the construction of Mexican border narrative identities. In this sense, the Chihuahuenses' joke about the best part of Juárez being El Paso hurts a great deal, because an important part of the Fronterizo identity is built upon that relationship. Of course, although the Fronterizo identity is built upon the relationship with the United States, this is not accomplished without contradictions. If many Fronterizos construct their identities *in relation to other Mexicans* using the United States as a point of reference, we are going to see in this chapter that they define their profile *in relation to the Americans* drawing heavily on their Mexicanness.

As we saw in Chapter 1, some of our interviewees acknowledged (and enjoyed) influences from the United States. Those influences range from moral values ("we are more liberal than the people from the South because of the American influence") to attitudes about work ("we are more work oriented because of the American influence") to religious practices (*el día de la coneja* [Easter bunny], Halloween, etc.) to food and dress. All these influences play a very important role in the construction of a Fronterizo identity that differentiates Juarenses from the other social actors on the border. But these influences do not mean that Fronterizos *are* Americans. Here is where national identity displaces regional identities in the process of identity construction, and where the American appears as the "other."

Therefore, some of our Juárez interviewees, when contrasting themselves with Americans, emphasized attitudes and behaviors they share with all Mexicans, regardless of state and region. The implication was that, compared to the Americans, non-Fronterizo Mexican nationals still have some "good" characteristics, even though in other contexts they are the lowly *"gente del sur."* Those attitudes and behaviors that supposedly separate Mexicans from Americans in toto are intertwined in the way gender, regional origin, religion, age, class, and ethnicity overlap with national ways of classifying human actions.

Chapter 2

THE MEXICAN SIDE
DISCOURSES OF NATION

In many of my interviews a topic that appeared prominently with very negative implications was the sense of superiority some Americans display in relation to Mexicans. According to some interviewees, that sense of superiority is one of the most important reasons Mexicans dislike Americans:

> **Agustín:** I see in this photo rebellion and vandalism. Even though you're from here, and you don't have any intentions to go there as a "wetback" or to earn dollars, but you only have to be casually there and to see that there is a fence . . . damn gringos and down you go! [he refers to the continuous acts of vandalism against the metallic fence that separates both countries in many places of the U.S.–Mexico border] [laughs]
> **Rafa:** It's not that, we have also seen how they treat us, damn it! And no, no no and no. But what do these assholes think! These assholes depend on us as much as we do on them! And you can see how they treat us! Bad, damn it!! They think they're gods . . . !

Some interviewees believe that such a sense of superiority is related to the negative image Americans have regarding Mexicans. Here is where the important narrative plot that establishes that "all poverty is Mexican" appears.

How Some Juarenses Think Americans See Them

I pointed out in Chapter 1 that in the case of references to Mexican nationals, the construction of a Juarense or Fronterizo identity took into account "how I think other Mexicans see me" (where the negative image of Juárez was widely acknowledged by our interviewees). But in the case of references to Americans, some of our Juárez interviewees also took into account the way they think Americans see them (a very negative image also). As Ernesto, one of the students in the vocational school mentioned in Chapter 1, pointed out:

> **Ernesto:** And the pure American who has never traveled outside the U.S. . . . . They still believe they can see a Mexican dressed in cotton cloth, with a *sombrero* and a bottle of tequila in his hand! I was told by a friend, that an acquaintance of his who came for vacation (never, never had he gone out of the United States, a pure American, right?), and they visited what was Mexico from north to south, right? They came back, and he was disappointed! Why? He said because he didn't find anything! The Mexican has more progress now!! He hadn't found the Mexican dressed in cotton

cloth with the big *sombrero de charro* and a bottle of tequila and *guaraches* [Indian sandals] with three holes!

In this short narrative Ernesto is not only referring to the negative image he knows many Americans have about Mexicans — drunken peasants wearing Indian sandals — but he is also implicitly denying that such a negative image applies to Juarenses. Consequently Ernesto is mixing two prominent plots of the border, one that stresses that "all poverty in Juárez is Southern," and another asserting that "all poverty is Mexican." This is because the negative image Ernesto is telling us Americans have about Mexico corresponds to the commonsense description (widespread in movies, television, and jokes all around the United States) of a Mexican from Central or Southern Mexico, not one from the North. Thus, the "*sombrero de charro*" reference is playing the same role here as the allusion to Jorge Negrete played in the previous chapter, that is, to depict a Central or Southern Mexican, not a Fronterizo.

It is important to point out here that at least in Juárez the idea of "how Americans see Mexicans" is not a metaphorical idea, because one of the distinctive features of the U.S.–Mexico border is that Americans can physically *see* Mexico. It was not by chance that in some interviews the "bad" image of Mexico Juarenses acknowledged was related to the way Juárez is physically seen from El Paso.

Alejandro: What kind of image of Mexico do we give people when one comes from California and the first thing they see is those streets [he shows photo 3, shown below] [laughs], those houses and one says: "That's Juárez, we've arrived." So we give that image of Fronterizos, of people who don't advance. They come annually, pass by there and say the same thing: "They don't advance, they don't advance at all." But we give a wrong image of the city. And we have the opportunity to give a good image here, but we don't, and that's strange, because Interstate 10 from California to El Paso is the only place from where Mexico can be better seen, where one can better visualize what the city is like, too bad it's the worst kept part of the city.

The issue of the "image of Juárez for Americans" (which in the deepest sense is the "image of Mexicans for Americans") seems to be so important that it has been addressed by the Mexican government. In April 1993 I attended a conference on environmental issues on the border sponsored by the Chihuahua government in Ciudad Juárez. At the conference one of the projects presented was the urban renewal of Puerto

Anapra (the poor neighborhood travelers see from the highway mentioned by Alejandro). Puerto Anapra was the only poor colonia (of the many Juárez has) that was going to be renewed, and the justification for that project, which included model houses, trees, paved streets, and the like, was not to improve the life of its residents, but to present a better image of the city to those who travel on Interstate 10. My joke that day was that a Hollywood set all along the highway would cost less money and would give a better image of the city.

The "image the others have about me" is a crucial element in the construction of identities. What many interviewees were claiming when they referred to this topic was that Americans have a distorted image of Mexicans because they equate Mexico with Puerto Anapra, and this equation is not fair, because it is to equate the poor inhabitants of that colonia with Mexicans in general, or still worse, to confuse Fronterizos with Central Americans or Southern Mexicans. This was what happened in our interview with the Oliva family. Don Librado is sixty-one years old. He was born in Guerrero but has been living in Juárez since he was fifteen years old, and is retired from a government position. He defines himself as "Christian" and has completed high school. Teresita, his wife, is a fifty-three-year-old native Juarense who works at home; like her husband, she has completed her secondary education. Talking about the picture of Puerto Anapra, they commented:

Teresita: This photo shows the division of both *pueblos* [meaning here "towns," but also "people"].

PHOTO 3

A panoramic view of Puerto Anapra, Mexico, taken from I-10.

Librado: This is the division of both *pueblos*. This photo was taken with a lot of malice.

Pablo: Why?

Librado: Yes, they put the ugliness on this side [toward the Mexican side] [laughs]. First of all, professor, human settlements in that area have not been controlled by anybody. Look at how Ciudad Juárez has been settled, professor: this is the train,[1] the train has fifty wagons; as you go into the black bridge,[2] the brakeman begins—hey, let's go! . . . So then, these men who come here, some jump over here, and some jump over there. The ones who jump over here enlist in the CDP [Comité de Defensa Popular], professor. There, they are taken in by Matus and his people.[3] The ones who jump over there come and see what they can rob and see if they can jump to the other side [the United States]. Unfortunately, that's the influx of people we have.

Pablo: And where are these people coming from?

Librado: They may come from El Salvador, from Nicaragua, Guatemala, Costa Rica (no, no, there are very few *ticos* in poverty, there aren't many Panamanians and Costa Ricans) . . . So, then, professor, these people also come from Durango, Guanajuato, parts of Jalisco. Jalisco is one of the states that supplies more *braceros* [field-workers], they are more active. And these go to the U.S. with phony passports and with cars. They live all over the state of California, those from Jalisco; but Durango, la Laguna, that area from Torreón. Ay, professor! That's how this town is, it's plenty of . . . people from Central America and Southern Mexico!

Don Librado and Teresita claim that the inhabitants of the poor colonia that so badly depicts Juárez are not people like themselves, Fronterizos, but people from Central America and Southern Mexico who come to Juárez to join the ranks of the leftist political parties that take advantage of their poverty to advance their agendas (the CDP in this testimony and many others in the same vein). Or, still worse, Puerto Anapra inhabitants are Central Americans and Southern Mexicans who come directly to the border to commit their delinquent acts against Juarenses. In order to stress the force of their argument and to show how different they believe they are in relation to those people coming from Central America and Southern Mexico, Librado and Teresita advance a phenotypical description of those immigrants:

Teresita: Also the Guatemalan and the Mexican, and the Salvadoran . . . they're very similar.

Librado: They have the same accent . . .

Teresita: It's a matter of knowing them well that you can tell the difference, because the Indians from Chiapas talk very similar to the Guatemalan.

Librado: Look at their profiles, professor, look at their profiles, they're Mayan! It's undeniable, and they're Mayan from Chiapas to Peru; if you observe them, they have the same features.

As we can see, much of the identity construction discussed in the previous chapter, that is, how some Juarenses construct Southerners as the stigmatized other, is directed not only toward other Mexicans, but also toward Americans, showing that Juarenses are "another kind of Mexican," suggesting, in Ernesto's, Librado's, and Teresita's way, that the negative image of Mexicans many Americans have applies to those "from the South," but not to themselves.

American Consumerism as a Characteristic of the "others"

In the process of constructing the Americans as the "others," many of our interviewees were also very critical of American consumerism and work attitudes. Such comments appeared in categorical discussions, metaphors, and narratives used by my interviewees, and emerged in most of our interviews, regardless of class, age, gender, or time of migration, as in the interview with the Universidad Autónoma de Ciudad Juárez students:

Josefina: My sister is studying in Los Angeles, and it's been two years and she hasn't come back. So then my mother calls her on the phone and says, "Aay, you don't want to come back, everybody tells me that you're there to stay permanently." So then my sister says, "No, Mom, how do you think I'm going to like staying here! If you could only see what it's like to be here; people really think this is heaven, but it's not. Here, nobody knows each other, nobody talks to me, here you are nobody, here you are one in a million, here you don't do anything, you only work and work." Look, my sister is in Los Angeles, and she has to work very hard if she wants to do something! And here, well, with little things, and working for three, four days, and you still enjoy the money, and oh, it's great! And over there you don't, if you want something you have to work every day, every day! Or go to school, and there's nothing else you can do.

In this short story about a conversation between her mother and her sister, Josefina is advancing a narrative theme that was very prominent in most of our interviews: "Americans are slaves of consumerism and their work attitudes." Thus, most of our Juárez interviewees believe that in the United States people work without any possibility of resting to enjoy the product of their work. On the contrary, some people in Mexico claim to be smarter in their balancing of leisure and work, allowing themselves free time to enjoy what they have acquired through work. To Josefina the five-day work week is what she considered as working "too much." Instead she proposed the "Mexican way" ("And here, well, with little things, and working for three, four days, and you still enjoy the money, and oh, it's great!") as the "proper" way to enjoy life.

Very similar kinds of comments appeared prominently in the interviews we conducted with Robustiano and Margarita, as well as in the interviews we had with Ana, Leonor, and Isabel. These women live quite precariously in a newly formed colonia without running water and sewage. They are "invaders" who have no legal title to their lands and always live with the fear of being evicted. Leonor is forty years old, and Ana is twenty years old. The former moved to Juárez from Coahuila three years ago, and the latter from Madera, Chihuahua, fourteen years ago. Leonor completed two years of high school and Ana has only completed elementary school. Isabel is a forty-year-old housewife who has some high school education; she was born in Zacatecas and has been in Juárez since 1973.

Ana: Over here in Juárez, I think it's better. There are more opportunities over there [in El Paso] and more ways of earning money, but I think it's so awful . . .
Isabel: Over there you work a lot . . .
Ana: Yes, and then you have what you have and you're always *endrogado* [in debt].
Isabel: Yes, all your life.

Robustiano: In the United States you *do* work, I mean, there's no time to rest or any of that, I mean all the people there are *endrogada*. So, then if they don't work one day, they are ruined, because life is very hard in the U.S., and here in Mexico, well, we are satisfied with beans and tortillas, and that's it, right? And here we get into debt according to how much we make so that we don't come off badly, and over there you don't, with the tale of luxury, and the easiness of getting debts, people are inclined to become *endrogados*.

These testimonies reveal what seems to be a particular vision of the "good life" among some Juárez low-income people. To have a certain amount of free time is vital for this version of "Mexican" lifestyle. These interviewees stressed that Americans work harder ("In the United States you *do* work") than Mexicans because they are more consumerist ("with the tale of luxury"). But, in order to have access to this higher level of consumption, Americans incur debts, usually beyond their real potential for repayment ("all the people there are *endrogada*"). Many Juarenses, on the contrary, would avoid going into debt. Robustiano gives two reasons for this. First, they resign themselves to lower levels of consumption ("here in Mexico, well, we are satisfied with beans and tortillas, and that's it, right?"), and second, Mexicans would have more *"vergüenza"* (pride, in this context) than Americans, and as a result try to avoid the shame of not being able to repay a debt ("to not come off badly"). In this kind of narrative, Americans are slaves to consumerism ("their debts make them work, and work, and work") who work constantly, senselessly, without leaving any free time to enjoy the products of their labor:

> **Robustiano:** There was a guy I met there in El Paso, and I said to him, "OK, so why do you work even on Sundays?" He said, "Because I'm very much *endrogado*," and I asked him, "How much do you owe?" And he said, "Fifty-eight thousand dollars." And I was almost off for the weekend, and the guy was only twenty-two years old and even had to work on Sundays, he didn't have any days off . . . but he surely lived in a lot of luxury [jokingly] . . .

These testimonies, like many others in the same vein, express the high value these interviewees place on retaining control of their destiny. And this is something that, they believe, Americans have lost due to their predisposition to consume beyond their means. This vision of Americans is nicely captured by the word *"endrogarse,"* a term that is extensively used in Central and Western Mexico (Michoacán, Jalisco, Guanajuato, Querétaro, etc.), but that on the border is particularly well suited to describe the "American way of life." The expression *"endrogarse"* astutely combines *"drogas"* [drugs] with *"deudas"* [debts] to draw an implicit parallel between *debts* and *drugs*,[4] where the entire weight of meaning of the word "drug" (illegal drugs on the border) critically modifies the meaning of the word "debt." A "drug/debt" is something that provides a brief moment of euphoria at the expense of a later, disproportionate cost, thus transforming the "debtor/addict" into a sort of "debt/drug" slave. The repeated use of this word to refer to the American way of life is a powerful criticism of American culture as a whole. In this phrase, American culture is implicitly condemned as one without real roots, one which prefers immediate pleasures to those that are more profound if less intense, and one that uses whatever means necessary to achieve immediate gratification. As Robustiano put it: "Over there in the United States you suffer a lot, you think that you will enjoy it and all that, no, there's nothing like being in your own home." Therefore, the word "*endrogarse*" on the border acquires its full meaning within a narrative plot asserting that "Americans are slaves of consumerism and their work attitudes."

But the consumer attitude promoted by American culture, something these interviewees try to avoid by all means, also has other bleak ramifications; for instance, it negatively influences the well-being of children. This point was prominently made in an interview we conducted in a working-class neighborhood with a group of housewives. These women are in their thirties and forties; all of them were born in Northern Mexico (Edelmira and Nivia in Juárez, Adela and Concepción in Delicias, Chihuahua) and work at home taking care of their children. Adela is illiterate, Edelmira and Nivia have completed only their elementary education, and Concepción has had some secondary education. These interviewees (like Margarita, Robustiano, Ana, and Isabel) would not want to be in the shoes of some of their family members who have moved to El Paso and have already succumbed to the American consumer attitude.

> **Edelmira:** I'm much better off here in my humble home than my sister-in-law in El Paso. Look, my husband works as a waiter and he doesn't have a salary, only tips, and my brother (the one who lives in El Paso) has a job. He makes $250 a week and he has all kinds of *drogas* [debts] . . . and they don't know how to pay the rent, they don't know how to pay this, how to pay that. And I, on the other hand, struggling, but I *come out ahead*. The credit collector is not after me *pestering and harassing*.

They do not want to be in their family members' shoes because they value greatly being with their children to supervise their education and growing up, something that, according to them, their family members who have moved to El Paso and are already *endrogados* cannot do anymore because, to keep pace with their debts, both members of the family have to work.

> **Edelmira:** And over there children are ruined faster because both parents work and they're never home. Even if the kids are in first grade, they're alone, all alone and they have no one to look after them.
> **Pablo:** And do you think that in the U.S. there are more couples whose two members work than here in Mexico?

Edelmira: I think there are more over there; usually they're forced to . . . both parents are forced to work over there!

For these interviewees the increased female participation in the job market that characterizes American culture is not seen as women's advancement, but as a negative by-product of one of the worst characteristics of that culture: its wild consumerism.

As noted, the criticism toward the American "endrogado" attitude does not recognize class boundaries; we found a very similar criticism in our interviews with middle-class groups. As one of the UACJ students put it:

Juan: It is easier for them to acquire things, even when they're *embargados* [indebted to the point of asset seizure] for the rest of their lives! That culture of consumerism is going to continue devouring them. And they are tempted to become part of that culture to acquire goods (that many times are unnecessary), but with the condition of having that dream of luxury, that American dream of having everything without any cost. Well, without any cost in parentheses!

We have here again the "endrogado" criticism cited previously, with the difference that these highly educated students think the word "endrogado" lacks "status," and they replaced it by the more "prestigious" word *"embargado."* Regardless of the use of another word, the discourse is the same: the consumer culture devours Americans because they become slaves to their seemingly endless desire for consumables—consumables which most of the time are unnecessary, and supposedly acquired without any cost, but that finally cost a lot because of the weight of the debt incurred. Thus, according to Ana, Isabel, and Leonor:

Ana: I think the ideal for me is to work over there and live here. To invest what you make over there, here.
Leonor: Well, it's that here there are two options. Here there are some people who already live like that, and here there are other people who don't. For example, look at the ones who have their houses with gas hook-ups, telephone, everything, if you have it, you have to pay for it. And, for instance, like we're here, well, here we don't have water, we don't have electricity, we don't pay for anything. But if we were in a colonia over there, one that has gas hook-ups, that has telephone lines, that has . . .
Isabel: We would already be paying for it, and . . . we would be the same as over there, the same and only working to pay for those things.

Here, these interviewees want the best of both worlds. On the one hand, they like the Mexican way of life; on the other, they prefer the American income. But when it comes to the moment of decision, these interviewees seem to claim they would live without basic utilities—water, electricity, gas, telephone—rather than taking on the debts required to enjoy them. Hence, our interviewees' comments are directed not only at the Americans, but also at the "Americanized" Mexicans who live on the southern side of the border. It is precisely in relation to both sets of actors that our interviewees want to differentiate themselves, constructing a particular identity of Mexicans living on the border.

> **Robustiano:** And you work and work, and the money doesn't buy you anything. Over there everybody pays rent, and the telephone bill, and the gas bill and here it's not like that. Here, you get used to the little bit that you have, but over there you're required to have all that. If you rent an apartment, they rent it to you with everything included, and then you're obligated to pay for all those utilities; why? because they're already hooked up. That's why, in the United States, there's a lot of slavery.

In the experience of these interviewees, in the United States there are more constraints on people's ability to make autonomous choices about their lifestyles. In Juárez people can live without gas, telephones, and the like, if they prefer to do so in order to maintain control over their lives. It is impossible to do this in the United States, where a "standard" level of comfort is socially imposed. These interviewees see the consumer pressure as so strong that it forces a very high minimum standard of living in the United States. It makes people living there see as natural and absolutely necessary things that, viewed from the Mexican perspective, are nonessentials. Due to the income level of a great portion of the Mexican Americans living in El Paso, this standard level of comfort is in fact difficult to reach without becoming indebted. Accordingly, the decision to live in the United States is seen as the decision to lose a certain amount of control over one's destiny, a control that these speakers value highly, and whose lack is expressed in Robustiano's words as "enslavement."

Of course, the materialistic and racist attitudes of some Americans are not the only things many Juarenses dislike. Another feature some interviewees used to establish their distance from the Americans was their character. This difference was usually summarized by the metaphoric use of the terms *"fríos"* [cold] or *"secos"* [dry].

> **Jesús:** For example, what you're saying . . . that the people are very dry over there, in December of last year, I spent a week's vacation in Los Angeles, with some uncles, and I noticed that in Los Angeles . . . It looked like living [there] was very fast-paced. Because as you can see here now, at this time there are a lot of people on the street, but not over there, only the people who come out of work and go home . . .
>
> **Felipe:** And they're very cold . . .

If Americans are depicted as cold and dry, Mexicans are implicitly understood as warm (or hot in some cases) and wet. Here the metaphor refers to the way people interact with each other, the place of leisure in everyday life, and the collective or private character of that leisure. Using this kind of metaphor, Juarenses depict themselves as being people-oriented, party lovers and more public in their lives than Americans. A concept that is intimately related to this kind of behavior is expressed by the word "*convivio*," whose roots are from the verb "*convivir*," which means to live together, but also to live together on very good terms. As we are going to see in the next section about Fronterizo identity construction in relation to Mexican Americans, some of my interviewees believe the latter share with them some characteristics that distinguish both from white Americans. *Convivio*, while absent among white Americans, is thought to be still alive among Mexican Americans.

> **Felipe:** And they're very cold . . . [but] in certain areas, in certain areas, because you go to the Second Ward [one of the poorest and more Mexican neighborhoods of El Paso] and there they do know each other and they live together like . . . not like here, but more or less the same. But for instance, if you go to Coronado [the richest and "whitest" part of El Paso] and in Coronado, and there everyone . . . He's a professor, and, do you know that he's a professor, why? . . . Well, who knows! [laughs] . . . But in Coronado, in those sections where it really is American-style . . . But here in the Second Ward it isn't, nor is it in the Lower Valley . . . because it's the Mexican section, right?
>
> **Jesús:** Because they're Mexican neighborhoods . . .

But several interviewees pointed out that being cold and dry is not only a characteristic of Americans, but also of the "Americanized" people on the Mexican side, where a national identity overlaps with a class identity.

Consequently, to be warm and wet is not a characteristic of Mexicans in general, but only a characteristic of low-income people, both in

El Paso (because most of the Mexican Americans there are working class) and in Mexico.

The Mexican American as the "other"

Introduction

If all those living on the other side of the border are points of reference in the construction of some Fronterizo and Juarense identities, Anglos are not the only important mirror to look at in constructing one's identity. As a matter of fact, Anglos are less important than other border actors in the Ciudad Juárez–El Paso area, because nearly 70 percent of El Paso's inhabitants are of Mexican origin. Accordingly, in the particular case of Juárez the Mexican Americans living in El Paso are a constant point of reference in the construction of identity. As in the case of Fronterizos in relation to Anglos, the construction of a Juarense identity also requires the simultaneous establishment of closeness and distance in relation to Mexican Americans.

Some of our interviewees considered that Mexican Americans were very similar to themselves. This is what happened in one set of interviews where the "anti-Southerner" stance was more prominent, with the students in the vocational school mentioned above. This did not happen by chance, because through their narrative plot those students were desperately trying to prove that Juarenses were a very particular kind of Mexican, closer to Americans than to other Mexicans living in Central or Southern Mexico.

> **Pablo:** And what do you think of all those Mexican American kids from El Paso who come to have fun here, but don't want to live here?
> **Abigaíl:** As long as they bring us currency. [laughs] Besides they are . . . we are Mexicans!! Only that a . . . little different. We are also different. I think that the border here is different from the rest of the country.

Hence, according to Abigaíl, both Mexican Americans and Fronterizos are a "little different kinds of Mexicans." To reinforce her argument she uses a metaphor that while very popular in Juárez is hardly ever heard in El Paso, that of the "sister" or "twin" cities. This metaphor is very important in the process of identity construction of many Juarenses because metaphors in particular (and tropes in general, as stated in the Appendix) have the capacity of "ordering" social reality selectively, making it much easier to buttress the fictional character developed in any narrative identity.

The "sister cities" Metaphor and the Feeling of Closeness

Nowadays this metaphor is an integral part of the hegemonic discourse that has its gravity center around the maquiladora industry in Juárez. I am referring here to the myth of the "twin plants," which in most cases refers to a factory in Juárez that employs thousands of workers, and a warehouse in El Paso that employs only a few.

> **Abigaíl:** I consider the border different from the rest of the country. Logically, we have the influence of the U.S.! We're two joined cities and there has to be a certain *exchange* because we're united, because . . . it's the same people. We speak, . . . um, almost the same language! More than 50 percent of the people in El Paso speak Spanish! Fortunately, many Juarenses here speak English or are learning English!

If the metaphor of the sister cities was present in several interviews in my sample, it emerged strongly among some middle-class Juarenses and it was central in their construction of identity. According to people who use this kind of metaphor, Juárez and El Paso are in fact only one city divided by a river. They do not consider Juárez different from El Paso; on the contrary, they believe they are very similar to each other. Of course this kind of discourse does not forget the important *economic* differences that separate Juárez from El Paso (the basic nodal point of the opposite narrative, to be discussed in the case of the American side of the border). However, it chooses to focus more on the commonalities Juárez has with El Paso—particularly their similarities in terms of *population and culture*. This type of metaphor notes that on both sides of the border, most of the population is Mexican; Juarenses are highly influenced by Americans, while the latter are also influenced by Mexicans; Spanish is spoken on both sides of the border, and so forth.

This was what happened in one interview I conducted with a group of female professionals living in Juárez. They are in their late thirties and were born in Juárez, except Esperanza, who was born in Jalisco but moved to Juárez when she was four years old. As one of those interviewees pointed out:

> **Esperanza:** I experience Juárez and El Paso as if they were the same city. I start marking a difference from Chihuahua City to the south and from Las

Cruces to the north. If I cross the bridge I go downtown and I see a lot of Mexican people. I go to UTEP [University of Texas at El Paso] and there are a lot of Mexican people; I go to the stores and there are a lot of Mexican people, and if I want to feel that I am among the same people, I can feel it at certain times. I've lived in Las Cruces for a while and I noticed a great difference in the language. Here, I don't notice language differences. When I am saying that Juárez and El Paso are the same cities, it's mostly due to the people. It's mostly because how we look, the language . . .

This interviewee not only identifies Juárez and El Paso as "the same city," but she also clearly specifies where the "difference" from the "others" starts: in Chihuahua City to the south and Las Cruces to the north. The construction of the "us" in this kind of narrative contrasts people living in both border cities with people living not only in the interior of the United States, but also inside Mexico! In other words, the "Mexicans closest to us" are the El Pasoans of Mexican descent, not the inhabitants of the state capital to which Juárez belongs: Chihuahua. This kind of Fronterizo identity clearly differentiates itself from both the Americans and the other Mexicans not living on the border.

The other participants in the same interview went a step further than Esperanza and expressed their feelings of total connection with El Paso using the word "symbiosis":

> **Grisel:** I very much agree with Esperanza. There's an important symbiosis between Juárez and El Paso. Juárez couldn't live without El Paso, nor El Paso without Juárez . . . they're irremediably joined. It's rare for someone not to have relatives in El Paso and for El Pasoans to have family in Juárez, that's common as well.
> **Milagros:** Well, they're so close together that there shouldn't even be bridges.[5] If it weren't for drugs, right?

A similar argument was used by other interviewees in my sample. This happened in an interview I conducted with a group of Juárez attorneys, some of them highly involved in politics in the city. Gerardo, who is in his fifties, was born in a small town in Chihuahua, but moved to Juárez when he was fifteen years old. Esther is a thirty-year-old native of Camargo who also moved to Juárez when she was fifteen. Dolores and Carmen are in their twenties, were born in Central Mexico, and moved to Juárez eight years ago.

> **Gerardo:** Ciudad Juárez and El Paso are one and the same community. It's very difficult to just speak of Ciudad Juárez or just El Paso. I understand

that this is the case much more in Juárez–El Paso than in Tijuana–San Ysidro or Reynosa–McAllen. Here, they're totally sister cities. All Juarenses who have been here for some time have relatives in El Paso.

According to this discourse, Ciudad Juárez and El Paso are the only "real" sister cities on the border, due to the intense family contacts across the line, something that, according to Gerardo, is not happening elsewhere on the border. In this sense, both cities are "sisters" in a very profound sense, that of housing the same family in two different (but intensely connected) places. The metaphor of connection is so strong that it has a physical nature: Gerardo does not hesitate to identify places in El Paso that *are* Juárez, that is, they are actually a continuation of Mexico:

> **Gerardo:** I have selected some characteristic shots of El Paso . . . because the Segundo Barrio [Second Ward] is precisely the union of Ciudad Juárez with El Paso, the union of Mexico with the U.S. It's more than a continuation of Mexico, only with a . . . moderation in its appearance, right? That geographical connection of Mexico with the U.S.

For some participants in this interview the feeling of closeness is so important that even though they recognize that the cities belong to two different countries economically (one to the Third World and the other to the First), they are surprised that people on either side of the border can live such similar lives.

> **Esther:** You can't say that it's possible to separate one city from the other. They are sister cities. The only thing that divides them is a bridge, but sup-

PHOTO 4

A mural located in the Segundo Barrio, El Paso.

posedly El Paso is a first-rate city because we're from the Third World. How is it that the lives they lead are so very similar one to the other?

In another middle-class setting, the sister cities metaphor also appeared and with it the feeling of intimate contact and closeness that some interviewees used to construct their Fronterizo identity. This happened in an interview I conducted with the Figueroa family. Héctor, the father, was very emphatic in claiming that the inhabitants of both cities are really brothers:

Héctor: Here in Juárez, we realize that both countries need each other. But both countries are also proud and don't want it known that they need each other and that they're vitally important to each other. Those who show their friendship are the inhabitants of both countries. In reality, those who are fraternal are the inhabitants who seek the common good. Then, how wonderful it would be if those same interlocking hands existed between governments!

In this type of narrative, people in Juárez and El Paso already acknowledge what their governments (and, as we will see below, what some El Pasoans) still hesitate to admit: that both cities are linked by intense bonds of brotherhood and solidarity.

In some other interviews the trope of "sisterhood or brotherhood" was more focused, claiming that Fronterizos and Chicanos (not El Pasoans or Mexican Americans in general) are very close to each other. This was what happened in the interview I conducted with the university students in Juárez. These students did not have any problem in making a parallel between their Fronterizo identity and the experiences of Chicanos living across the border:

Esteban: Fronterizos and Chicanos are very similar in that both seek their own cultural identity. *Not* like people from the North, let's say from Chihuahua City, from Hermosillo do. In those places the thing is to live. If they have problems, they never worry about seeking out the reason, the roots of those problems. In contrast, the Fronterizo and the Chicano, they do. The Fronterizo says: "Well, I have *cholos*, why is it that I have *cholos*?" The Chicano says: "All right, I'm considered a marginalized group within North American society. Why am I considered thus?" Someone from the state capital never asks her-/himself, "Why are there castes in Chihuahua City?" "Why is there such a difference between rich and poor?" It's as if being close to the U.S., seeing the problems, there are some people seeking their identity . . . and the Fronterizo seeks his own identity, but not over there!

José: Then, do you think the Fronterizo has created his own culture or that we don't have a culture?

Esteban: No, on the contrary! The Fronterizo has much more culture than non-Fronterizo Mexicans.

José is a native Juarense. With all the regional resentment that exists between Juárez and Chihuahua, that last statement, coming as it did from a native-born Chihuahuense, surely sounded like music to José's ears. After all, what Esteban was arguing is that Fronterizos possess the most important feature any culture can aspire to: reflexivity. According to Esteban, that is something that seems to be lacking in his hometown, Ciudad Chihuahua, which is supposed to be the repository of culture in Northern Mexico.

These are only a few examples of a variety of narratives that have the same goal: to prove that Juárez and El Paso are, in reality, the same city divided by a river/bridge; that their inhabitants are so close to each other that they can be thought of as "brothers" or as belonging to the same family. Using these metaphors, some middle-class Juarenses construct their identity as Fronterizos, that is, as people who live near the U.S.–Mexico border, focusing on the commonalities they feel they have with people on the other side of the border. As we will see in the next chapter, quite a different kind of identity is being constructed by many Mexican Americans living on the other side of the border, who identify the Mexican national as the "other" with the widespread narrative asserting that "all poverty and social problems are associated with Mexican nationals." Some Juarenses are aware of this narrative and, also being cognizant of how discriminatory some Mexican Americans are regarding Mexican nationals, they construct a very anti–Mexican American stance, where the "other" is the Mexican American categorized as *pocho* [a highly Americanized Mexican] or as a *malinchista* [a traitor].

Mexican Americans as *Pochos*

The complex intertwining of love and scorn toward Mexican Americans was expressed in an interview we conducted in Juárez with the Oliva family. In that interview Teresita first addressed how much she likes Chicanos:

Teresita: Well, this is the gathering place for Chicanos [she refers to the picture of "Centro Chicano," El Paso, shown in Chapter 3]. Do you know what I see in the Chicanos? (You are Chicana, right?) [she asked my colleague, Yvonne]. The search for their identity, that's why they get together. And it's that they don't feel they're from here or from there, and I like Chicanos so much! I like them so much because they love Mexico very much, and, on the other hand, they also love the United States.

But Don Librado quickly put in:

Librado: They love Mexico very much, but they don't love Mexicans . . . ! [laughs]
Pablo: Let's see, how is that? What do you mean they love Mexico but they don't love Mexicans?
Librado: You look at the members of LULAC [League of United Latin American Citizens], you see a clear specimen of the Mexican, you see the Indian types and those with big mustaches. But it seems that these people are descendants from those who one day went over there [to the U.S.] fleeing from something over here, and they have a resentment toward what was left here. For example, they say, "You know, so-and-so was caught by immigration." Who told on him? The Chicano, that one! The Chicano versus the Mexican . . . of course there are very good Chicanos . . .
Teresita: Yes, I think there are all kinds.
Librado: But there are Chicanos like that Corona, that Corona who used to hire workers . . . that man killed about 118 workers after they collected their salaries.
Teresita: He had his own cemetery, he buried them there.
Librado: The dead were all Mexicans, what's the problem?
Pablo: There's a contradiction, right? To love Mexico and hate Mexicans?
Librado: No, not the Mexican, not the *bípedo* [human being]! [laughs] The nation, yes, the nation, yes . . .

We can see here something that appeared many times in our interviews in Juárez. According to many of our Mexican interviewees (on both sides of the border!), it seems that some Mexican Americans mistreat Mexican nationals to different degrees. What Don Librado was mentioning regarding the border patrol—that Mexican American border patrol agents are harsh with Mexican undocumented workers trying to cross the border—was repeated in much more detail in the trade union interviews.[6] In one of our reunions Jesús told us a very interesting story to illustrate his point about many Mexican Americans being *sangrones* (conceited but also discriminatory) regarding Mexican nationals. Jesús' story repeats a narrative theme that appeared many times in our interviews: "If a Mexican has the bad luck of being caught by the border patrol in his attempt to cross the border, it is much better if the agent is an

Anglo than if it is a Mexican American, because the latter treats Mexicans much worse than the former."

> **Jesús:** I used to cross as a wetback and I would go as a wetback all the way to San Antonio, Fort Worth, since there's a lot of work on that side. One of those times a Gabacho [Anglo] security guard saw me and let me get on the train . . . and well, I arrived. The following month I came back and I said, "This is easy." And I left Mexico again and a security guard saw me, but he was Mexican, and he got me down. "Where are you going?" [he asked] "No, right now we're going to San Antonio, there's a lot of work on construction now . . ." If we arrived, well, the work was waiting for us. "No, man!" he said, "No, no, no, it's that you need papers." And I told him, "No, it's that I don't have any." "All right then . . . but, back you go." Then I thought and said to myself: "If this guy is Mexican, he messed up also" because, it's more . . . how can I tell you . . . [laughs]
> **Angela:** No . . . tell me . . .
> **Jesús:** . . . well they're more surly with us, because if a Gabacho, because I saw him, right? I saw him when I was hanging onto the train to get on, and I told my companions: "Do you know what? We've been spotted by the security guard, let's see what happens." Well, nothing happened, the first time was easy, but the second time it was a Mexican and he got us down and held us for immigration. Meanwhile, as the *perrera* [the border patrol van; literally, "dog kennel"] was getting full he was there talking with us. Then I said to them: "But, why . . . if you are from the same race, are you such bastards to us?"

But it seems that such mistreatment is not directed only toward illegal Mexican immigrants. According to some interviewees, both border patrol and custom agents of Mexican descent also mistreat Mexican nationals who are law abiding and want to cross legally. Anglo border patrol members, by contrast, are kinder and always trying to help them with their paperwork. This type of commentary was prevalent in our interview with Edelmira and her friends.

> **Concepción:** When one goes to obtain a permit to go to . . . to Los Angeles or any other place, and one gets a Mexican immigration agent . . .
> **Edelmira:** . . . uuuy, he sends you flying . . . !
> **Nivia:** And one knows, no, it's better to return because you know that he's not going to give you the permit.
> **Concepción:** And if you get an American, a Gabacho, well right away: "There's your permit, and have a good time." Very friendly, very friendly . . . !

Edelmira: And to simply get the local passport, or certain papers, if you get a Mexican he even asks for the least important paper that you might need, but if he's a Gabacho, no . . . because, look, as Mexicans they should help one. Isn't it true that they should help one? Because they're of the same race as us, nevertheless, they mistreat us a lot, those ungrateful ones. However, a Gabacho doesn't. They question us, right? Why this and that, and once you explain it to them it's all right. I came across several when I got the local passport, a Mexican didn't want to give me a permit to go to the United States, so I went to another bridge and this time I got a Gabacho, and he gave it to me right away! He didn't even ask me for a single paper, none. He said, "Why are you going?" I said, "Just to visit," "Here you go." And the Mexican, "Why are you going?" I said, "Just to visit." "Do you have money? Show it to me." I showed him what I had. "Do you work?" I gave him all the papers he asked me for. He said, "No, I can't, I can't give you a permit." I had everything he asked me for and he didn't want to give it to me!

Concepción: And a Gabacho puts up less obstacles . . .

Having worked as maids in El Paso at some time in their lives, these interviewees also referred to the mistreatment they have received from Mexican American housewives in El Paso, to the point that they claim to prefer working in Anglo households rather than in Mexican American households, because Anglo housewives treat them better.[7]

Concepción: Over there sometimes the bosses are very *fijadas* [picky, but also discriminatory] and they tell you: "You know what? You can only eat that, and you don't get any of that." One can starve to death over there! And over here people aren't *fijadas*, but over there they are.

Edelmira: But the women of El Paso that are *fijadas*, are the Mexicans.

Pablo: How is that?

Concepción: Let's say, they aren't real Americans.

Edelmira: They're Mexicans born here and *arregladas* [with American visas] and those are the ones who look more. Well I know because of my mother, because she talks to me, right? And she says that the Mexicans are stingier than the Gabachas.

Nivia: The people that go from here are more despotic than the American men and women, because I have also had some bosses like that.

Many of our interviewees, regardless of class, cannot understand why, if Mexican Americans are from the same *"raza"* as themselves (where *"raza"* in this context means "people"), many of them mistreat Mexicans more than Anglos do. Looking for an answer to explain the unexplainable, many interviewees argued that some kind of resentment against Mexico must be present in those Mexican Americans:

Librado: How strange, right? They say that dogs don't eat dogs [laughs], however, here they do, dog eats dog I don't know . . . there's rancor. Let me tell you, in the year of 1910 began the largest exodus in our country, above all from Central Mexico to the north. We're talking about Zacatecas, Guanajuato, Jalisco, Durango, Coahuila, Nuevo León, where there was a massive exodus that fled from the revolution of 1910, a revolution that began here in Juárez. Then the people leave and leave with their full knowledge or ignorance . . . and they started thinking: "I won't return, and I won't write because they can find out where I'm at." Logically, the ones that left were the sons, or the relatives, or the wives of the lieutenant, the sergeant, the captain, the major, the general of the army that lost. And all those people fled, they left and began a new life on their own terms. They are those who built the San Antonios, built the Houstons, built the El Pasos, large communities, but, they are the ones that today say: "Don't go with the people from Juárez, son, don't go with the people from Juárez! Because they're bandits, they're bla, bla . . . the bandit." You have to take a look at how these men use the word bandit, because they considered that the Mexican revolutionary was a bandit, a robber. And it seems that they grew up with that ideology, these people who are the grandchildren of those people who left Mexico during the revolution. And today, even now, they still come to Mexico to visit and they keep thinking that's it's like that, like the Spaniards think that we still have Indians with feathers. And this is the resentment that those people have.

Thus Don Librado claims that resentment is the main cause of the discriminatory behavior many people witness in some Mexican Americans. According to his testimony, that resentment is linked to the fact that those Mexicans were forced to abandon Mexico against their will, because they were the losers of the Mexican Revolution. Accordingly, Don Librado goes back to the Mexican immigrants' supposed position *against* the Mexican Revolution to back up his claim about their status as traitors and anti-Mexicans in the present. Also apparent is the anti-Southerner stance discussed above; according to Don Librado, most of these Mexican Americans who now discriminate against Mexican nationals are the heirs of the *Southern* population that was forced to migrate due to the revolution! In this sense Don Librado is claiming that these Mexican Americans are not real Mexicans like himself. First, they are the heirs of those who were against the most important achievement of Mexico in the twentieth century, the Mexican Revolution; second, they are not really "one of us, Mexicans from the North" ("a revolution that began here in Juárez"), but descendants from those despised Mexicans from the South and Central regions who we already know are the "others" for many Fronterizos.[8] After this kind of portrayal, it is not by chance that Don Librado finally laughs about what his wife first celebrated: the search for their Mexican roots by the Chicano movement:

> **Librado:** They dream about Aztlan. Historians here have not yet come to an agreement about whether the famous Aztlan ever existed or not, and they're fighting about it!

Hence, what started as a celebratory comment toward Chicanos (perhaps influenced by the presence of Yvonne, who is a Chicana) ends as a fierce criticism of the lack of identity and problematic nature (drugs, mental problems, crime, etc.) that supposedly characterizes Mexican Americans in the United States:

> **Librado:** This is not a joke, it's serious, in Los Angeles we met a guy by the name of Juan Palomares and over there his name was John Dovecote [laughs]. It's not a joke, it's serious! They charged him three dollars to change his name, would you believe it? And they gave him his papers, he changed his name to John Dovecote.
> **Pablo:** And why do you think he changed his name?
> **Librado:** It's an inferiority complex . . . his inferiority complex! I assure you that if we could psychoanalyze those people right now, or just talk to them, and ask them: "What did your father do? Why did you flee from your hometown?" Was it just because he was hungry or were there other things? Why did he want to completely lose his identity?
> **Teresita:** I believe that the problem of family breakup is as important as poverty or misery! So they have very low self-esteem, then they're satisfied with whatever they're given.
> **Librado:** But not just that, they also change their identity . . . *chin*! If you change your name . . .
> **Teresita:** . . . they accept everything! They feel so inferior that they accept everything.
> **Librado:** And here in this picture it says: ". . . Help us fight drug addiction" [Don Librado refers to photo 5, shown below] [laughs].
> **Pablo:** Why are you laughing?
> **Librado:** We're back where we started, the "Juan Puentes" who changed his name to John Bridge, or the "Juan Venado" who changed it to John Deer, if they left Mexico they must have left something similar to this, with these kind of legends, with these slogans.

The heart of Don Librado's explanation of the discriminatory attitude of some Mexican Americans is resentment; the workers in the trade union focused more on egoism:

Angela: Why do you think they're that way?

Jesús: I think that because a lot of times they must have suffered a lot, or they must have struggled a lot to get to where they are, or to get their immigration papers, right? I think that's why. When they see a wetback

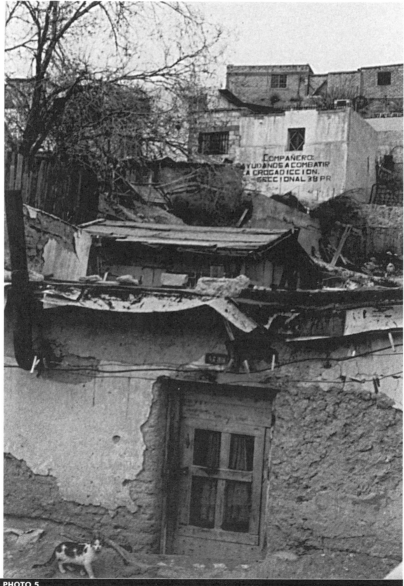

PHOTO 5

A shanty town in Puerto Anapra. On a wall there is a message: "Compañero, ayúdanos a combatir la drogadicción."

they try to vent their anger. I think that's really why . . . they try to get
even . . .

Felipe: I think that . . . we're very selfish . . . I already obtained it . . . well,
don't let him obtain it, because then he might even surpass me . . .

Angela: Do they see it as a competition?

Felipe: Yes, exactly.

Secundino: They defend themselves from future competition.

A similar argument was made by Edelmira and her friends; that is, many
Mexican Americans would not want any competition coming from
Mexican nationals because they are afraid they might be displaced by
the newcomers.[9]

We are going to see in detail in the following chapters what kinds of
narratives some Mexican Americans (and Mexican immigrants, too)
use to explain why they do not want more Mexican immigration (legal
or illegal) in the United States. Here I only want to present a brief testimony to show how the complaints of many of my interviewees were
not out of place. As one Mexican immigrant said:

Rosario: The problem is that before there were fewer people, right now
there is no room for more people here . . .

Therefore, it seems that not only many Mexican Americans, but also
some Mexican immigrants, discriminate against Mexican nationals. For
some of our Juarense interviewees, this kind of immigrant was also
considered the "other."

Mexican Immigrants Living in
the United States as the "others"

Some of our Juárez interviewees, who take pride in their Mexican border identity, look askance at immigrants who, becoming Americanized,
appear to have renounced their old affiliations and loyalties. And aware
as our Juarense interviewees are of the real poverty in which many of
these immigrants live (for instance, Rosario lives in one of the poorest
colonias in El Paso, which for more than twenty years was without running water and sewage), some were particularly irritated by what they
experience as the disdainful attitude many of those who have moved to
the United States hold toward Juarenses. As Margarita put it: "They
used to eat beans with their bare hands and now they use a fork!" [¡Es-
tán impuestos a comerse los frijoles a puño y ya agarran tenedor!].

The main claim in some testimonies is that emigrants seem to want, by the most obvious means they have available, to show how well they are doing in the United States. And what is more obvious than a big new car?

> **Robustiano:** One thing for sure, you even see the guys without shoes, but the damn cars they drive, man!
>
> **Margarita:** Forget that they're barefooted, they're starving! Let them bite into their cars!
>
> **Robustiano:** Yes, they leave Mexico and in about two, three months, they're driving these big and fancy cars, that, damn! But, poor guys, they're so pitiful.
>
> **Angela:** And the fact that they're living in the United States changes that, or were they people who were always trying to buy a car here?
>
> **Robustiano:** No, they're poor people, like us.

Our interviewees do not "buy" the deceit these emigrants want to sell them, and are totally aware of the masquerade some of these emigrants try to put on stage.

> **Robustiano:** They go over there, they work and in a few months, right? They come back with these big cars.
>
> **Pablo:** And why do you think they come back in those big cars, what do they want to prove?
>
> **Robustiano:** Since here in Mexico there's no opportunity to advance, they go over to the United States. Over there in the U.S. he can save, let's say, about five hundred dollars. Then he goes to a car lot and takes out the car, and well, while he's paying for that car, he can go barefoot, without one dollar in his pocket.

Hence, Robustiano and Margarita firmly believe, all the effort made by these emigrants seems to be in vain, because they are as poor as they were when living in Mexico. The only difference, according to our interviewees, is that in the United States they can *endrogarse* — take advantage of a credit system that does not exist in Mexico, a system that, as we have already seen, our interviewees consider one of the worst characteristics of the "American way of life."

Another thing these emigrants seem to use in staging their "American dream" show is to exhibit their command of the English language.

> **Pablo:** But, why do people change so much when they cross the river?
>
> **Feliciano:** Because they get their feet wet . . . Now they're from over there, they even throw English at you, they come back talk-talk-talk [English].

Thus, according to these interviewees, some Mexican emigrants returning to their hometown not only want to prove how well they are doing in the States, but also to show that they are fully integrated and really *belong* to the States. In this case, to speak English while in Mexico is perceived by Feliciano as a way of saying: "Right now I am a Mexican American." And this kind of self-identification, or how some Mexican emigrants show it (driving big cars and using English while in Mexico) is felt by some of our interviewees to be a form of aggression:

Angela: And why that change, what causes it?

Margarita: They want to humiliate.

The point that "they want to humiliate" is a very strong criticism toward some emigrants who, according to Robustiano's family, not only try to prove that they are better off than the Mexican nationals who decided to stay home, but also try to establish a hierarchical relationship with their old friends and acquaintances.

Robustiano: We're here in Mexico, we don't have opportunities for any of that, so then we go to the U.S., we come back in an old car, we think we're better than others, so then the people who you knew, you look at them differently because now you're in a car.

Pablo: From top to bottom . . .

Robustiano: Yes, you've gone up more.[10]

It is important to point out here that some of our interviewees know that the "American dream" show is only a performance, but they also acknowledge that, even though it is only a show, it modifies many of the interactions between those who remained at home and those who emigrated.

Margarita: When they're here, they talk to us, but when they go over there they don't talk anymore.

Margarita jokes about a way to avoid talking to other women in the colonia: "I am going to send my husband over there, thus I will never again talk to the other women in the neighborhood!"

We found similar kinds of criticisms in many of our interviews in Juárez. For example, Edelmira and her friends interpreted the attitude of the emigrants as arrogant:

Nivia: A lot of people who live here, just because they *arreglan* [legalize their documents], they feel superior to us.

Edelmira: Just because over there they're residents, or because over here are persons who have gone over there, and it is true, they change a lot.

Concepción: And then they don't talk to us.

Nivia: They come speaking English.

Adela: They don't even know you anymore.

Edelmira: One of my sisters-in-law changed, she was from here, my brother took her, he *arregló* her papers and everything, but now she's very different, now she thinks she's better than us. She dyed her hair blonde . . . No, I am joking. Well, there she is, she lived in my house, she doesn't like Juárez at all. She says she doesn't like it, that it's ugly, and I say, "Well, you ingrate, you were born here, what do you mean, you don't like it?" What's more, she was born in Zacatecas, imagine . . .

Concepción: It's much worse than over here . . .

Edelmira: "You're getting airs," I tell her. "You would be better off in Juárez." "No," she says. "I'm very happy here." To each his own, right? But she *developed airs* going there, I don't talk badly about her, but it's true.

Concepción: When you go to their house, they treat you as if you were a beggar . . . just because they have their papers, they think they're something else.

Very similar kinds of arguments appeared in the interview we had with a group of *cholos* in a lower-middle-class colonia in Juárez. These young people are in high school or have already dropped out, and they are working in different maquiladoras and service jobs. All of them were born in Ciudad Juárez.

Reinaldo: They go over there and they think they're bigger than the people here . . . they feel more accomplished over there.

Cata: And here they come . . . [Cata mockingly speaks a couple of English-sounding words] like a bunch of *clowns*.

Lety: They come back speaking more English than Spanish, imagine!

According to some interviewees, the "American dream" show can sometimes resemble a circus . . . with clowns included. Additionally, they believe the show almost always hides the real situation of poverty and, sometimes, desperation, that many Mexican immigrants experience in the United States.

Pablo: And why do you think that happens, that they cross the river and they become another type of person?

Reinaldo: They think they're going to get more money, and they don't get anything! Just vices!

Daniel: Just watch out for the children of vice . . . they come back addicted to drugs, and not over here . . .

Nevertheless, to many of our interviewees, the ostentatious behavior of some Mexican emigrants is directly related to coming back to Mexico, because they do not behave in this way (in relation to other Mexicans) when they are in the United States. It seems that the point is to perform the "American dream show" at home, where supposedly you can sell your deceit to those who decided not to emigrate. You cannot perform the show in the States, where the other Mexicans know the real situation that you and many other Mexicans endure there. Consequently, Robustiano's family criticisms were predominately directed against the Mexicans who return to Mexico to lord it over their Mexican compatriots. They were not directed toward those same Mexicans when they were living in the United States:

Pablo: And how did you deal with all those people who thought they were so high and mighty, with your friends at work?
Robustiano: Well, do you know what? Those of us who went across as wetbacks would get together . . . they're different over there, when they come over here is when they think they're superior.

Working in the United States without legal papers, in a stressful and discriminatory environment, Mexican illegal immigrants tend to consider themselves equals, not strangers. But to go back to Mexico is, among other things, to return to a country where the lines of social classification are drawn differently than in the United States. Thus, Robustiano's criticism is directed toward those emigrants who return to Mexico and use their sojourn in the United States as a means of socioeconomic advancement within Mexico; toward those who, experiencing exploitation, poverty, and racism in the United States, attempt to belittle their compatriots upon their return.

As we can see, in addition to using the regional system of classification, some Juarenses use a *national* system to separate themselves from the various actors living across the border. Among these actors, some interviewees particularly resent the behavior of some transitory migrants who go back and forth along the border. They claim these migrants have already changed their culture, and some interviewees believe they "want to humiliate" those who do not cross. For others, Mexican Americans are regarded as the principal "other." Finally, many Mexican border residents also differentiate themselves from Americans in general, aside from ethnic background. In so doing, they paint a bleak picture of "*endrogados*" who have lost control over their lives.

The above-quoted testimonies show clearly how complicated the process of identity construction is on the Mexican side of the border, where "us" and "them" move constantly along regional, national, ethnic, class, gender, and religious lines. Those different categorical systems confer meaning to attitudes and behaviors that require diverse types of explanations, explanations that are provided by the narrative plots different border actors advance to "order" their surrounding social reality in this precarious negotiation of meaning that is any social identity. In that process of negotiation, for some middle-class Juarenses, the metaphor of the "sister cities" is very important for buttressing a claim of similarity regarding the inhabitants of the American side of the border.

Introduction

A peculiar characteristic of the U.S.–Mexico border is that people changing countries are not only crossing from one country to another, but are also moving from one national system of classification to another—both systems in which they have a place. In changing their country of residence, immigrants expose themselves to a new set of expectations about their attitudes and behaviors, expectations to which they must respond by constructing a social identity that has meaning in this new social context (Vila 1997b).

Imagine, for instance, a resident of Ciudad Juárez from Mexico City who moves to El Paso. In the regional classification system of Juárez discussed in Chapter 1, the inhabitants of Mexico City are called "Chilangos," and the narratives people tell about them construct them as being smart, sharp, arrogant, that is, clever rascals. As some of our interviewees put it:

> **Ana:** The Chilangos are very determined. They are very hard workers, they're very tenacious . . . they are very slick talkers.
> **Leonor:** Well, it's just that someone who is born in Mexico City is very clever, because that city is so big, right? Because they know how to live and they know how to survive!

However, as soon as our imaginary Chilango crosses the border, he/she enters the ethnic classification system of the United States. Ergo, in the eyes of some people in the United States (to whom the label "Chilango" has no meaning), he/she becomes a "Mexican" or a "Mexican American" (if he/she lives in the Southwest) or a "Hispanic" (if he/she lives elsewhere in the United States). In this new system, the person is classed not only with other Mexicans—including those who only a few years ago supported the "be a patriot, kill a Chilango" slogan—but also with Cubans, Puerto Ricans, Peruvians, and so on. And a new label is not the only thing he/she acquires; accompanying it is a discrete set of assumptions about who he/she is and how he/she behaves. Thus, the "ex-Chilango" is transformed into a Hispanic or Mexican American and into an image opposite from what he/she had in Mexico. He/she is no longer seen as being smart, arrogant, sharp— a clever rascal; on the contrary, many perceive him/her as being a

Chapter 3

THE EMPLOTMENT OF THE MEXICAN ON THE U.S. SIDE OF THE BORDER

person without ambition, because this is the usual image that repeatedly appears in many narratives in the United States. The problem is that our emblematic Chilango, in one way or another, has to respond to this new set of social perceptions, creating a self that relates in some way to this new mirror (Vila 1997b). The complex and sometimes contradictory responses to having lived through this transition from one classification system to another and from one set of narratives to another can be seen in a letter to the editor of the most important newspaper in El Paso:

> Mexicans come to the United States and take everything away from us, things that we worked so hard to get . . . I was born in Mexico, but I worked my way here. . . . I was born in Mexico and I know the way most of the people over there think. Those people don't know anything about responsibility. (Magdalena García, *El Paso Times*, December 26, 1992)

The question of who I am is never separated from whom I see as the "other," nor from how those "others" see me (or, more accurately, how I *think* they see me). The move from one side of the border to the other adds a new set of mirrors; at the same time, that continuing closeness of Mexico ensures the ongoing presence of old ones. Therefore, the border offers many possible mirrors that can be used to generate images, which then can be utilized to narrate oneself and "others." In this sense, to be a person of Mexican descent living, for example, in Chicago is quite different from being a Mexican living in El Paso. The essential difference is that Mexico (the country, the origin of Mexican American ethnicity) is *there*, literally visible from El Paso. For Mexicans living on the U.S. side of the border, the *source* of their difference is always present, a constant reminder (Vila 1997b). As Wilson and Donnan point out (1998, p. 13):

> One of the most obvious, and perhaps most problematic, situations in which people's national identity must be negotiated is where a border is drawn with little reference to the ties of blood and/or culture which in some cases bind those across its reaches . . . those living in these border areas must evolve a *modus vivendi* which incorporates contradictory identities.

Accordingly, Mexicans living on the border deal with the meaning of their identity both as an ethnic group and, simultaneously, as a nationality. It is no coincidence, thus, that it was the Mexican immigrants and the Mexican Americans [1] in my study, rather than Mexican nationals or Anglos, who constructed the most complicated and contorted narrative identities.[2] Narrative identity construction is difficult for them because they constantly mix classification systems in order to make sense of themselves and "others" (Vila 1997b). They use nationality to detach themselves from Mexican nationals and to open a gap "inside" the Mexican ethnic category. But they also use ethnicity to differentiate themselves from Anglos. Due to the vast array of narratives people develop to make sense of themselves and "others," this section will address only *selected examples* of plots that organize the process of identity construction on the U.S.–Mexico border. Other interviews surely will reveal other plots, and we already know some of them that are missing in this section, for example, that of Anglos who construct a very romanticized image of the Mexicans and that of African American native El Pasoans who also have a positive image of Mexico and Mexicans.

Race, Ethnicity, and Nationality:
The Volatile Construction of Social Identities in El Paso[3]

On the American side of the border, *racial, ethnic, and national* discourses organize social identity; regional distinctions, in a city where more than 70 percent of the population is of Mexican descent, are less important (Vila 1997b). And this is not because regional identities are unimportant in the United States. American discourse is rife with allusions to "liberal Californians" and "aggressive New Yorkers," but ethnic and racial identities are stronger still.[4] If an Anglo Californian encounters an African American New Yorker, the latter's "race" is a more important datum by which to classify him/ her than his/her New York origin.[5]

In El Paso, as in other areas of the country, the discourse of race and ethnicity is pervasive. Nevertheless, here it combines with a discourse of nationality in a volatile mixture that, for many people, marks almost anything that is stigmatized as Mexican. Poverty is named in Spanish in El Paso—and in El Paso, Spanish signifies Mexican.[6] For instance, the poor neighborhoods of the city are known not as neighborhoods, slums, ghettos, or shanty towns but as "colonias."[7] This is the case irrespective of the language spoken or the ethnicity of the speaker. Similarly, the Second Ward—one of the oldest and poorest Mexican neighborhoods in the city—is habitually referred to by the name "Segundo Barrio" by everyone and in all contexts—and the name "Segundo Barrio" has come to be emblematic of poverty in El Paso. In this context, the use of Spanish kills two birds with one stone, for Spanish is both the language spoken in Mexico and the cultural marker of a great part of the Mexican American community in El Paso. Consequently, the use of Spanish to name poverty in El Paso is part of a local hegemonic discourse invoking both national and ethnic classification systems (Vila 1997b).

A controversy over the billing statements of the most important public hospital of the region is a good example of this discourse in practice. The hospital's bill reads:

Courtesy reminder. Please remit full payment due today. Contact the business office regarding your account.

Si no le es posible hacer pagos en sus cuentas de servicios medicos posiblemente califique para recibir ayuda financiera. Por favor llame al 534-5908 o 534-5918 [If you cannot pay your medical bills you may be eligible for financial assistance. Please, call . . .]. (*El Paso Times*, March 9, 1993)

The hospital's bills carry a bilingual message, but the message in the two languages is not the same. The English version asks for immediate payment, assuming that Anglos can do this. The Spanish version informs its clients that they can receive financial help if they need it, assuming implicitly that Mexicans or Mexican Americans are the *only patients* who would need this help. Not only does the double version of the bill discriminate against poor monolingual Anglos,[8] it also expresses and reinforces an integral part of El Pasoans' "common sense": poverty, for many people, is synonymous with Mexican (Vila 1997b).

Constructing the Mexican as the contemptible "other" has a long history in the border region. According to Jane Hill (1993), it is one aspect of the creation, in the Southwest United States, of a durable regional political economy based on a racial hierarchy that requires Anglos to produce and reproduce the subordination of Spanish-speaking and Native American populations who have a prior claim to the area's resources. Margarita Hidalgo (1995, pp. 34–35) refers to the long history of this construction in El Paso:

The history of the city implies that El Paso was born and evolved with a strong anti-Mexican /anti-Spanish sentiment, due not only to the presence of South El Paso [El Segundo Barrio], but to the incessant migration of Mexican descent that "took over" the city starting in the early 1900s . . . At present . . . In El Paso, Spanish is no longer the focal point of intense *overt* conflict, although ambivalent attitudes toward Mexican normative values and identificational orientation remain a source of *covert* conflict.

Regardless of a possible discussion about how *overt* or *covert* the conflict around the Spanish language is in El Paso, the process described by both Hill and Hidalgo is currently related to a new and broader one that appears to be threatening well-established social identities anchored in the traditional nation-state. As Stuart Hall (1996, p. 4) points out: "We need to situate the debates about identity within all those historically specific developments and practices which have disturbed the relatively 'settled' character of many populations and cultures, above all in relation to the processes of globalization, which I would argue are coterminous with modernity . . . and the processes of forced and 'free' migration which have become a global phenomenon of the so-called 'post-colonial' world."

Of that process of globalization, NAFTA is the local example. I agree with Michael Kearney (1991) that transnationalism implies a blurring, a reordering of the binary cultural, social, and epistemological distinctions of the modern period, where the nation-state established a well-marked difference between "them" and "us." Today, though, we are witnessing what some have called "peripheralization of the core," that is, millions of people from Third World countries are taking up residence in Western Europe and the United States. In this context, the U.S.–Mexico border plays a very special role. In Kearney's words (p. 57): "In recent years the Border Area . . . again becomes contested terrain. Now, however, it is not territory *per se* that is being contested, but instead personal identities and movements of persons, and cultural and political hegemony of peoples." I think that English Only, Operation Blockade, Proposition 187, and the congressional legislation that took away welfare from *legal* immigrants are some of the devices proposed to regain control over the identity construction process, to differentiate again between "them" and "us" during an era when "they" reside among "us." Of course, there are several "them's" and "us's" to be constructed, and hence, several narratives to be told (Vila 1997b).

Many people on the American side of the border constitute their identities against this backdrop. Needless to say, in this context, the constitution of a valued identity is relatively straightforward for middle-class Anglos and relatively difficult for many people of Mexican descent, regardless of class.[9] Using an *ethnic and racial classification system*, many Anglos (and those from other ethnicities—including Mexican Americans—who share with them this particular way of understanding identity) tend to conflate Mexicans and Mexican Americans because both belong to the same "ethnic" category. Most people from Mexican descent, on the other hand, constantly mix classification systems in order to make sense of themselves and "others." Many Mexican Americans tend to use nationality to detach themselves from Mexican nationals and race and/or ethnicity to differentiate themselves from Anglos. Mexican immigrants, on the other hand, have to confront the fact that they "are" Mexicans in both senses of the term, as a nationality and as an ethnicity.

The difficulty is even more acute for those who have decided, for varying reasons, to avoid the two prestructured narratives that are readily available to them: the "melting pot" ideology that calls for acculturation and assimilation, and the Chicano discourse that stresses the discriminatory character of American society.

The "all poverty and social problems are Mexican" Thematic Plot

Anglos, African Americans, and Mexican Americans: The Blurring of the Difference between Mexican Ethnics and Mexican Nationals

I will start by following the process of identity construction in a couple of Anglo interviewees, as their narratives most closely embody the hegemonic discourse described above. From there I will go on to explore the more constrained efforts of those of Mexican descent in the same context.

If Anglos decide to attune themselves to the local hegemonic discourse that equates poverty with Mexicans, they have an entire array of highly structured and consecrated discourses at their disposition (Vila 1997b). They do not have to prove that the negative images of Mexican nationals and Mexican Americans are wrong; on the contrary, they have only to confirm what is already there. This is what happened in some of our interviews with an Anglo family in Fabens, a city fifteen miles east of El Paso. The family included Carol, who had been born in the Midwest seventy-five years before and who had come to El Paso during the Depression. She had finished middle school and identified herself as "Methodist." Her daughter, Debbie, was a forty-five-year-old native El Pasoan who worked as a clerk and had a high school diploma (she was a Baptist). Carol's grandson, Larry, was a community college student in his twenties who was also a native of El Paso and a nondenominational Christian. Following the local hegemonic discourse I described above, many interviewees depicted poverty as being Mexican (Vila 1997b) and believed that most of the photographs portraying poverty had been taken on the Mexican side of the border, even though some of them had been taken on the American side.

> **Carol:** Well, what about these people in cardboard boxes? They're in terrible shape, huh?
> **Debbie:** Heh, heh . . . I don't know. There are lot of things that fall back to being poor.

Carol: That's right. Truckloads after truckloads of boxes stacked in these old trucks go across the river. [They refer to photo 9, page 96.]

Carol: Oh goodness!! That's what you call the pits. Heh, heh, heh. Isn't that terrible!? [Carol mistakenly locates in Juárez photo 6, depicting a poor, abandoned shack, actually located in "America," a poor American colonia.]
Larry: The freeway right there and the *rio* is the only line that lies between this kind of poverty and then right here there is like awesomely nice houses, businesses, communities, everything is like worlds just separated by . . . some pavement and a little bit of water. [He is describing photo 3, of Puerto Anapra, shown in Chapter 2.]

Here we encounter what was prominent in most of our interviews with Anglos: the idea of "otherness" they feel in relation to Mexicans is so profound that it is not enough to talk about El Paso and Juárez belonging to two different *countries*. They have to remark that both cities belong to two different *worlds*. As Robert[10] pointed out in another interview (trying to describe the shock of arriving in the Southwest for many Anglos who migrated from other regions, attracted by the industrial development of the border):

Robert: I used to take my family to Mexico, I used to like to take 'em to Zaragoza or up through there. It's a different world altogether.

PHOTO 6

An abandoned shack located in "America," a colonia in El Paso.

For Robert, as for Larry, to call Juárez another country is not sufficient to capture the gap he perceives between the United States and Mexico — to adequately express his experience of difference he needs an entire *planet*. As we will see below, the trope of the "First World versus Third World" plays a very important role in the construction of this sense of otherness.

The clarity of Robert's sense of difference is such that he also destroys any possibility of recognizing internal differences in the "other." He, like many Anglos we interviewed, never referred to the inhabitants of Juárez as either Juarenses (the way they refer to themselves) or "Juareños" (the slur some Mexican Americans use to depict Juárez inhabitants), but as "Mexicans." Thus, in this kind of discourse, the "other" is not the Juarense in particular, but the Mexican in general. From his perspective, the entire laboriously constructed Juarense self-image as a "different kind of Mexican" becomes invisible.

But if geography serves the purpose of stressing the difference from Mexicans, time can also help in the process: many of our interviewees were skillfully addressing the Mexican not only as belonging to another *world*, but also as belonging to another *time* dimension, another phase in history.

> **Larry:** It's just that one little boundary, and it's wild to just drive around right there and you go around UTEP [University of Texas at El Paso] and then it's almost like uh . . .
> **Carol:** Being in another town, eh . . .
> **Larry:** Not another town! It's just like if you just shot into a different phase, and you just drive along and you're back over there by Sunland Park into another rich area. [Larry is describing the surroundings not revealed in photo 3, of Puerto Anapra, shown in Chapter 2.]

Robert also "completes" his picture of Mexicans' absolute "otherness" by claiming they operate with a sense of time different from his own.

> **Robert:** I'm comin' from New Jersey so I'm comin' from a lot different environment. I had culture shock for like the first three or four months. We had an engineer here that was from the middle of the state where I'm from and he says: "Juárez is just like what Smithville, New Jersey, was like forty or fifty years ago." It's a whole different world . . .

Larry's and Robert's experience of "cultural shock," of "living in another world," does not seem to be unique. Robert and his co-worker Albert told us how many Anglo managers could not survive that "shock":

Robert: When I first came here the philosophy was: If you're here two years, you did a good job. Most Americans burned out or had heart attacks or were fired or got sent back to their parent companies.

The sense of otherness is so profound that, of course, these interviewees have no room whatsoever to even imagine they could live like the Mexicans do.

Debbie: I can't see how these people in Mexico live, but I guess they survive.

Carol: I'd hate to have to live like that!

Debbie: When you're coming from the west side over the freeway you can smell the garbage in the air just in that certain area around ASARCO and down that way. [She refers to the Mexican colonia Anapra.] It's unbelievable!! I couldn't imagine living over there!

Looking for an explanation of the absolute "otherness" they feel separates them from Mexicans, and well attuned to the local narrative theme "all poverty is Mexican," these interviewees use the readily available discourse of Mexican laziness ("Mexicans are poor because they are lazy and not work oriented, as Americans are") to explain the levels of poverty they see in Juárez.

Larry: On our side of the bridge people are more situated in their minds to what's, you know, work, life . . . maybe they're life themselves [*sic*]. Whereas over there they would be also, but maybe not being so stressed about it.

Some of our interviewees continue to use a narrative plot they themselves know is a mere stereotype:

Robert: Like, when I first came here, I expected to see the Rio Grande you know, half a mile wide and the bridge to be like the San Francisco bridge and John Wayne is riding across [laughs]. Especially, I'm speaking for myself because I'm from the North and you stereotype the area, the Mexican people. You know, everyone has a *sombrero* and everybody is sitting out there drinking their *tequila* and taking their *siesta* and me working in the plant.

Despite his own sense of the stereotypical and unrealistic nature of his "old" image of Mexicans, he cannot abandon the thematic plot that establishes that "Mexicans are poor because they are lazy":

Robert: It's hard to believe that you got kids that are fourteen, fifteen, sixteen years old and, I know what I was like when I was fourteen, fifteen, sixteen years old, I was rebellious and here you got kids that are working on production lines and . . . their father's home and he's taking it easy! They may have four, five kids in the family working. Their father's home and he's the *Don* and everybody brings their money home to give to the father and . . . so you know it's a culture shock for us.

In more than eight years working among Mexicans, Robert has changed his vision of "the Mexican" very little. He cannot describe the workers he actually knows as lazy, so instead he attributes the laziness to their fathers. The Mexican who wears a *sombrero*, takes a *siesta*, and drinks *tequila* has not disappeared, he has simply been displaced a generation. Ultimately, however, Robert's logic is less circuitous than this. Later in the interview he interprets the workers' actions — in this case absenteeism at the maquila — within the same schema of *siesta*, *tequila*, and *fiesta* that he originally brought with him from New Jersey.

> **Robert:** On Mondays if you don't have 10 to 15 percent absenteeism you're very fortunate. And after a holiday it's worse. And you take a Mother's Day when it happens during the middle of the week, forget it! You might as well write that day off. And Monday is going to be a waste . . . And you're gonna get like 60 percent absenteeism. And then Tuesday is gonna get better. And then Wednesday or Thursday is usually a bad day, for whatever reason. For sure Friday's your best day because that's the day everybody's gonna get paid but you don't get the work out of the people after a certain amount of time because ah, Friday's the day everybody's getting charged up to hit the road at 3:30 or 4:00 to go out and have a good time. It's a complete different world!

Thus, according to his "new and improved" vision of Mexicans, Robert still believes that they prefer leisure to work, and he associates absenteeism with weekend parties and drunkenness. Here we encounter again the discussion about morals and values discussed in previous chapters. Just as some Juarenses wanted to separate themselves from Southern Mexicans, and construct a valued identity of being a more "Americanized" kind of Mexican, where "Americanized" refers to American morals and values, here Robert is doing the same in relation to Mexicans in general. The moral side of identity is again overlapping with the main system of classification, in this case, an ethnic and racial one.

Hence, despite his own sense that he has changed, Robert's image of the "other" has been little affected by more than eight years of daily contact. On the contrary, the stereotype has been elaborated, without being modified in terms of its essential assumptions. The "Mexican" in general (not Norteños, Juarenses, Mexican Americans, and the like) has been and still is the category that absorbs the potential human foibles from which he wishes to distance himself. Robert does so by balancing the understanding of the reality that surrounds him always in the same direction. Although he knows his workers work hard, he blames their fathers for not working, or ultimately the workers themselves for being absent from the factory so often.

Even if Robert is totally aware that American factories are moving to Mexico not only because of its low wages and loose environmental laws, but also because in some cases productivity and quality are higher in Mexico than in the United States, he does not credit Mexican workers (who he feels are lazy by definition):

> **Albert:** Believe it or not, in Mexico now the quality of the work [chuckles slightly] is better than in a lot of places, including the States! I know the plant that I work for, the TV service area, a lot of the work that used to be done in Missouri is now being done in Juárez because the quality now is better. They're actually ahead of the Americans.
>
> **Pablo:** The productivity is better in Mexico than the States?
>
> **Robert:** By far. One of the main reasons here, though, is that you try to break down the lines. The specific jobs as far, as low as you can. 'Cause of the high absenteeism rate and everything else. You try to break the job down and you get good quantities. Where I come from, the plant in New Jersey, if you get a job for a thousand pieces, God! The plant would go crazy! It would be the greatest thing in the world! And that thousand pieces, maybe a person would have to do three hours worth of work themselves for each one of those thousand pieces. Here, to me, I'm in production control right now but when I had lines I loved to have lines with a thousand a day! And you broke that thousand a day down so a person only had two or three minutes worth of work or seconds! Even to do the job and I think that's one of the big reasons. I think that's a big difference between our production in the States and here.

Therefore, it is not Mexican hard work that is behind high quality and productivity, but American ingenuity. Here again Robert does not allow any room for the appearance of the "good side" of the Mexicans, that side with which he might sympathize and use as a bridge to close the enormous gap he feels separates him from the "other." On the contrary, Mexicans are again portrayed as lazy, and in trying to cope with that laziness ("'Cause of the high absenteeism rate and everything else"), American managerial ingenuity supposedly has improved productivity in Mexico.

If Mexicans are lazy and poor by definition, how can people make sense of the visible signs of wealth some Mexicans display on both sides of the border? Here again, the hegemonic discourse of the region offers these interviewees the clues they are looking for to make sense of this contradiction between laziness and wealth: if Mexicans have money it is due to their corruption and delinquent activities, like drug dealing and stealing cars (Vila 1997b).

> **Debbie:** I think everybody probably blames Mexico for a lot of the drugs that are here.
>
> **Carol:** Well, they are bringing it across. . . .
>
> **Debbie:** Five years ago, all of the cars in Mexico were old cars. If you see what they're driving now it's because they're stealing one hundred cars a week from here to take over there![11] It's sad to think that they're coming over here to steal the cars and really to see what they're driving now. It's amazing to me because I know what they drove five years ago, and they were all wrecks!
>
> **Carol:** Go to Sam's and you see these cars with Mexico license plates on 'em. They're all pretty good looking trucks and cars.

According to these Anglo interviewees, Mexicans bring all these negative characteristics to the United States in their process of migration. Accordingly, since by definition poverty is Mexican and not American, poverty in El Paso is the product of the presence of Mexicans in the United States; in other words, poverty in El Paso is still Mexican (Vila 1997b).

> **Debbie:** You've got all those people that came from Mexico that live over here now. So . . . their standards of living are gonna be pretty much the same. That's the reason the condition [she refers to photos 6 and 13, depicting poor houses in El Paso] is the way it is, because those people came from over there, and all they've done is bring this side down. They think maybe they can . . . live off welfare.[12]

As we can see, these Anglo interviewees are following, almost without modification, the script the local hegemonic discourse has written for them to make sense of their identity, where the stigmatized "other" is the Mexican in general, understood as both an ethnic and a national entity. Consequently, these interviewees are not only mercilessly destroying the laboriously constructed identity of the Juarenses as a "different" kind of Mexican, but also the endless effort we will see many Mexican Americans go through to demonstrate to Anglos that they are *not* like

Mexican nationals. And this is so because for most of our Anglo in-terviewees to talk about "Mexicans" is, primarily, to talk about ethnic-ity. Mexican nationals, according to this kind of ethnic logic, are ethnic Mexicans who were born in Mexico, and therefore they have been less exposed to Anglo influence and preserve more of the original charac-teristics of their ethnicity. Mexican Americans are ethnic Mexicans who were born in the United States and were more exposed to Anglo culture, and they have lost, to different degrees, the original features of their ethnic group. Thus, the main difference between Mexican nationals and Mexican Americans is the time of exposure to American culture, but both remain essentially ethnic Mexicans.

Of course, not every Anglo in my sample worked with the narrative theme that "all poverty is Mexican." Some Anglos I interviewed had a very positive attitude toward Mexicans and recognized that there is poverty on both sides of the border. Whereas Carol, Debbie, Larry, and Robert tended to locate all the photographs that depicted poverty on the Mexican side of the border, even though half of them were taken in El Paso, those Anglos who did not construct their identities using the "all poverty is Mexican" plot were more accurate in locating those pho-tographs. This was what happened with the Williamson family and their friend Jacob.[13]

Jacob: I'm not sure which side of the border either one of these photo-graphs is on, but you know, on both sides there's poverty or people living below what we consider the poverty line. And, you know, they look to other people for their handouts and . . . to put food on the table . . . [Jacob is referring to two photographs from Juárez (photos 8 and 9) and two photographs from El Paso (photos 6 and 13).]

According to this kind of discourse, poverty is everywhere, and not by definition uniquely "Mexican." Hence, it is not by chance that Jacob hesitated before claiming that those photos were taken in either Juárez or El Paso. At the same time, if for these interviewees not all poverty is Mexican, laziness is not an intrinsic Mexican characteristic either. They may have other defects, but laziness is not one of them:

Joe: I pulled this photograph out because even though they're poor people (I assume this is in Mexico, too, looks like that), they're very reli-gious people. 'Cause of the picture of the Mother Mary in the background. So, you know, I think the people that I've had the opportunity to know and work with are very hard working, very honest! I think they're nonassertive, nonaggressive, they're very passive at the same time.

Something similar occurred with some of the interviewees in another group of Anglos I contacted in El Paso. Arthur and Helen are in their late twenties. She identified her occupation as "mother," and her husband is in the military stationed at Fort Bliss. They have been in El Paso for three years (Helen lived in El Paso in her childhood, too). Bridget, Helen's sister, is a secretary married to a Mexican citizen; they have been living in El Paso for the last thirteen years. Arthur, who is in the military as well, identified himself as a Lutheran, and Helen and Bridget put "none" for the question about religion. Arthur holds a bachelor's degree, Helen a high school diploma; Bridget went for a year to college. Again, these interviewees (above all Bridget) were not using consistently the "all poverty is Mexican" plot, and thus they were not locating all the photographs of poverty in Juárez (except for Arthur, who was the most inclined to use the theme "all poverty is Mexican" and who mislocated all but one [photo 10] of the photographs of poverty in Juárez).

> **Helen:** Where is that? Is that in Juárez or . . . That could be in El Paso also.
> **Bridget:** I'm not sure but I would venture it's Juárez.
> **Helen:** And yet, you know, those could be the colonias over here also. Have you ever been out there?
> **Bridget:** Yeah, but that's not the colonias because they don't have water [she laughs, because the picture, shown on page 95, portrays very prominently stagnant water all over the street]. My assumption is that this is in Juárez.
> **Helen:** I think this is El Paso.
> **Pablo:** Why?

PHOTO 7

An altar surrounded by hanging clothes in a poor tenement house in Ciudad Juárez.

Helen: It looks like a place I saw, actually, the colonias. It could be out there in the Lower Valley. But we went out there . . . by Montana Vista. And we saw mobile homes out there and a little bit of construction like this, like a cinder block building. [Helen is describing photo 13.]

Arthur: No, I think they're both in Juárez, yeah, definitely.

Bridget: OK, see, I think this is Juárez and this one is El Paso.

Arthur: No, but you know what? Up here in the driveway, with the trailer, . . . looks like a Texas license plate.

Helen: That could be either way.

Bridget: Your second clue is the trailer. They don't have trailers in Juárez.

Arthur: Damn, man. It's a shame. Both places are El Paso.

As we can see, these interviewees take their time to decide where the shots of poverty were taken, without immediately assuming (as Carol, Debbie, Larry, and Robert did) that they were taken in Juárez. Thus, it is not surprising that Bridget, looking at the photograph I thought everyone would put in Juárez due to the degree of poverty it showed (a photo that usually — and in this interview, too — triggered a lengthy discussion about the difference between poverty and messiness), still did not automatically locate it in Juárez.

Bridget: I haven't been in many places where I've seen the slums and this. But the mess! I'm a very compulsive person. This sort of leaving junk and crap outside . . .

Helen: Be poor but why do you have to . . . [simultaneously with Bridget] be messy! Why do you have to be so dirty?

Bridget: And like I say, I don't know where it is . . .

PHOTO 8

A street, with plenty of mud and trash, located in colonia "La Perla," Ciudad Juárez.

Pablo: Where do you locate it? In Juárez or El Paso?

Bridget: I'm gonna say this is in Juárez only because they don't make fences like that too much in El Paso. Over there everything's made out of cinder block. They're actually better constructed than my piece of plywood I live in! But, I mean, that would be my only reason, not for any other . . . Not for anything else but just because of the cinder block wall.

Notice that, pushed by me to finally locate the photo somewhere, Bridget still addresses architectural issues and not poverty ones to place the photograph in Juárez and not in El Paso. Additionally, she does not lose the opportunity to praise Mexicans for the quality of their materials compared to American ones!

Therefore, if on the one hand not all my Anglo interviewees used the hegemonic discourse "all poverty is Mexican" (talking about Mexicans in general, as an ethnicity and as a nationality), on the other hand it wasn't only Anglos who used that thematic plot; as I explain in the Appendix, there is no such thing as an "ethnic interest" that determines a particular ideology. We found a very similar hegemonic discourse among middle-class African Americans in El Paso. Miles is a U.S. military officer who was born in South Carolina forty years ago. He holds a master's degree and identifies himself as Baptist. His wife, Billie, works at home and has completed three years of college education. Their friend, Bessie, is married to another U.S. officer; she is thirty-five years old, was born in Kentucky, and is also a Baptist. She has completed high school. These interviewees, without being as discriminatory against Mexicans as Carol, Debbie, Robert, and Larry, still predominately used

PHOTO 9

A very poor hut against a cinder block fence, with some clothes hanging outside and a nylon roof, located in colonia "La Perla."

the "all poverty is Mexican" discourse in the construction of their narrative identities. These interviewees, most of whom had never crossed the border in more than two years living in the area, had a very negative image of Juárez and could not imagine how Mexicans who work in El Paso could go back to such a depressing situation:[14]

> **Miles:** The photographs were really depressing to me. And I try to picture what people feel like when they come over here to work and have to go back. You come over, things sort of brighten up, you leave, and you go back into a depressive state, so . . . I see people who, heading back in, kind of dreading having to go back into this type of life but they have no choice . . . so, they must go.
> **Bessie:** Well, it's just a good luck of being an American . . . [laughs] When I went to Juárez I was ready to come back in ten minutes . . . [laughs] Ah, it's painful! You know, you come here! And then you go over there and look around . . . I don't know, it's just, for me it was *painful*. Kind of like . . . like you say two places are so close together but just so different.

Working with the hegemonic thematic plot that states that "all poverty is Mexican," and without really knowing Mexico, they comment that the pictures showing poverty "resemble" Juárez without seeing how absurd it is to claim something resembles some other thing they know nothing about. In this sense, resemblance is a conformity, but to what? To an identity. Now, this identity is imprecise, even imaginary, to the point where I can continue to speak of "likeness" without ever having seen the model. I can only spontaneously claim "likeness" in a photo because it conforms to what I expect of it (Barthes 1991). If this is so, it is not by chance that the hegemonic plot guided these interviewees in their perception of the photographs, in such a way that they totally confused the location of some of them. This happened with photographs of cemeteries of the region. One of the photographs depicted a very old cemetery in a ruinous state, totally abandoned, without any flowers on the tombs and without any visitors. Another portrayed a cemetery very well kept, with many flowers, well-preserved tombs, and many visitors. The third one depicted the Jewish part of El Paso's cemetery (in the middle of the Concordia cemetery). People usually concentrated on the first two photographs, and did not comment on the third one.

For those whose narrative identities revolved around the "poverty equals Mexico" idea, there was no doubt that the first cemetery was in Juárez (Vila 1997b). This was what happened with Carol and Debbie:

Carol: Is that our cemetery?

Pablo: You must guess what photograph corresponds to Juárez cemetery and what to El Paso cemetery.

Carol: Well, my opinion, probably this one is Mexico.

Pablo: Why?

Carol: Uh . . . well, it's a little in bad shape for one thing and it's just scattered.

But the same also happened with Miles and his friends:

Miles: Ah, this is sad. We know people are buried on top of each other, but it shows you that, they're buried and then, it's kind of forgotten. Because of the hustle and bustle of life, ah, doesn't require you to look back, you gotta always look forward.

Pablo: And where do you locate the photograph?

Miles: In Juárez.

Billie: Once again, the contrast, the landscaping, you know? One as opposed to the other, totally different. *Totally* different!

Pablo: And how do you compare this cemetery [the unkempt one] with this one [the well-kept one]?

Miles: See, you can tell a lot of effort has been made to keep this in some semblance of order, ah, so that you can come through any time and reflect on your relatives who have passed away, but, with that one, . . . I don't see that.

All these interviewees (and many others working with the same basic plot, equating poverty with Mexico) had no doubt that the unkempt

PHOTO 10

Concordia Cemetery, El Paso.

cemetery was the Mexican one and the well-kept one was American. In fact, the ugly one was Concordia Cemetery, the most centrally located cemetery in El Paso, impossible to miss from I-10, while the well-kept one was Tepeyac, a Juárez cemetery. Consequently, "resemblance" here was not in relation to a model but to a preconceived discourse establishing that "all poverty is Mexican."

It was not surprising then, that those Anglo interviewees who were not working at all with the "all poverty is Mexican" theme (like Bridget), or who were more ambiguous in its use (like Helen and Arthur), did not have any difficulty correctly locating the cemeteries.

Pablo: Where do you locate these two cemeteries?
Arthur: This [the ugly one] is the one that I was thinking, here in El Paso, where the bridge turns.
Bridget: Yeah, that's it . . . Concordia.
Helen: Concordia? I thought it looked nicer than that.
Bridget: No, you're thinking of the B'nai Zion, the other one, the Jewish cemetery. This is the public cemetery. And that looks an awful lot like the cemetery in Juárez, except the one in Juárez has no cement. They have wood crosses and they're buried, like, four or five deep.
Pablo: And what do you think about the other one [the well-kept cemetery]?
Helen: It could be anywhere, to tell you the truth.
Arthur: Oh, that's in Juárez, no doubt.
Bridget: Why?
Arthur: Because of the, the colors that are in there.

PHOTO 11

Tepeyac Cemetery, Ciudad Juárez.

Bridget: This, I would say Juárez 'cause of the crosses. They put a cross down right away. It's not like here.

If, as I try to prove in the Appendix, there are no "structural" interests linked to particular ethnic groups beyond their articulation in a peculiar narrative, then it is not surprising to find that the hegemonic discourse was also repeated, in some instances, by Mexican Americans themselves (Vila 1997b).

This happened in an interview we conducted with a group of young, first-generation Mexican American El Pasoans. Cristy and Tom are UTEP students. Lucy is a teacher and Tom is a driver. Susie is trying to complete her GED program and Arturo is a fifteen-year-old high school student. All of them are Catholics. Talking about their personal experiences with people living in government projects (some of them have lived part of their lives in those projects), these interviewees did not hesitate to identify them as being "Mexicans" (conflating ethnicity and nationality in their interpellation):

> **Cristy:** I'm a teacher and at the school where I teach, half our students come from the projects. Most have single mothers and, if there is a father, he's often alcoholic, well, I speak from experience . . . and the older brothers are in gangs.
> **Pablo:** And to what groups would they belong? Black, Mexican, Mexican Americans, Anglo?
> **Cristy:** Unfortunately, here in El Paso, I think they're just Mexicans.
> **Susie:** Ninety-nine percent [laughs].

Having identified the "other" that the hegemonic narrative prescribes (the Mexican in general, without differentiating it in any other dimension: nationality, class, religion, gender, or age), these interviewees repeat once more the major theme of the hegemonic plot: Mexicans are poor because they are lazy.

> **Pablo:** And why do you think that so many Mexicans live in government projects?
> **Cristy:** Because many times you become complacent and when you see that help is available, you say: "Oh!" . . . Well, that they're . . .
> **Tom:** I think that a lot of those families lose their way at a certain place. They suddenly become lazy, they get used to it. And it's very easy for me to do it too. If you get everything for free and I don't have to pay for anything. [laughs] . . .

Susie: We lived in those projects for thirteen years, and, well, life was very sad . . . My sister and I saw things in front of the house where we lived, where all the *cholos* would gather . . . deaths that would occur and drive-by shootings. And you need to remember that they were all Mexicans, all the people who did that wickedness were Mexicans, Mexican Americans, Mexicans. The ones who did it were Mexican. And it's very sad because one is also Mexican American.

If they used, without any modification, the hegemonic theme establishing that "all poverty — due to laziness — is Mexican," I think it is understandable why these interviewees also mistakenly placed the unkempt cemetery in Juárez and the well-kept one in El Paso:

Susie: How nasty! This one reminds me when one dies, one isn't anything anymore. They don't even respect tombs! And it's in Juárez. You can tell right off.
Pablo: And why do you think it's Juárez?
Susie: Because of its ugliness and because all the tombs are unkempt and they don't respect over there any longer.

As we can see, these interviewees (Anglos, African Americans, and Mexican Americans) are following, almost without modification, the script that the local hegemonic discourse has written for them to make sense of their identity, where the stigmatized "other" is the Mexican in general, understood both as an ethnic and as a national entity (Vila 1997b).

The Chicanos as the Mexicans to Whom the "all poverty is Mexican" Narrative Should Apply

It is precisely in relation to this hegemonic discourse stating that "all Mexicans are equal — all Mexicans are poor" that Mexican Americans have to construct their identities. One route is that followed by Cristy and Susie, accepting that their ethnic group is responsible for its own problems. If they accept that without questioning it, it is not surprising that some interviewees, using a similar logic, constructed the "others" as those Mexican Americans who refuse to acculturate and assimilate to American society, that is, to abandon the culture that is supposedly damaging them. In this example of identity construction, we can see how some Mexican Americans who have "made it" in class terms can choose to build their identity outside the context of their Mexican ancestry (considered in both its national and ethnic versions). Thus, many Mexican Americans seem to renounce their ethnic ascription and accept the "melting pot" ideology, constructing a valued identity based on a claim of belonging to the American polity in which the "others" are those who supposedly do not accept this possibility. As Albert [15] put it:

> Those [Albert refers to photo 12] are the bad guys in my opinion, those guys who find it very easy to blame someone else and don't have any initiative to

PHOTO 12

102

Centro Chicano, El Paso.

better themselves! Those are the guys who sit and complain day after day, night after night and then go home and have a fix or a six-pack of beer, then wake up the next morning, the next night and start all over again!

He perceives Chicanos as crying discrimination in order to avoid confronting their personal failures. For him, they are the sort of people who build a whole political argument simply in order to hide their true nature — as laggards and drunks who are unwilling to work hard (as he did) in order to succeed.[16] The option taken by this interviewee was individual, not collective, and in order to show the superiority of his choice, he described his own family's trajectory from poverty to relative comfort through individual effort:

Albert: I think feeling sorry for yourself is not where it's at, you just gotta take [it]. My mother lived there [in Chihuahuita, a poor Mexican neighborhood in El Paso] for forty years, but she finally moved away. My mother's a teacher. There were those people who wanted to better themselves and then there are those people who just saw it as a way of life. I know there's a lot of people who love Chihuahuita. But, if Chihuahuita is all you want for the rest of your life then you're not gonna accomplish anything.

The barrio as a way of life is rejected by this upper-middle-class Mexican American who grew up in Chihuahuita, but now lives in an expensive house on the west side of El Paso. The barrio as a way of life — with all its connotations of preserving traditions from Mexico, such as big families, free time, leisure, and friends — is part of the past, and it is the credo of the kind of people who, according to Albert, do not want real progress in their lives, that is, the Chicanos. The barrio is also *his* past, and in his narrative identity Albert constantly emphasizes how far he is from that past and how his future is going to be still farther away. According to Albert, to accomplish something in American society, getting out of the ethnic ghetto is a *must*. People who remain in Chihuahuita are, according to him, people who have done nothing with their lives, who have wasted their lives.

Pablo: Do you think that people who live there are going to live there all their lives or do you . . . ?
Albert: Yes! [curtly] I would say that a good 40 or 50 percent have no aspirations of leaving. I have a cousin, believe it or not, who—here it is thirty-four years later—still for some reason finds it necessary to stay in that damn corner there. I don't know what his purpose in life is, you know. He's grown up and now he has little boys who are fifteen, sixteen. And this guy who is probably thirty-five and still has a reason, I don't know what

the hell his reason is, but he still finds it necessary to stand at that corner, you know, on Friday nights. I, shit, I don't know. We all have priorities. I guess I have different priorities.

If the ethnic barrio is something of the past, then for Albert Chicanos are not an ethnic "vanguard." On the contrary, they are representatives of a twofold past. On the one hand, Chicanos are the spokespersons of those Mexican Americans who want to hide inside ethnic boundaries — who are afraid to go out into the "real world" outside the barrio, in which they would encounter and have to compete with the Anglos. On the other hand, Chicanos are representatives of the past because, in not taking responsibility for their individual destinies, they behave like children:

> **Albert:** ¡No crecen! They refuse to grow up and assume responsibilities! It's a way to live in the past and kind of forget all your problems and, yeah, forget the responsibilities you should have as a father or a mother or, you know . . .

Albert's "they do not assume responsibilities" theme does not take into account group responsibilities. According to Albert the most important responsibility is in relation to your own life and family, not to your ethnic group. Accordingly, Albert thinks the Chicano movement and ideology ("I've read the literature") is an easy escape ("a lot of people find the easy way out") from everyday life responsibilities, that for him, above all, are individual responsibilities. Therefore, Albert cannot understand why some people freely choose, in the sense that they *can* choose another option, to live there instead of moving to a more "middle-class," Anglo environment.

> **Albert:** And then, believe it or not, my cousin was an accountant and he lived on the third floor! My cousin had a civil service job who at the time *ponle que* [let's say] he earned thirty-eight thousand dollars. This goes back twenty years ago . . . and I still have family who live on Charles Road, people who could've *done* something with their lives but who chose not to, just live on the very minimum. Some people refused to leave, refused to let go, grow up. You know, there's a whole world out there, just, people don't want to see it.

His only answer, again, is that they have a childlike mentality, a traditional one that does not embrace change. And this "mentality" somehow also impinges on those who have tried to leave the barrio, undermining their possibilities for success in the "real" world, that is, the Anglo one.

Albert: You gotta keep on trying, man! See, I grew up there and just because I grew up there doesn't mean I was gonna stay there! And I'm twenty-eight years old and it doesn't mean I'm gonna stay at this level either all my life! I'm not gonna stop trying! But I know I'm gonna have to work harder than somebody else to get that opportunity. And more importantly, in those instances when we got an opportunity, being referred to as a Hispanic . . . The two times I saw somebody get an opportunity, they both failed, they both came back home. And that goes back to our upbringing. Where we didn't want to leave or didn't . . . we were intimidated.

Hence, Albert thinks that there is something in Mexican American culture that plays against Hispanics when they attempt to escape the ethnic enclave to venture into the "real" world. Here we finally encounter the hidden side of the "melting pot ideology" so well learned by Albert: successful adjustment to American society is presumed to necessitate complete dissociation from Mexican American culture because the origin of the Mexican American problems lies in the culture itself. Albert, who not by chance refers to himself as "Hispanic," having embraced the acculturation-assimilation discourse, identifies the Chicanos as the "others," because many Chicanos are precisely those who reject that kind of discourse and advance another possible explanation of the problems Mexican Americans face in American society: discrimination (Vila 1997b).

The Chicano Discourse: "All poverty is Mexican" because of the Discriminatory Character of American Society

In this sense, the Chicano narrative also uses "Mexican" as an ethnic label but advances very different claims in relation to Mexican American ethnicity, while constructing Anglos as "others." However, the Chicano movement has lost much of its power in recent years, and its decline is especially marked in El Paso.[17] Nevertheless, a "Chicano voice" did emerge in several interviews. César is a Vietnam veteran born in El Paso who works in a federal government warehouse. He is in his late forties, holds a high school diploma, and is a Catholic. César, from the beginning of the interviews, stressed his close relationship to Mexico:

I was born here in Chihuahuita, but my grandmother, whom I wish she were alive more years (but she was really old), in order to . . . my children . . . how do you say it in Spanish? *"Exposen"* to her life . . . to them to see how it is life over there . . . that way they would learn the Mexican customs. Because my grandmother . . . her name was Guadalupe . . . and on the day of the Virgin of Guadalupe she would dance with the "Matachines," until she couldn't dance anymore. She stopped dancing with them when she was eighty-something years old.

He is not a Mexican native, but his grandmother was, and he wishes she were alive so she could teach his children the Mexican heritage first-hand. But still more important for his Chicano narrative, he is particularly proud of the *mestizo* character of his heritage:

> She was a descendant of the Yaquis Indians . . . and I am proud of that Indian heritage. I took from her her Indian blood, and there are people who are ashamed of that. And to me . . . on the contrary! I am very proud of that! I try to explain this to my children, but for them it seems that it is hard to accept that fact.

What he is offering us is the Chicano version of his "Mexican heritage," in which references to the Indian legacy are much more prominent than in the Norteño or Fronterizo version. But César offered us not only a Chicano version of the Mexican heritage, but also an analysis of why he claims for himself the term "Chicano."

> **César:** Here they treat us as . . . because today there are so many Cubans, Puerto Ricans, and people from South America . . . they call us "Hispanic." Before they never called us "Hispanics," they called us: "those Mexicans." They put us together in the same group. I do not consider myself a Hispanic. I know that in Mexico they would call me *"pocho,"* but first of all . . . if they want to put a label on me, I would call myself Chicano. . . . I am Chicano. Well, the label is not very common nowadays. I am very proud of my Indian blood. I could call myself *"mestizo,"* too, because that is what I am. It is the most correct label. But, if they wanted to put a label on me, I would better call myself Chicano . . . Chicano-*mestizo*, but not Hispanic. Hispanic means to be already grouped. Anglos have grouped us that way.

As we can see, he is quite aware of how some "others" label people like him. Who are these "others" on this occasion? On the one hand, the "others" are some Anglos who use what he considers politically loaded labels that contribute to the maintenance of their power, and on the other hand they are many Mexican nationals who use pejorative labels stressing that they do not consider him a Mexican anymore. In his reference to Anglos, what he does is describe how the ethnic classificatory system works in the United States and how some Anglos, the intellectual authors of the taxonomy, have acquired the privilege of not being referred to as an ethnicity, while all the other groups in the taxonomy are described as ethnic groups. César is extremely clear in his argument: the Hispanic label is an imposition originating in the power some Anglos have "to label" others: "Here *they* treat us . . . *they* call us . . . *they* put all of us in groups." According to his argument, to accept the label "Hispanic" is to accept being named by the "others" in power and in this way to reproduce one of the sources of their power: the ability to name, to decide which people are going to be considered "the same," to mark off the boundaries between those who can address the "others" and those who have to accept the label they have received, to offer for commonsense appropriation the starting point for an equivalence between name, attitude, and behavior, which is the basis of negative images and racism. Of course, he does not feel represented by the label and prefers the Chicano name instead. César also alludes to his awareness of the weakness of the Chicano movement in El Paso today: "the label is not very common nowadays . . ." However, Anglos are not the only "others" César refers to in his statement. The "others" are also the Mexican nationals who call him Pocho. This is the other social group to which the veteran tries to address his version of his Mexican heritage. On the one hand he complains that some Anglos are blurring his Mexican identity behind a dubious "Hispanic" label; on the other hand he criticizes many Mexican nationals for their unwillingness to consider him a real Mexican.

In this way, César is talking about his Mexicanness in ethnic terms, and in preferring the label "Chicano" to "Hispanic" or "Pocho," he is stressing the peculiar character of his identity:

> **Angela:** And if people were to ask you what it means to be Chicano, how would you explain it?
> **César:** That I'm a Mexican born in the United States, that's what I'd like. But really, really, I am first . . . American . . . We use the American ways. I was born here, my military service was in the United States. For me the United States is the most perfect government . . . the best democracy of the world.

César refers to himself as an American in national terms and as a "Mexican" in ethnic terms; thus he can claim simultaneously loyalty to his heritage and to the country where he was born and of which he is a citizen. Hence, he does not feel any contradiction in saying, in the final part of one of the interviews, that he is, first, "American," after almost four hours of conversation in which he has not only always addressed himself as a Mexican born in the United States, a Chicano, but also constructed the "*Americanos*" as the "others." And this reference is a very interesting one, because being a person who fought a war for "America," César almost always preferred to use "Americans" instead of "Anglos" as the label for the "other."

> **César:** When I was in junior high school, in the sixties almost 50 percent of the students were Mexicans and the others were Americans or Anglo Saxons, and now there isn't any more Anglos in San Elizario. Now there are only Mexicans. Then where are the Anglos now? They simply moved out.

> **César:** Look, the older people are the worst, as far as Americans, in discriminating.

> **César:** It's an attribute of the American, like the song says: "To make money, there is no other like the American."

> **César:** In the summer, I cut my own grass, I prune my own trees. I take out my radio, my beer, and my neighbor (who is Mexican but very Americanized) tells me: "Are you having a party?" And I tell him: "Ya, it's a one-man party because if nobody throws me a party I throw it for myself!" [laughs] I have my Broncos and those from the North . . . Los Tigres del Norte [two very Northern Mexican bands], I like them a lot.

We can see how César, being himself a plain American in national terms, uses almost the same kind of words people from Mexico use to depict the "other," the American. And not only that, but all his references to popular culture as an authority for his sayings, above all, music, are references to Mexican popular music: *corridos*, Los Tigres del Norte, and so on. Besides, he is in total agreement with the comments of some Mexican immigrants in El Paso who perceive that Americans do not like them, and as soon as they have the opportunity, they move from the neighborhoods that have become "Mexicanized." César, being himself an "American," is no less poignant in his remarks about the cleavage that exists between ethnic Mexicans and ethnic "Americans" (i.e., Anglos).

> **César:** Then, where are the Americans? They started moving because what we call *la raza* started moving in, and they want to separate themselves.

His reference to "*la raza*" here is a very important one. On the one hand, it is part of his Chicano credo, the acknowledgment of the brotherhood/ sisterhood that supposedly exists between Mexicans and Mexican

Americans. On the other hand, it is the recognition of who is the "other": the Anglos or Americans who are not from *mestizo* heritage.

The "Mexican" of the "all poverty is Mexican" Thematic Plot Is the Mexican National

Still, Mexican Americans have other resources with which to build a more or less valued identity. If you are a Mexican American and have two Mercedes parked in the driveway of a mansion on the west side of town, words are not needed to prove you are a different kind of Mexican: the cars and the mansion are discourses in themselves. But most Mexican Americans in El Paso do not have Mercedes or mansions, so narratives must occupy the place of expensive cars and houses: they have to "convince" people that the "all poverty is Mexican" narrative theme does not apply to them but applies to the "other." One obvious possibility for Mexican Americans living on the border is to open a gap inside the Mexican ethnic category, addressing the differences that supposedly separate Mexican Americans from Mexican nationals. According to these kinds of narratives, the "all poverty is Mexican" plot really applies to "them," the Mexicans living in Mexico (Vila 1997b). Therefore, the category "Mexican" is not used by these interviewees in ethnic terms but in national terms. This happened in an interview we conducted with a group of first-generation Mexican Americans who work in a variety of manual and semi-skilled occupations and who belong to a Christian church group. Joel, Mike, and Bob are native El Pasoans in their twenties. Joel is in college and Mike and Bob have finished their high school education. Ramón and Mary were born in Juárez but moved to El Paso more than fifteen years ago. Both hold high school diplomas. Alvaro (Ramón's brother) was born in Chicago, but moved to El Paso with his brother more than fifteen years ago. Like earlier interviewees, these interviewees mistakenly assumed that a photograph from El Paso was taken in Juárez. In this case, it was not a cemetery but a house in a run-down state that they, following the "all poverty is Mexican national" theme, automatically placed in Mexico, considering it the epitome of Mexican poverty (the same photograph that those Anglos who were not working with this narrative correctly located in El Paso):

Joel: That's the situation in Juárez. Not everybody but almost 99.99 percent of the people are in that situation [the one showed by the photograph . . . of El Paso!]. I mean that, that bad.

Advised of his mistake (the photograph prominently shows a mobile home, and in Juárez people do not live in mobile homes), he still claimed that the photo reminded him of Juárez:

> **Joel:** No, that's what I see in Mexico every time I go see my grandma. That's what I see.
> **Pablo:** But you placed this photo in Mexico. And you think that 99 percent of the people are being . . .
> **Joel:** I've been all over Juárez. It reminded me of a situation over there. I didn't see the mobile home, I just saw . . .
> **Bob:** Dude, but now, what did you say, 99 what?
> **Joel:** It's a lot of people, I don't wanna, I'm exaggerating it, but a lot of people, most of the people there.

The need to see poverty as foreign to their daily lives is so profound that when advised of their mistake, these interviewees reinforce rather than shift the essential logic of their basic plot: "All poverty is Mexican (national)." Accordingly, Joel and Ramón try to prove that El Paso's poverty is clearly different from Juárez' poverty. Nevertheless, since they cannot locate *all* poverty in Juárez, and since they have no choice other than to accept that poverty also exists in the United States, these interviewees begin to differentiate *degrees* of poverty. While Mexican poverty is "extreme" poverty, where people live in cardboard houses without water and electricity, practically starving, American poverty is *not* extreme and people live in projects with air conditioners:

PHOTO 13

A very poor hut at the center of the photo and a mobile home at the upper side located in "America," El Paso.

Ramón: When you're poor over there you live in a house made out of car-
ton or cardboard. And over here in El Paso, if you're poor, you're in the
projects, which is a house with air conditioners.

When I pointed out that the photograph Ramón and Joel selected as
the epitome of Mexican poverty was from El Paso and was, in fact, not
a shot of the projects, they tried to solve the puzzle using, once more,
the "all Mexicans (in this case, Mexican nationals) are lazy" plot.

Pablo: But this is not the projects.
Ramón: Well, you know. I think this is their own choice, wherever that is.
I guess he likes it there, or be lonely, or be . . . being messy probably. More
than being poor, you know what I mean? Because you can keep it clean,
let's say you have a trailer, just like that one. That looks trashy. Poverty in
El Paso is not poverty compared to Mexico because when you say they're
poor in Mexico that means they don't have nothin' to eat. That means you
don't have water, that means they don't have a toilet. In El Paso, there's no
poverty . . . unless, you're a bum and you *choose* to be like that. You don't
wanna work, you don't wanna pay no taxes. It's laziness, it's not poverty.
I mean the people, poor over here, they're rich compared to Mexico, you
know, you get *food*, what's poverty? You get food, they give you clothes,
they give you . . .
Alvaro: There's a Salvation [Army] for the clothes.
Ramón: . . . yeah! They, they give you clothes, they give you food, they
give you those houses over there that you pay fifty dollars, or whatever.
Mary: Thirty-one dollars . . . they are paying thirty-one dollars. If you
don't look for it, or maybe if you don't live here *legally* there might be
some poverty but just as long as they're trying to reside in El Paso, they'll
get benefits.
Bob: Don't you think that's bad?
Joel: I mean that's our tax money, there.

"Real Mexicans were those of the past"

Another interesting identity option we found in El Paso was that some
Mexican Americans tried to distinguish themselves from other Mexicans not only in national terms (like the interviewees mentioned above),
but also in ethnic terms. On the one hand they claimed that the "all poverty is Mexican" plot does not apply to them, but rather to Mexican na-

tionals (Vila 1997b). But, on the other hand, they alleged that the narrative theme also applies to other Mexican Americans of first- and second-generation whose relatives migrated to the United States more recently than they did (third- and fourth-generation Mexican Americans). This was one of the paths we found in our interviews with third- and fourth-generation Mexican Americans who no longer maintain contact with Mexico, but who still stress pride in their Mexican heritage. These interviewees are dealing with a particular feature of the border, where the statement "being proud of your Mexican heritage" has to be constantly actualized by the *real* presence of Mexico next door. To the Mexican Americans living along the border, the possibility of relating to an "ideal" Mexico far away and that few people besides they and their families know firsthand (like Poland for the Polish, Italy for the Italian Americans, etc.) is more difficult because Mexico is *there*, and what some people see on a daily basis across the border (poverty, corruption, etc.) is not well suited to construct "pride in your heritage" (Vila 1997b).

However, you *have* to point out the reasons for the pride you feel in your Mexican heritage if you use this argument to support your identity as a Mexican American. How can a person do that and detach, simultaneously, from those things he/she does not like about Mexico and Mexican culture? One way some interviewees accomplished that in El Paso was to detach themselves from the "real" Mexico and "represent" a Mexico to which they could proudly relate. And because people using this narrative cannot negate the real Mexico that the others (and themselves) see everyday across the border, they displace geography by history and link their pride in Mexico and its culture to a Mexico and culture that no longer exist, a Mexico and a Mexican culture of the past. This happened in an interview with a group of middle-class Mexican Americans of third, fourth, and fifth generations.[18]

From the first interview they recognized how difficult the construction of a Mexican American identity is for those, like them, who have no ties with Mexico anymore. As Alfredo put it:

> I think every one of us is left to our own world and the way we interpret . . . our Mexican American culture, heritage, world, . . . whatever you want to call it. It's a little different because there's really not ties left to Mexico, at least for me . . . so I think it's nothing like the Jewish that have, . . . I mean, it's just one strand period and it runs through history and wherever they are, it's the same and they can contact each other, and build a house together . . . But all of us are left to our own design, our own education, our way to do things, our morals, our ethics, wherever they came from and go.

And it's a little unusual, it's not the Anglo traditions. We're making inroads, and whatever we come to make inroads into, but we are in this country, this is our country.

According to Alfredo, for those without real ties with Mexico, the so-called Mexican American heritage becomes a matter of interpretation, not a brute fact coming from a real experience. Then for these third- and fourth generation Mexican Americans, it makes no sense to contend (as many scholars do) that the continuous immigration from Mexico to the United States keeps Mexican culture alive among Mexican Americans. We can even claim the opposite argument: for some Mexican Americans, not only is the relation with Mexican heritage a matter of interpretation (i.e., a symbolic construction that does not need any actual, current element coming from Mexican culture to be fed), but also the presence of "real" Mexicans can undermine such symbolic constructions, for they are a constant reminder of the "real" contemporary Mexican culture that these persons want to detach from. This was exactly what happened with one of the families in the interview who had the brilliant idea of "importing" a nephew from Mexico to "teach" their children their "Mexican heritage": the experience was a disaster. They rapidly discovered that their nephew's Mexicanness was totally at odds with their own sense of what it is to be a Mexican.

Alfredo: I got the bright idea: I wanna teach my kids some of our heritage, some of our culture, and I'm gonna bring in my nephew from Guadalajara into our home for a year as an exchange student. So here comes Raúl. . . . Quite an experience that was! [laughs] It was very horrible, we had experiences like, uh, one day, in the *middle* of the night, his brother showed up and he had with him the son of the secretary of the army, or the military, something or other, right from Mexico City. So here comes this *arrogant* kid. [laughs] . . .
Fanny: He would not even speak to me. . . .
Alfredo: Oh no! you can't talk to a woman . . .
Oscar: That's below them, yeah . . .
Fanny: Oh, absolutely!
Alfredo: It was midnight: "Hey, hey" [snapping his fingers] "*¡Hágame algo de comer!*" [Make me something to eat!] "*Y aquí está mi ropa para lavar*" [Here are my clothes that need to be washed] . . .
Fanny: "*Y esto se haga* [sic] *en seco, y esto*" [This has to be drycleaned] . . . he gave me instructions on how to do his laundry! And this was like: "Well, where's my coffee?" And *I* have *never* felt like a servant like I did when those boys were in my home . . .

Alfredo: To make a long story short. . . that was *real* confusion! I mean, I thought it was going to bring [laughs] our culture in, and show it to 'em! . . . It didn't quite work. He tested our *every* ethic and moral, for example, to go to church on Sunday. . . .

Fanny: Oh, we'd get into a violent argument . . .

Alfredo: They don't go to mass.

Fanny: First, he wanted me to prove to him that there was a God! Because it was . . .

Alfredo: He was this little, this little shrimp, you know, doing these things! . . .

Oscar: ¡*Un pedo*! [a fart!] [laughing]

The presence of the "real" Mexico in his house, instead of reinforcing the Mexican heritage as this interviewee understood it, threatened to undermine his family's most profound beliefs and values.

Pablo: And besides religion and all of that, what other features did you see as totally different from *your* culture?

Alfredo: They grew up entirely different, they grew up . . . very, um, pampered and with a lot of machismo. There are men that will *own* the woman, the woman is a property. Not in our family. Our women in our family are equals, they're supposed to go and do independently, they are not slaves. But, he grew up and I'm sure today, he's an accountant, he goes like that [snapping his fingers] to his wife . . . [everyone laughs].

These interviewees do not see any contradiction in stating that *their* Mexico of the past was a Mexico *without* machismo, for instance, as if machismo were a *new* feature of modern Mexico. Moreover, the "macho" style they hated so much in their "submersion" into the "contemporary Mexican culture" could have been described using some other explanation besides the "time/ethnic/national" one they offered in the interview. Thus, in the case of the "son of the secretary of the army, or the military" they could have offered an answer in terms of status, such as "all the military people behave in this kind of demanding and arrogant way," or in terms of class, such as "all these *juniors* [nouveau riche youth] in Mexico behave in such a way." The selection of the particular frame they used to explain the macho behavior of their nephew was not by chance. On the contrary, it was deeply rooted in the particular plot these interviewees were employing to construct their identity as "Mexicans of the past." We can also see in this example how difficult it is to separate the different subject positions people identify with. Alfredo's family criticism toward their relative is constantly mixing ethnic, national, age, and gender dimensions in a complex knot that can be separated analytically, but not factually.

Consequently, the construction of a valued identity of Mexican Americans assumes a double-edged form in these interviews. On the one hand, they revindicate their Mexican heritage, but stress that they are proud of the Mexico of the past, not the "corrupt, poor, violent, and machista" Mexico of the present. On the other hand, they separate themselves from the contemporary Mexicans, who they do not recognize as their own people. According to this kind of discourse, Mexicans living in the United States do not have "just one strand period and it runs through history and wherever they are, it's the same and they can contact each other, and build a house together." For these interviewees, Mexicans living in the United States who arrived into the country in different periods of Mexican history, and who came from very different Mexican regions, are not the same, and they cannot build a house together (a metaphor for solidarity). The comparison with the Jews that Alfredo made (and many similar comparisons made by other interviewees) is meant to prove exactly that: unlike Jews, who are supposedly *one* people, Mexicans living in the United States are many peoples.

Furthermore, homogeneity and heterogeneity are clearly social constructions, where *my* group always seems to be heterogeneous, and *the other* homogeneous. Hence, according to Alfredo, Mexican Americans are a very heterogeneous population, whereas Jews are homogeneous. It does not matter to Alfredo's argument that Jews arrived in the United States during several different periods, from different countries and speaking many different languages. To him, all are Jews and have what Mexican Americans lack: common ethnic morals and values.

But how did these interviewees construct their "old" Mexico, of which they could be proud? First, they offered an image of past Mexico that "was totally different" from the contemporary Mexico.

> **Rosa:** My *suegra* [mother-in-law] was from Coahuila and my *suegro* [father-in-law] was from Sonora, and all their deep roots *are* from there. We used to like to go over there. We would go at least three times a week, to eat mangos, and take 'em this and that. Every Friday was burrito day. And I still remember, it *has* been good, but it has changed a lot to the point that you just don't want to go over there anymore: the traffic, you know, the *mordelones* [corrupt policemen], you know, . . . so it scares you and, we have roots way back when, like you say, and it's not that we're ashamed, it's just that you get scared, you get scared.

Fanny: I'm very, very proud, and those memories are very beautiful memories, but *of back then*.

Rosa: Back then. Back then.

Oscar: A different time.

Fanny: Huh, huh, it's a different time . . . a Mexico of the past.

Everybody: Yes.

Fanny: It was beautiful.

Alfredo: These pictures here are representative of the Juárez I knew when we were growing up. It was the houses on 16 de Septiembre, representing the wealth that was there, you see very small pockets of it today. That's the Juárez we knew. It was a completely different Mexico. At worst case some of the poverty could be seen across from the smelter, the little houses up in the hills starting. But for the most part . . . oh, and then the only seedy part of Juárez was the back streets . . . where the houses of prostitution were . . . that's still there today, I'm sure it hasn't changed much, but basically that was the only seedy part of Juárez and that was kind of a Las Vegas-type thing in back, nothing like today. So from a past of *real* beauty . . . It was something else . . . the people . . . even the people were different and that's our culture, that's our heritage.

They see the Mexico of their past as a happy, wealthy Mexico, and even the infamous stigma of Juárez as a city of vice is downplayed by these interviewees, who argue that today's prostitution is much more open and public (not a "Las Vegas-type thing in the back" as it was before) than in the "golden years." And the argument goes on to explain that not

PHOTO 14

A mansion located on 16 de Septiembre Avenue, Ciudad Juárez.

only the country has changed, but also the people. And this Mexico of the present, from which these interviewees want to separate themselves in order to preserve their identities as "Mexicans of the past," is seen as so strange that it is "a completely different world" (just as it was described by some of our Anglo interviewees!). And these interviewees do not see any possible bridge that can close the gap between that golden past and this turbid present.

> **Alfredo:** My aunt is with immigration. She's been with them for years. And my aunt used to be a very *kind* individual (she still is, she has a very big heart), but her job has made her very, very bitter. It's a very *ugly* job, with no common sense to it: round 'em up, our own people, throw 'em back. And then sometimes she's on the front lines there, and the men from over there can be so abusive, and it's a completely different world! It's nothing, nothing like what we grew up in . . . even the *people* are different! Like they're off on a different mission. It's nothing as comfortable as when we were growing up . . . when the Mexican American was a *true* Mexican American. Today it's very divided . . . and the Mexican citizen can be very, uh, almost not Mexican-like, from another world.

This interviewee is denying the status of "true Mexicans" to those Mexican nationals of the present, as if the only bearers of the "real" Mexican heritage, that of the Mexico of the past, were third- and fourth-generation Mexican Americans, not contemporary Mexican nationals. Accordingly, Mexico becomes a concept, not a country, a way to understand morals and ethics, morals and ethics that allegedly were characteristics of a country named Mexico—but a long time ago. And if contemporary Mexican nationals are not "true" Mexicans, then most contemporary Mexican Americans are not "true" Mexican Americans either. Why? Because most Mexican Americans in El Paso are recent immigrants from Mexico who no longer carry the "authentic" Mexican heritage. Thus, it is not surprising that images of the illegal Mexican taking advantage of the American taxpayer, and the lazy first- and second-generation Mexican American living on welfare, appeared in this interview. The latter are the "Mexicans" to whom the "all poverty (due to laziness) is Mexican" narrative theme applies. This narrative does not apply to them; they are the bearers of the true Mexican heritage. As one interviewee pointed out:

> **Fanny:** I'm fourth maybe even fifth generation, and I remember *so much* of what my grandmother taught me . . . stressing to be educated and to be proud of your heritage and to live honestly and with pride, and to *work* for

everything that you want in life. My mother had a very, very *difficult* time when my father died . . . but God forbid that any of our mothers or any of us *would have dared* thought of going for help or asking for food stamps! Because there was so much pride, you'd never do that!

Alfredo: And today they exist on the system.

Thus do these interviewees, using time instead of ethnicity or nationality to mark their difference, and claiming that they are the *real* Mexicans, those from the old and good Mexico of the past, construct the "other" from whom they must separate. In the interviews we conducted with them, the first social actors they addressed as the "other" Mexicans were the poor Mexican nationals "taking advantage" of the generosity of the American people:

Fanny: I worked for the El Paso Independent School District for about nine years and in *those* years there were kids that would come across the border Sunday night or Monday morning and they would attend classes all week long, which I thought was wonderful, but what I have a hard time with is the attitude . . . the *attitude* infuriated me, they are very demanding, they weren't really here to learn, they found a way to get into the system . . . you know, the free lunches, and everything, the disrespect was there, and I tried my best to encourage them to learn to speak English . . . it will enrich your lives . . . and they demanded that *I* speak Spanish to them because that was *their* right, and that I could not force them to speak English because it was their right . . . and . . . I had a very hard time with that . . .

Rosa: I substitute with El Paso, too, and that's *exactly* what's going on with the students. Over there some of them are starving, that's why they probably came down here, and yet, the lunch, the free lunch, ooh! They push it away, "¡*Que fea comida!*" [What ugly food!]. And I tell 'em, "You know you are better off than over there, what is your gripe?" No . . . and they always, . . . they are demanding, they want everything.

Therefore, those kids who cross the border not to learn (they refuse to learn English), but to get free lunches, without showing any gratitude to the American system which is saving them from starvation, are the epitome of the *new* Mexican national from whom these interviewees want to separate themselves. The image of a child behaving in this "demanding," "disrespectful" way is a very powerful one: if children are behaving this way, what could we expect from their parents or the older generation? This theme also appeared in the interviews with these families, when Alfredo mentioned how the first-generation Mexican American (one of the "others" for these interviewees) adolescents behave:

Alfredo: You know that attitude that you all are talking about in the kids, it's worse in the young adults! The Lower Valley is *teaming* with gangs! . . . And for the most part, they are first-generation Mexican American people! . . . *Man* they are bad! . . . Their attitude . . . they own the Lower Valley! The other day at my client's hotel, there was a murder . . . one just decided to murder the other, two kids . . .

Then, the "attitude," the "mentality" these fourth- and fifth-generation Mexican Americans try to detach from is not only present in Mexican children, but also in first-generation Mexican Americans (i.e., not the "true" Mexican Americans), those who cannot bear poverty with dignity as our interviewees did in the past: "God forbid that any of our mothers or any of us *would have dared* thought of . . . going for help or asking for food stamps!" On the contrary, according to Alfredo and his family, first-generation Mexican Americans not only would go for food stamps when they need them, but also would take advantage of the system in very bizarre ways:

Fanny: I remember going to the Smith that was here, and there was a man with a basket full of the best meats, best fruits, cookies, dog food, and things like that, . . . and he had food stamps, and the checkouts girl at the checkouts stand said, "*Señor, esto* [dog food] *no se puede comprar con estampillas*" [Sir, you cannot buy dog food with food stamps] and the guy *dijo*, "*Ah, está bien, entonces le compramos fresco*" [OK, then we will buy fresh food for our dog]. He went back and *got fresh meat!* And I thought: *Lo que le compra a los perros* [What he is buying for his dogs] would feed my family for a week, it was a feeling in my stomach that turned, uh.

But these "attitudes," which our interviewees try to detach from, are not only present in children, adolescent, or first-generation Mexican American adults who buy fresh meat for the dog with food stamps, but are also present in rich Mexican citizens, because the problem is with the *new* Mexican culture and Mexican people, regardless of social class, age, gender, or citizenship. And here we observe in all its magnitude the idea of "invasion," the idea of "losing" El Paso to "Mexican invaders," that appeared prominently in some of our Mexican American interviewees. These invaders are coming from two very different fronts. On the one hand are the "illegal aliens" who are supposedly at the base of most of the social problems of the city, and who take advantage of the American taxpayer (the rationale that justified the amazing degree of Mexican American support for Operation Blockade in El Paso). On the other hand are those "rich" Mexican nationals who are "taking over" El Paso's economy through their buying power.

In relation to the rich side of the equation, what some Mexican Americans like Alfredo complain about most is their feeling of "displacement":

Alfredo: Another thing that is happening in our country and our city, uh, our stores right now are being supported by Mexican citizens, so the emerging rich class in Mexico has come over *here* and taken over. Our stores here on the border have survived only . . . because of their trade, it's the strangest thing.

Oscar: Especially downtown.

Alfredo: Huh, huh, now we get to go downtown and no one pays attention to us because we don't *look* like Mexicans [laughs], you go to the Popular, they could care less about helping you . . .

But in a way Alfredo takes it as an "honor" to not be confused with a "contemporary Mexican," because these Mexicans behave in a way that is not characteristic of a "true old Mexican" like himself:

Alfredo: And those people that come over can be so *pushy, pushy* . . .

Rosa: Very demanding. People that come from Chihuahua and all that . . . they bring cash, and they expect everybody to wait on them like queens and kings . . . [snapping of fingers in the background].

Fanny: I've got to learn how to do that 'cause it seems to work . . . [laughs].

Rosa: And they come and they take *three* baskets, *four* baskets, full . . . and everybody hates that.

Alfredo: But in a very pushy, arrogant manner . . . like they'll buy their thousand dollars worth of stuff at Dillard's and they care nothing about the wrappings that's left in the parking lot . . . to me, is left . . . to the morals and ethics we were taught by our parents, but they are *different*, they are *different* . . .

Fanny: . . . they are *different* . . . and, and I, I have a *real hard* time with that . . .

Thus, nothing is farther from "the morals and ethics" of the "true" bearers of the Mexican heritage than the pushy and arrogant behavior of some Mexican citizens (those "kings and queens") who seem to have taken over El Paso's shopping centers. In this sense we can see how the poor Mexican nationals and first- and second-generation Mexican Americans are those Mexicans to whom the "all poverty is Mexican" plot really applies. Neither do these kinds of interviewees see any contradiction in portraying the rich Mexicans as the "other," because the bottom line of their narrative plot is the construction of a moral barrier between them and all the other Mexicans who, for different reasons, do not hold anymore the "authentic" Mexican heritage.

According to these interviewees, the resentment between Mexican Americans and Mexicans can be so profound that they can, in some extreme occasions, hate each other:

> **Alfredo:** And my aunt, the one in immigration, she says crazy things like: "*I hate 'em, I hate 'em, I hate 'em!*" [laughs]. And she's become so *bitter*, so embittered with her job and what she sees that she'll say, "*I am not Mexican!*" [laughs] . . . so talk about confusion . . .
> **Fanny:** And my daughter says, "Alicia, excuse me, you are Mexican!" [laughs].
> **Alfredo:** And she says, "*No I'm not!*" [laughs].

These educated middle- and upper-middle-class Mexican Americans are totally aware of the confusion and ambivalence that pervade their feelings. Ergo, these interviewees felt that they were in a kind of "limbo."

> **Alfredo:** Talk about confusion on our part, I mean we get caught in limbo . . .

And the consistent answer to this state of "limbo" is, again, that they are Mexicans themselves, but Mexicans of the past, not contemporary Mexicans:

> **Fanny:** We have different attitudes, different values . . . But they did exist in Mexico, when there *was* that pride and that respect as we knew it, because our grandparents *came* from there, and it was there! It *was* a different Mexico!

Their own experience of discrimination *inside* the Latino community in the United States does not prevent them from doing the same things discriminatory people did to them, with those Mexican citizens and Mexican Americans they want to separate from:

> **Alfredo:** In Northern New Mexico, . . . Uribari, in Albuquerque is Uribarry, Romero is Romaro, they are *not* Mexicans.[19]
> **Oscar:** *Son Españoles.*
> **Alfredo:** They are Spanish [everyone laughing]. And they look down their nose at you [laughs]. But they are Mexican Americans! I mean they are not *Spanish* . . . you'll find a Mexican American over there . . . just cannot and will not, and *refuses* to identify with Mexicans . . .

What the group is referring to here is the well-known attitude of some Mexican Americans in New Mexico who refuse to acknowledge any linkage to Mexico, and trace their roots directly back to Spain.[20] These New Mexicans support their claim that they are Spaniards and not Mexicans because after Mexico's independence, and due to the political turmoil that followed it, what is now New Mexico was almost not touched by Mexican rule and authorities. Consequently, these New Mexico Hispanics argue that they came under American citizenship *directly* from colonial Spain, and never from Mexico as a country. But some of these "Spaniards" not only refuse to acknowledge their Mexican heritage, but also discriminate against Mexicans and Mexican Americans:

> **Fanny:** I was having a garage sale in Santa Fe once, and this older gentleman walked in and he heard me speak Spanish . . . *y me dice, "Oye pues, ¿De 'ónde eres tú?" Y le dije, "Señor, yo soy Tejana-Mejicana." Y me dijo, "Pues yo no sé qué estás haciendo aquí . . . aquí no nos gustan, ni los Tejanos, ni menos los Mejicanos"* . . . [and he told me, "Listen, where are you from?" I told him, "Sir, I am Texan and Mexican." Then he told me, "Then, I do not know what are you doing here . . . here we do not like Texans, much less Mexicans"]

But if these interviewees truly understand the absurdity of this kind of position, and how much confusion is going on in developing a Spanish identity in New Mexico, they do not grasp how similar the position is to their own. *Both use time* to separate themselves from those Mexicans they do not want to relate to. The New Mexicans recognize a Spanish heritage that is located in the first part of the nineteenth century. Our interviewees are proud of a Mexican heritage located in the first part of the twentieth century — the culture their grandparents taught them when they were growing up (and that they "tasted" for themselves during their childhood), which they identify as the "Golden Age" of Mexico. The only difference is that going farther back in time the New Mexican Spaniards can avoid the label "Mexican" completely, something our interviewees cannot, hence their necessity to differentiate between a Mexico of the present they dislike and a Mexico of the past they love.

But Mexican Americans like Alfredo and his family, who claim they are proud of their Mexican heritage, not only have to make sense of the Mexican part of their identity in order to detach themselves from the "all poverty is Mexican" narrative plot, but also have to "explain" to the Mexicans living on the other side of the border the *American* part of the category ("Mexican American") they have decided to identify with.

In this one and many other interviews, a recurrent question that many Mexican nationals posed to Mexican Americans was: Why do you fight and die for the United States if you are a Mexican?

Oscar: I had a friend of mine that he had cousins and they used to visit all the time from Sonora, they used to come up here and we used to lock horns. And one thing that they can't conceive . . . they see us or whatever as marginal men, and we are not Mexican, and we are not American, *y no somos tontos* or *pendejos* [and we are not stupid or fools], why are we loyal to the United States? And that gets to me, you know 'cause I served my country and it's in me, and I taught my kids, when I saw them tear that flag down, remember about ten years ago in Juárez . . . and I'm looking at it on TV . . . and I guess I saw red . . . you know you don't do that to my flag and stuff like that.

Alfredo: This *is* our country.

Oscar: It's in us you know, and nobody's gonna take it, either the Anglo, the *güero* [blonde] or nobody will take that away from us, you know, we are loyal Americans . . . and if people don't like it, that's too bad. And all our generation, we've served our country honorably, World War I, World War II, we got the most medals of honor in the war . . . in Korea, in Vietnam . . . and yet we still have our roots, you know, *así somos* [we are like that], whatever, you know, we have Hispano, Mexican, but when it comes down to that, push comes to shove, *somos* [we are] . . .

Alfredo: We are people that have principles, ethics and norms . . .

Oscar: When they push us, you know, this is our country, and everything else, you know . . .

"When push comes to shove . . ." these third- and fourth-generation Mexican Americans identify themselves as being primarily Americans.

As we have seen, in order for these interviewees to be proud of their Mexican heritage, they have to separate themselves from the Mexico of the present and construct an idealized Mexico of the past. As such, living on the border surrounded by Mexico's reality and *real* Mexican citizens is experienced as a detriment rather than an asset (Vila 1997b). If this is so, they understand why their children want to live somewhere else in the United States, far from the border, in places where there are not " . . . so many . . . people from Mexico . . ." Rosa explains,

I have a son who lives in Tennessee now and he comes for Christmas. And he says: "Mother, no offense, but if I didn't have to visit you and my dad I would not come back to El Paso, it is disgusting. And it's hard for me to say that because I was born in El Paso. But it's very sad, Mom. That I'm over there and I come and I can see the difference. . . . The people . . . how they treat you, there's so many . . . people from Mexico in El Paso, and those people . . . they don't have any manners or class or anything, they just shove you over, you're nobody. . . . And we were born here." Yeah . . . a lot of our kids . . . they don't want to stay here 'cause there's too many people from *that* side, and they're gonna move out of town as soon as they get a chance.

To claim that they are primarily Americans, to dislike Mexican nationals and first- and second-generation Mexican Americans, and to approve of their children's decision of living far from the border, where there are not "too many people from Mexico" does not contradict their claim of being proud of their Mexican heritage. Because that pride is not linked to a country but to a way of understanding morals and values that, some time in the past, but no longer in the present, were linked to a country named Mexico.

Tropes of Difference on the American Side: The "Third World country versus First World country" Case

As I point out in the Appendix, tropes play a very important role in the construction of identities on both sides of the border. We already discussed the importance of the metaphor of the "sister cities" in the construction of sameness on the Mexican side of the border. With some of the testimonies quoted above (and with others I will quote below), we can see a totally different picture, that is, how a trope of difference is used to mark the absolute otherness many Americans feel in relation to Mexicans. I am referring here to the widespread use of the "First World vs. Third World" trope by many of our interviewees who were working with the thematic plot stating that "all poverty is Mexican." Thus, if the "sister cities" trope is a metaphor that buttresses the construction of a Fronterizo identity on the Mexican side of the border, the "Third World vs. First World" is a contiguity trope, or, more precisely, an *inventory* that sustains exactly the opposite, that is, how different many Americans feel in relation to Mexicans.

We already saw how Debbie, Carol, Larry, and Robert separated Juárez and El Paso in terms of entire "worlds," where the "otherness" they feel relative to Mexicans is so profound that it is not enough to characterize El Paso and Juárez as two different *cities* or parts of two different *countries*. Indeed, they must go further and describe the cities as belonging to two different *worlds*. We also saw how Miles, Bessie, and Billie were doing the same thing. Here we will see how the logic of difference is named in terms of the inventory trope mentioned above.

Then, if all these interviewees were talking of differences in terms of worlds, why not identify those worlds? Hence the trope "Third World vs. First World," which many middle-class interviewees in El Paso (Anglos, African Americans, and Mexican Americans) used to depict the extreme otherness they feel separates themselves from Juarenses.

One extended way to use the trope "Third World vs. First World" is to use the term "underdeveloped" to describe Juárez. This happened in the interview I conducted with Miles, Bessie, and Billie:

Miles: As I look into the depth of this photograph, I see underdevelopment here . . . I see a depressive state and, it brings sadness to my eyes when I see this . . . people living like this, ah, unpaved roads and, houses with no windows . . .

Miles' wife, Billie, shares his sentiments. As a matter of fact, that is the major reason she wants to leave El Paso immediately, to be as far away as possible from the kind of poverty that only a Third World country can suffer. Because they are in the military and have traveled the world, it is not surprising that these interviewees compared what they have seen in the El Paso–Juárez area with what they witnessed in Berlin:

Miles: As I look here in this photo [photo 3, shown in Chapter 2], I reflect back to Berlin, leaving from West Berlin and going into East Berlin, the streetlights were nice and bright in West Berlin and you drive across this imaginary line and you got a, hung lightbulbs in there . . . that was really depressing to me . . . . I having lived in Berlin, this looked to me as like an imaginary wall . . . ah, the Rio Grande separating prosperity from despair, and I wonder just how many people put their lives on the line, to try to make it . . . try to make it to prosperity.

"First World vs. Third World", "development vs. underdevelopment," "prosperity vs. poverty," "hope vs. despair": these interviewees used all these images to express the sense of otherness they feel in relation to Juárez and Juarenses. It is a feeling well captured by Billie, when she commented, "Separation . . . close but yet so far . . ." As we can see, these interviewees have a very negative image of Juárez; it is depressing to them. They feel totally separated from Mexico and Mexicans. They cannot even imagine how people can live over there, and nothing seems more distant to their living standards than those of Mexico. This kind of narrative is not only an Anglo or an African American one, but also was used by many Mexican American interviewees. It is quite understandable that many Anglos and African Americans, due to the ethnic logic that underlies how some Americans construct identity, construct the ethnic "other," the Mexican and its country of origin, Mexico, with such overtones of "otherness." It is another matter when the same descriptions are offered by people of Mexican ancestry who claim pride in their ethnicity, as many Mexican Americans do. The following examples show, once more, how contradictory the narratives of Mexican Americans can be on the U.S.–Mexico border.

In an interview conducted with a group of first- and second-generation Mexican American professionals and clerks, the trope of the dramatic encounter between the First World and the Third World was prominent:[21]

> **Armando:** And when you think about the U.S.–Mexican border, there is no other place in the world where a First World . . . a first power of a nation as rich and everything as the United States borders what's considered a Third World nation. And the difference is very, very dramatic . . .
> **Sergio:** And you know, we even saw a lady living in between a crack in Juárez . . .
> **Serafín:** In the mountain . . . in a hole in the mountain.
> **Sergio:** On the rock wall . . . on the rock wall . . .

In this interview, instead of comparing the U.S.–Mexico border to Berlin, Armando used another dramatic geographical comparison to stress the extreme sense of separation he feels from Mexico: the border between Israel and the Arabs:

> **Armando:** I picked this photo because the disparity you see . . . one side, UTEP, and you see the other side, Juárez, and the disparity and all that . . .

PHOTO 15

University of Texas at El Paso.

and how poor, and all that . . . It reminds me and my friends of the West Bank and of Israel. You look at it on TV and all that, and it's *exactly* what that looks like. And no one makes comments about the disparity, the poverty . . . and they're worried about fighting for land that *looks* like that.

We can see how some El Pasoans (still those of Mexican ancestry) overlooked what they share with Juarenses in terms of their *population and culture* (the most important argument behind the "sister cities" metaphor). Instead, they focused more on the *economic* differences that separate the United States from Mexico. In this way, they tended to construct an identity as *Americans* based on the claim of belonging to American society, which they characterize as "totally" different from Mexico.

In this sense, like so many other aspects of human perception, homogeneity and heterogeneity are in the eyes of the beholder. We have seen in Chapter 2 how for many middle-class Mexican nationals, an important part of their Fronterizo identity involves stressing how connected they feel to El Paso and El Pasoans. To do this, they address an inescapable fact of border life: that most of the people are of Mexican descent, a large percentage of whom are connected by family ties, and who share some aspects of the Mexican culture. Instrumental in this kind of construction is the use (and abuse) of the "sister cities" metaphor.

By contrast, in the identity construction of many middle-class El Pasoans (regardless of their ethnicity), an opposite claim seems to be vital, that is, to stress how different they feel relative to Mexican nationals and Juárez. To prove their point, they stress the inarguably enormous economic differences that distinguish El Paso from Juárez. Important in this narrative is the use of the "First World vs. Third World" trope.

Which assertion is correct? The answer is neither and both. The fact of the matter is that no one is lying, nor is anyone telling the whole truth. Rather, this process of selective appropriation of reality is crucial for identity construction; by telling their stories, individuals make claims about the coherence of their lives. Further, what is included and omitted from their accounts renders plausible the anticipated future (Rosenwald and Ochberg 1992, p. 9). This issue — of what is included and omitted from the account — leads us to a crucial feature of narrative in the construction of identity: its selectivity. In the next chapter I will analyze the contorted narrative identities of some Mexican immigrants who have to deal with the fact that they are, in both ethnic and national terms, the Mexicans that the "all poverty is Mexican" narrative theme portrays so negatively.

Introduction

In the last chapter I mentioned that, due to the pervasive presence of the "all poverty is Mexican" discourse in El Paso, the constitution of a valued social identity is relatively straightforward for some middle-class Anglos and relatively difficult for many people of Mexican descent. We have seen how using an *ethnic classification system*, many Anglos (and those from other ethnicities — including Mexican Americans — who share with them this particular way of understanding identity) tend to conflate Mexicans and Mexican Americans because both belong to the same "ethnic" category. On the other hand, we had the opportunity to see how some Mexican Americans use nationality to detach themselves from Mexican nationals and race and/or ethnicity to differentiate themselves from Anglos. Mexican immigrants, on the other hand, have to confront the fact that they "are" Mexicans in terms of both nationality and ethnicity.

In this chapter I will discuss the problematic situation of some Mexican immigrants in El Paso. If they are poor, they have to follow a quite distinct path in the constitution of a valued social identity. They confront an ethnic and racial classification system that denigrates them without the escape hatch of economic success used, for instance, by Albert and Alfredo and his family. As a result, they have to deal with the fact that, at first glance, the hegemonic discourse seems to be confirmed. For poor Mexican Americans who, for a variety of reasons, do not consider the Chicano discourse theirs, the process of constructing a valued social identity is far more tortuous. Without the possibility of relying on a structured, social, and collectively developed discourse that blames poverty on discrimination, these interviewees nevertheless have to make sense of their situation. At the same time, if these interviewees still maintain family ties with Mexico, they have to make sense of contemporary Mexican poverty without portraying Mexican nationals as the "others," like Joel and his friends did, or inventing a Mexico of the past in the way Alfredo and his family did.

To complicate matters further, many of my Mexican immigrant interviewees still use Mexican and/or Fronterizo categories, metaphors, and narratives to construct the "other," mixing frames of ref-

Chapter 4

**MEXICAN IMMIGRANTS AND THE
"ALL POVERTY IS MEXICAN" NARRATIVE PLOT**

erence (sometimes in a single portrayal of the "other") to make sense of their identities. Here is where they have to rely on a very complex discourse to construct a valued identity as Mexicans living in the United States.

The Mexicans of the "all poverty is Mexican" Narrative Plot Are the Mexican Americans Who Live on Welfare

In one interview I conducted with a group of female immigrants in El Paso,[1] one of the interviewees told us the following story:

> **Norma:** A girl who lives here in the alley once got in a fight with a guy. She has a little boy and the guy has another little boy. They were there on the park slides. So, the guy goes over and gets the girl's little boy so that his kid can get on and he tells him, "Get out of here, scoot aside so my kid can get on." And she asked him, "Why are you taking him off?" He said, "You know what? This park belongs to those of us from here. You're from Juárez; you don't have anything to do here in the park." She said, "You know what? If I live here, all what I eat I pay for it . . . it's at a dear price, but not for you. The government supports you and your brat. I pay taxes, I pay everything and you pay for nothing." And it's true because everyone here has this many kids and food stamps for all of them! Look, they've never been able to give me any because I have this pittance of a house. My husband works. My husband's sixty-seven years old and he still works and I work and that's why they don't give us any. And I tell him, "You should quit working now. You are elderly, and can no longer work." I say to him, "There are many young people and they are resting in the park," and I say to him, "They are the ones that the government is helping and maintaining, people who are strong, and people like us who give more and more to the government are the ones who have more taken away through taxes." Listen, why is it that way?

This is a complete narrative with plot, characters, a sequence (a beginning, middle, and end), and a moral stance about what is being told. In this story Norma claims that the "all poverty is Mexican" hegemonic thematic plot really applies to Mexican Americans, not to Mexican immigrants, who are not allowed to use the American welfare system. Accordingly, Norma strongly identifies with her neighbor's answer to the Mexican American man. In this sense, Norma has a very developed plot about her previous Juarense and current Mexican immigrant identities, attuned to the hegemonic "all poverty is Mexican" discourse (here pointing out that the "Mexican" of the sentence actually applies to the Mexican Americans), and illustrated by the complete narrative shown above. Norma's story corresponds to what van Dijk calls "lack of Resolution" in minority stories: we do not know what finally happened between Norma's friend and her Chicano opponent. According to van Dijk (1993, p. 135): "This lack of a Resolution . . . in stories . . . is rather typical . . . an expression of the lack of a solution in the underlying model: The complicating event is interpreted as an unresolved predicament, which makes the whole story take the form of a complaint-story . . ." The lack of resolution in stories about the "other" means that ethnic events are essentially problematic, that there *is* no solution for the storyteller.

The theoretical point I want to stress here (and that I develop in full in the Appendix) is that the non-narrative descriptions about herself and "others" that Norma gave me in the interview are also narrative-laden. In other words, when Norma is talking in pure categorical terms or using metaphors to refer to herself and "others," she *still* has her basic identity plot in mind, and she also is performing her "Mexican immigrant who works and does not use welfare" character. Importantly, the *evaluative criteria* that guide any narrative construction still work in truncated, unfinished narratives like the ones people use when addressing the "others" in categorical or metaphorical terms. In Norma's case, the basic thematic plot Norma used to compose her story also organized her other statements about her Mexicanness and the difference she sees between Mexican immigrants and Mexican Americans. When Norma used other non-narrative discursive devices to talk about the differences between Mexican immigrants and Mexican Americans (categorical references to Mexican Americans and the use of some metaphor to refer to them—*ratas* [rats] in the testimony cited below), she was doing that from the selective point of view of the "Mexican immigrant who works and does not use welfare" character she had constructed for herself during the interview process. And, of course, the categories and metaphors she used helped her to buttress the narrative character she wanted to portray before me.

> **Estela:** Let them take away welfare and let everyone work. We have to work anyway.
> **Norma:** Well, look, there's gonna be more *ratas* [delinquents] because most of the people here are not used to work.
> **María:** That's true, now they sell stamps to buy beer.

Norma: They've come to sell stamps to me. They've come to offer me forty stamps for twenty dollars . . . just so you give them cash, they give you double the amount.

Pablo: And the people who are on welfare are those born here, that is, Mexican Americans born here or people from Juárez?

Estela: No, no, people born here.

The reference to the lack of morals that supposedly characterizes some Mexican Americans, who take advantage of the welfare system to satisfy their vices, is in line with one of the key features of any narrative. This is precisely the characteristic that differentiates narratives from other discursive devices; that is, narrativity proposes a particular order of meaning that, as I point out in the Appendix, is always a moral one.

Therefore, when Norma and her friends stated that they were Mexicans (and when other interviewees were saying they were Anglos, African Americans, Chicanos, Hispanics, or Mexican Americans), they were not just saying that they were strongly attached to this particular ethnic identity by chance, but that this particular ethnic identity provided them the frames within which they could determine where they stood on questions of what is good, worthwhile, or of value.

Consequently, these women, knowing that many Mexican Americans try to deflect from themselves the "all poverty is Mexican" stigma by arguing that the really poor people are the Mexican nationals on both sides of the border, counterattack by claiming that if all Mexicans are the same (using "Mexican" as an ethnic term), the really problematical people in El Paso are the Mexican Americans, not them.

Norma: You know what makes me really angry? That they say: "people from Juárez." All the people over here are just Mexican people, just people like us. And even though we live on this side we will never cease to be Mexicans. And people from here, just because they were born here say: "Oh, we are Americans." They're darker than I and they say they're Americans! That's awful and all the people from here call those of us who come from Juárez: "Oh, these Juareños, since they arrived this place has gotten worse and worse." And if you say something, they say: "Oh, like for instance I was robbed once, . . . oh, it's the people from Juárez!" "No," I said. "It's not the people from Juárez! It's the people from here because the people from here know how things are here. The people from Juárez cross and they cross desperate to go through to the interior. They're not gonna stop and rob them." Ah, but everyone here is very *malinchista* [unpatriotic]!

Norma lives in a very poor (and almost totally Mexican) neighborhood in El Paso, and despite the fact that she has been living in El Paso for almost ten years she still considers herself a *Mexican*. Not only that, she also feels that *all* her Mexican American neighbors are essentially Mexicans. In this sense, she has constructed a category that includes both Mexican nationals and Mexican Americans; that is, she utilizes "Mexicano" as an ethnic, not as a national term. This adoption is not by chance; it allows her to strongly reject the national logic of classification we have seen some Mexican Americans try to use to separate themselves from Mexican nationals: "And people from here, just because they were born here say: 'Oh, we are Americans.'" According to the ethnic scheme she has adopted, place of birth is less important than skin color, and Mexican Americans could never go outside their ethnicity regardless of their efforts, because their dark skin would not allow them to do so: "They're darker than I and they say they're Americans!"

According to Norma, some of her Mexican American neighbors use a national frame of reference to separate themselves from the Mexicans coming from Juárez. Thus, they attribute (as many of our own interviewees did) "poverty without dignity" to the Juarenses: "Oh, these Juareños, since they arrived this place has gotten worse and worse." "And if you say something, they say: 'Oh, like for instance I was robbed once, . . . oh, it's the people from Juárez!'" In turn, Norma rejects their complaint using an ethnic point of reference. However, after living in the States for a while, she is aware of the ethnic and racial classification system working in the States and uses it to deny her Mexican American neighbors' claim of separation from "Mexicans." She then pushes her argument further, pointing out that the real "poor without dignity" on the border are the Mexican Americans themselves: "'No,' I said, 'it's not the people from Juárez! It's the people from here . . .'"

Finally, to complete her argument, she needs to explain why the Mexican Americans are those "poor people without dignity" from whom she wants to distinguish herself—although she insists, *not* for the reasons advanced by the Mexican Americans themselves (i.e., because they are "Americans," and she is not). She finds this explanation by the Mexican Americans lacking in ethnic loyalty: "Ah, but everyone here is very *malinchista* [unpatriotic]!" Her usage of the word "*malinchista*" to refer to the Mexican Americans who complain that robbers are Juarenses is very important. It is another way of saying that Mexican Americans are Mexicans in spite of their desires, because this word is used *in Mexico* to describe a traitor to his race or ethnicity, and it makes sense only in the context of the inner group.[2] In this way, Norma is claiming that in her barrio all her neighbors are "Mexicanos," some of them loyal to their heritage, and others *malinchistas* [traitors]. In this way, the use of the word "*malinchista*" helps her to make a distinction within "her" ethnic group. This line would separate those who are proud of their Mexican heritage (like herself) from those "others" who are in the process of selling out and forgetting their heritage (like her Mexican American neighbors).

We can see how one of the "others" that appeared in the Juarense discourse, the Mexican American, is still present in the narrative identities of these interviewees who currently live in El Paso. Accordingly, these women are still constructing their identities using a Mexican frame of reference, that is, Juarenses against Mexican Americans, but they have already incorporated some elements coming from the ethnic classificatory system of the United States, and therefore they use that system to construct their identity. They characterize Mexican Americans with the commonsense images lifted from some versions of the American ethnic discourse: Mexican Americans are lazy drunks and drug addicts who do not want to work and who live off of welfare.

> **Norma:** For people in this barrio, it's rare for them to have a job. It's rare . . . they live off food stamps and off of . . . stealing and selling clothes.
> **Estela:** And some other little things that seem to also mix in, right?
> **Norma:** Yes. They sell drugs, they steal and . . . off of stamps and off of welfare.

As we can see, these women are very clear in their arguments, and all the time they conclude that the real "poor people without dignity," those to whom the "all poverty is Mexican" narrative plot really applies, are the Mexican Americans, not themselves, as many El Pasoans argue. In Norma's account the lack of ethnic loyalty supposedly showed by many Mexican Americans transform them into *malinchistas*, that is, into traitors to their own race. That treachery seems to be linked, at least implicitly, to the delinquent behavior they supposedly show, as if the lack of "Mexican morals and values" were the moral barrier these Mexican Americans have lost in their process of Americanization. We can see how Norma is constructing an argument very similar to Alfredo's (the "other" is the Mexican who has lost the "real" Mexican system of values), but, in this case she applies the argument to people like Alfredo himself.

The complexity of their identity construction is such that, confronted by "data" that could undermine their well-developed "all poverty is

Mexican American" plot, they do not hesitate to take advantage of the Fronterizo regional system of classification to make sense of that "anomaly." Because these women are in a group in transition from one country and one culture to another, it is not surprising that they mixed systems of classification and narrative plots to make sense of a situation that, at first glance, undermines their claims and their construction of the Mexican American as the "other." I am referring here to the fact that many El Paso's beggars (at least until Operation Blockade started in September 1993) were Mexican nationals. The women's solution to the "puzzle" was quite simple: they recognized the obvious, that beggars were Mexican nationals, but they rapidly pointed out that beggars were Mexicans, but not Juarenses, that is Mexicans from the South, or, still worse, not Mexicans at all, but Central Americans (as Estela commented: "They are really not people from Juárez, actually, they are people who come from the South . . . many from El Salvador, from Guatemala"), taking full advantage of the Fronterizo plot asserting that "all social problems in Juárez are caused by Southerners."

Estela: They are not exactly from Juárez . . . they are from further South.

The Mexican Americans Who Discriminate against Mexican Immigrants as the "others"

Another set of interviews where the Mexican American was also portrayed as the "other" from a quasi-Juarense point of view was one we had with a group of women in San Elizario (an El Paso suburb). In those interviews we could hear the voice of those Mexican immigrants who, without having lived in El Paso much longer than Norma, were more Americanized, but who still, in some circumstances, portrayed the Mexican American as the "other."[3]

Pilar: What happens is that many times, when one crosses the bridge from there to here, the Anglo inspectors are very pleasant and treat you well, but there are times, when they are Mexicans, and they treat you very badly! They even search your purse and everything! And they are from our own race!

Pilar is repeating here what many of our Juarense interviewees had told us before (see Chapter 2): it seems that frequently Anglo customs agents treat Mexicans better than Mexican American agents do. And the interviewee cannot understand, either, since they come from the same "race," why Mexican Americans are so mean to their own people.

In order to find an answer to this "weird" behavior, Pilar again repeats some of the commonsense explanations we have found on the other side of the border: these Mexican American customs agents "feel" they are Americans, not Mexicans, so they discriminate against the latter; they want to prove they have the right to live in the United States, and that "other Mexicans" do not have the same rights.

In this type of discourse, the "others" are those people of Mexican origin who discriminate against Mexicans, because they reject their Mexican heritage, supposedly because they were born in the United States or because they were raised in the United States from childhood. Then "they are raised with the idea that they are Americans." In this way Pilar traces a line inside her own "race" (as Norma did before), where she is on the side of those who do not discriminate against other Mexicans, because they do not reject their Mexican heritage (supposedly because they came to the United States as adults). But not only do many Mexican immigrants feel rejected by some Mexican American custom agents; they also feel the tension that separates them from many Mexican Americans in other everyday life situations in which they interact with other people of Mexican descent. And here the reference is not toward the "mean" Mexican American housewives who "starve" Mexican maids, but toward some Mexican American customers and co-workers who somehow "punish" Mexican immigrants for not being completely bilingual.

> **Rosalba:** Where I work very often I have problems with Mexican people . . . people who are obviously a hundred percent Mexican![4] I say to one of my co-workers who speaks English, "Look, here's a young lady who speaks English." And in just a little while she is speaking with my co-worker in Spanish! Why couldn't she talk to me in Spanish?!
>
> **Pablo:** And why do you think that they won't talk to you in Spanish?
>
> **Rosalba:** Well, I do not know, I think that they want to brag that they know English. Or I don't know if they realize that I am struggling because I don't know English . . . They are supposed to speak Spanish, but they don't do it, and then I go and call someone who speaks English and Spanish, and they start out speaking English but I see them ending up in Spanish!! Yes, one feels bad.
>
> **Francisca:** . . . and we take it as a humiliation.

Hence, Rosalba and Francisca feel "humiliated" (like Margarita when she referred to the emigrants who go back to Mexico with big cars and speaking English all the time) by the behavior of these Mexican Americans who claim: "You do not know how to speak English." What these customers seem to address is the issue of the marked language difference that separates many Mexican Americans from Mexican immigrants. Thus, it is not uncommon that the customer in the story asked for an English-speaking clerk and finally continued the conversation in Spanish. This is because bilingualism (where speakers are more fluent in English than Spanish) seems to be the cultural marker these Mexican Americans use to separate themselves from the "other," in this case, the Mexican immigrant who is either Spanish monolingual or bilingual with more fluency in Spanish than English.

The Mexican Nationals as the "other" for Some Mexican Immigrants

The issue of who is the "other" can have different answers even within the same family, sometimes clearly along gender lines, but not generational ones (Vila 1997b). This happened in our interview with the López family.[5] All the female members of the family had a pronounced anti-Mexican nationals discourse, whereas all the males supported more of an anti-Anglo narrative, even though some of the sisters had been born in Juárez and all of the brothers in El Paso, and both parents, Horacio and Mónica, had been born in different Northern Mexican states. Here we will see how the female members of the family are using, almost without any change, the "all poverty is Mexican national" hegemonic plot, while the male members prefer to criticize some aspects of the American way of life from a Fronterizo perspective (above all religion).

> **Mónica:** What do you see in it? What does the photo remind you of?
> **Laura:** Well, just that, mom. Juárez . . .
> **Rick:** Photographs of poverty—such as these—remind you of Juárez?
> **Horacio:** I think that you need to know the outskirts of El Paso, because there there are places like these ones . . .

When the females mistakenly located the photograph with the trailer in Juárez, because it looked very poor (the same mistake we have already seen with most of the people who utilized the "all poverty is Mexican national" theme), the males discovered that their female family members consistently located all the photographs depicting poverty in Juárez and reacted as follows:

> **Horacio:** And this place, where do you think it is? . . . Just you, ma'am.
> **Mónica:** Juárez.
> **Horacio:** No . . .

Rick: As soon as you see an unpainted wall without stucco, it right away makes it Juárez! [laughs]

Horacio: For people in Juárez it's easier to build a room than buy a trailer. It's easier to build a house. Where does your uncle live? In one of those . . . [Horacio is talking about photo 13, shown in Chapter 3.]

This discovery triggered a family discussion about an issue they had not been aware of previously: how different they were in relation to their ethnic identity.

Horacio: Why do you relate every kind of poverty with Juárez? Because it often seems to me a certain inclination to discriminate toward the people of Juárez. Which isn't something pleasant for many people and anything positive for your own mentality, because you need to be a little more open. Center yourself, put your feet on the ground, and see the reality of each thing, *m'hija*.

That difference in their ethnic identity relies, among other things, on whom each constructs as the "other," which in the case of the female side of the family is clearly the Mexican national (regardless of the fact that some of them are Mexican nationals themselves). Mexicans are depicted in two negative but contradictory ways. They are portrayed as the really poor people to whom applies the "all poverty is Mexican" thematic plot, but are also those who have more money than the Mexican Americans, which they arrogantly deploy in front of the latter, showing off their superior buying power (Vila 1997b):

Rick: What do you feel when you see a person getting out of a car at Cielo Vista [one of the most important malls in El Paso] and has Juárez plates . . . What do you think? Does it anger you?

Laura: Hmm . . . sometimes.

Rick: It angers you, right?

Rosenda: Yes, it angers me!

Rick: Why? Do you think he's come to take advantage of something which has cost you a lot of effort?

Mónica: Like, when you have seen at the store that they take all the shampoos.

Guillermo: And you say: "Juareños!"

Laura: Or like at Wal-Mart, when they take all the hair sprays. Now, that is mean! No [laughing]. I mean . . . you go and you go to get one single hair spray and you look and the shelf is already empty and then you turn around and you see a shopping cart full of hair spray. That's when I do get angry!

Horacio: Look, daughter, I don't know if you've been affected because I often make comments (or your mom) about . . . the people from Juárez, or the Juareños. But that has always been jokingly. I mean, if it has become very inscribed in your mind . . .

Laura: No, because I've seen it. That's what I see.

Horacio: But don't forget, for example, that just as they are clients who are going to buy, you could come in as well and buy a . . . whole box.

Laura: No, I don't have the money to buy a whole box! [laughs]

Horacio: Then it's hard for you that a person from Juárez has enough money to buy all that but not you. [laughs]

Guillermo: Laura, don't forget that you also came from Mexico . . . you're really part Mexican.

Laura: I'm not going to say anything about Juárez anymore.

Trying to make sense of the profound gender differences the males suddenly discovered in the process of identity construction within their own family, they try to figure out what has caused such differences:

Horacio: What does it tell us about a person that's thinking in such a manner? What does it tell us, for example, about the person's behavior? Is she resentful? Has she forgotten her roots? Can you tell us?

After discarding the possibility that Horacio's jokes were the cause of such profound resentment again Mexicans ("Rick: Paul's asking why the rest of us didn't take it seriously"), the López family attempted other types of explanations. Not surprisingly, the females went back to their previous claim: they are anti-Mexican because they are the ones who really know how Mexicans behave. However, the males did not accept that answer and tried the "Americanized" explanation: their sisters are anti-Mexican because they are more Americanized than the males; for different reasons, they have decided to reject their Mexican heritage in a way the males have not:

Rosenda: But we're the ones who've seen that when we go to look for hair spray, there isn't any, and the ones that more often see that the Mexicans . . . the ones that come from Juárez are the ones who are taking it.

Rick: I think that in a way my sisters have become more Americanized.

Guillermo: They don't remember where they come from.

Rick: They prefer to speak just English, and to speak Spanish in front of a large group of people seems to them like embarrassing—for people to know that they know Spanish. And I don't think like that, because I have been proud of where I come from and of who I am since many years back.

Horacio: Your roots.

Mónica: Not them. They've always said . . .

Rick: Oh, how embarrassing!

Mónica: They don't see . . . we're American. And no, they're not American. We've made that clear to them. They're Mexicans born here, but their roots are wholly [giggles] Mexican. And all three of them are the same.

Paul: Yeah, but they've gone back on it, that's what you are saying?

Mónica: Yes . . . that they want . . . they would have liked to be only . . . to not have anything . . . Mexican.

Rick: It's like they've lost their culture, right?

Mónica: Yeah.

Paul: OK. And where does that problem stem from? When did you most notice that the problem began? At school, at church?

Rick: At the schools.

Horacio: Yeah, at the schools.

Rick: Yes, I mean, like from sixth grade to junior high, right, Laura? It's like they became Americanized.

Mónica: And they saw a very big difference between themselves and their cousins living in Juárez and they wanted to see themselves higher up, they rebelled.

Laura: It's that we didn't like how the girls dressed over there.

Horacio: They've been growing with those prejudices. I even went as far as to tell them (it's been a while since I told them): "The sons and daughters of Mexicans are Mexicans, daughter." We're all Mexican! You are Mexicans from this side, because you were born over here, but that doesn't take away your Mexicanness.

We can see how difficult the process of identity construction is for some first-generation Mexican Americans and Mexican immigrants. In the same family we have identified constructions of two different "others" (the Mexican nationals for the females, the Anglos for the males). This leads to the use of the label "Mexican" in two different ways, as a nationality for the females and as an ethnicity for the males: "You are Mexicans from this side . . . but that doesn't take away your Mexicanness."

Mexican Immigrants and the Construction of the "Americans" as the "others"

So far we have seen how the different "others" people construct on *both sides* of the border can appear, sometimes simultaneously, in the narrative identities of many Mexican immigrants in El Paso. Norma and her friends, from the point of view of Juarenses living in El Paso, addressed the Mexican Americans and the Southern Mexicans as the "others," mixing both systems of classification (the regional and the ethnic) and using metaphors accordingly. On the other hand, the López family was more consistent, at least along gender lines, because the female members (some of them Mexican nationals themselves) consistently addressed Mexican nationals as the "others," while the males had a more pro-Mexican attitude.[6] But I also found that the prominent "other" whom many Fronterizos depicted constantly — the "Americans," which in the border context means "Anglos" — also appeared in the narrative identities, metaphors, and categories of the Mexican immigrants I interviewed in El Paso.

This was what happened in our interview with Martín and Patricia, who were in the group that included César — the Vietnam veteran who claimed the Chicano identity. Martín is a forty-year-old worker who was born in Rio Bravo, Tamaulipas, and who arrived in El Paso ten years ago. He completed his elementary education in Mexico. His wife, Patricia, is a bank clerk. She is thirty-eight years old, was born in Durango, and arrived in El Paso thirteen years ago. She has some middle-school education. Both, Martín and his wife (who define themselves as Catholics) lived in Juárez most of their lives before coming to El Paso.

First, these interviewees constructed their Mexicanness in relation to the "Americans," and not so much in relation to the Mexican Americans, like Norma and her friends did. They did this even though Martín and Patricia are naturalized Americans, and César was not only born in the United States, but also fought for his country during the Vietnam War. Thus, they are still using one of the "others" many Juarenses use in Mexico: the American other. Doing that, these interviewees, to different degrees, constantly mix the ethnic and the national American systems of classification when they address the "other"; they constantly put together "Anglos" with "Americans."

> **Martín:** Why is it that when a Mexican moves in, they all begin to arrive, and arrive, and arrive . . . they begin to buy, and buy, and buy, and the Americans start moving out of there?

> **Patricia:** If an American marries a Mexican, or vice versa, now it is more acceptable.

> **Martín:** In the Dairy Queen, there was a group of old men, you know, Americans . . . and when we arrived they got up and changed tables . . . we ordered a soda and they wouldn't give it to us . . .

As we can see, Martín and Patricia (like many of our interviewees in Juárez) continually establish the difference between "us" (the Mexicans) and "them" (the Americans), although other ethnic groups (Blacks, Asian, etc.) may appear in the statements.

When these interviewees were asked why they thought Americans and Mexicans were so different, Martín did not allow any area where both groups could share common characteristics:

Martín: Well, they have other customs, other religions, other ideas. I don't think they share the ideas of . . . another race, another race that is not their own. They understand one another, they are their own . . . well, no comment.

Hence, according to Martín, Americans and Mexicans differ in almost everything: customs, ideas, religion. The sense of separateness is so intense that it is put in terms of race against race, where Martín utilizes the term "*raza*" so important in the construction of the Chicano and Mexican identities. Here he is using the label "Mexican" clearly in ethnic and racial terms, a way to encompass both ethnicity and nationality.

Patricia follows her husband in her social identification: she is a Mexican *living* in the United States, and she differentiates herself from the other participants in the interview — César and her son — who were *born* in the United States.

Patricia: It's very different from his situation [she refers to César] . . . and it could be different from his situation as well, right? . . . [she refers to her son Juan]. Because, we, no matter where we are, are Mexicans. Well, he [César] says he is Chicano.

She is also, as her husband stated before, Mexican in the double sense of the term — ethnically and nationally — and she constantly remarks that she is *only living* in El Paso (not even in the United States, but in one of the poorest and more "Mexican" cities of the Southwest) and not a Mexican American:

Angela: But if someone introduced you: "Look, I would like to introduce you to so and so who lives in the U.S . . ."
Patricia: No! I would like her to say that I live in El Paso, and nothing more, not that I am Mexican American . . . simply and plainly that I live in El Paso.
Martín: "Look, this is my friend, we went to school together . . ."
Patricia: . . . in a Juárez school . . .
Martín: ". . . it's been many years ago. My friend was born in Juárez, she lived in Juárez for many years and then she left to come and live in El Paso."

Patricia: That would be the introduction that would make me feel fine, more comfortable.

As we can see, to stress her Mexican identity over her present status of being an American citizen, she is very careful to point out that she went to school in Juárez, and that she was born over there and lived there for many years. Consequently, in this particular testimony, Patricia emphasizes the national character of being a "Mexican." Martín supports his wife's claim and tries to push the issue of their national Mexicanness *first* in relation to their American citizenship.

Martín: Look, it's that we haven't changed a bit ourselves! I still have my Mexican military I.D. card and I have my official I.D. card, the one the Americans give! [laughs]

And all these moves are not by chance; what Martín and Patricia are doing (like many Mexican immigrants I interviewed) is constructing their identities as Mexican immigrants through a constant imaginary "dialogue" with the native Mexicans living in Mexico, continually explaining to them that they (emigrants) are "still" loyal Mexicans, not traitors or Pochos. Here we are dealing again with the "double mirror" in the process of identity construction: the way I think the "others" see me. This double mirror is an inescapable feature of that process; my comments about the "other" are usually highly influenced by the way I suspect the "other" sees me. In this sense some interviewees seem to be asking the Mexican nationals not to think about the emigrants as the "other." Their wish is still to be considered part of the Mexican national "us."

Therefore, being so proud of their Mexican heritage, having changed so little after living in the United States for so many years (if one were to classify people by the way they dress, Martín could have been described as an undocumented Mexican just arrived from one of the poorest colonias in Juárez!), this couple cannot understand how some Mexican nationals can think of them as traitors.

Patricia: Many people think that . . . as the years have gone by we have changed. They think that because one came to live here, that one has rejected Mexico . . . no. Us, at least, to us it is exactly the same . . .
Martín: I have a *compadre* who is so ignorant! Listen, I have another gossip for you . . . [laughs]
Patricia: This man is again talking about personal things! [laughs]
Martín: When we became American citizens my friend came to me and said: "And this and that, and we *la raza*, and stuff." And he says: "Now,

just because you became an American citizen, you're going to spit on the Mexican flag." [laughs] "Gosh, compadre . . . why did you do that [becoming an American citizen]?" I don't know where people come up with that, it's ridiculous.

Angela: And your compadre, how does he see you today, how does he take you as an American citizen?

Martín: Fine! But when he's very drunk, he starts all over again . . . good grief! [laughs]

Patricia: There are many people who think of you as if you were . . .

Martín: . . . like someone who has turned his back on them.

We heard dozens of stories like Martín's, in which a Mexican national is testing the loyalty of a Mexican immigrant or a Mexican American through statements about the flag, or questions such as "if there is a war between Mexico and the United States, for which country would you fight?" But not only in tense situations like that does the importance of the Mexican nationals living in Mexico appear as a kind of ghost presence in the identity construction of this couple. All the interviews with them were plagued with references to those who remained in Mexico, who, Martín and Patricia believe, look askance at them for living in the United States.

Martín: I know a family in Juárez that has never been able to get ahead, and has remained poor, and every time I see them, they are poorer. And they didn't want to get ahead, and they have stayed there. These people have never made it to school, so they simply remained ignorant . . . and they live in a neighborhood that is crumbling, and they don't want to leave because it's theirs, and then their sons drink a lot . . . everything is a disaster! And so when they come here and see us . . . they see us as wealthy, I suppose! And they say we don't want to talk to them anymore because we have money, and that . . . well, now I'm gossiping, right?

Angela: No its OK, its OK! . . . [laughs]

Martín: Let them hear me . . . Yes! That is what they think, but we are the same, they are the ones that hide, the ones that don't want to talk to us, . . . they start to avoid you, . . . we continue to be the same . . . We invite them to big parties . . . a birthday party, a debutante party, and no . . . they always say they don't have anything to wear. They didn't come . . . and after a few months, I bump into them and ask: "Why didn't you come?" "Oh, I didn't have anything to wear." They are lying!! They avoid us. Possibly because they feel ashamed.

In this short narrative about acquaintances who are ashamed to go to Mexican immigrants' parties in El Paso, we encounter the "other side of the coin" in relation to Margarita and Robustiano's claim about those Mexican emigrants who want to "humiliate" Mexican nationals upon their return to Mexico. Martín and Patricia feel that it is the Mexican national who does not want to talk to them anymore.

But Martín and Patricia seem to make endless efforts to "prove" to some Mexican nationals, most of them their friends, that they have not betrayed their old Mexican lifestyle. This effort requires showing the Mexican nationals that they have not changed beyond a mere physical move from Juárez to El Paso; but the effort also entails a constant "monitoring" of their behavior through the eyes of the "others" in order to avoid any "deviance" from the Mexican way of life. Thus, to "fully" prove they have not changed due to their move to El Paso, our interviewees used different devices. First, as we saw above, they claim and offer "proof" of how little they have changed. Second, they offer evidence of their effort to keep alive both Mexican traditions (above all the Spanish language and Catholic customs) and ethnic pride in an environment that continually undermines that effort. Here again — as I will discuss in greater detail in *Border Identities* — Mexican traditions are equated with Catholicism, as if Mexicanness and Catholicism were synonymous.

> **Patricia:** We have taught them [our children] a lot about what it is to be Mexican, right? Here we speak Spanish, we relate to Mexico, they have been taught the Mexican traditions and customs. We go to where Martín's family lives, with the annual traditions . . . for example, Christmas time, they have spent Christmas there, those traditions . . .
>
> **Martín:** *Posadas* (a nine-day Christmas festival), the town squares, the churches, everything!
>
> **Patricia:** They know all of that, and we have always taught them that they are Mexican.
>
> **Angela:** And why do you maintain this situation? Why do you want to keep all of this?
>
> **Patricia:** Why? It's pride, it's an honor for them to know where they came from. When we came over to the U.S. one of the things I was always against was them speaking only English . . . that they would not know how to speak Spanish . . .

They also talk about how important it is for them to maintain close relations with their families living in Mexico, and to achieve that, they struggle to keep their children's Spanish alive.

> **Martín:** It's a shame that after coming here, and bringing the children, and then visiting the family over there, that they can't communicate with

them anymore . . . with their aunts, and their grandparents . . . that's when one becomes full of oneself, when one speaks only in English, when they begin to attack us. And then you go back to the South, and then their cousins, who are the same age, encounter each other after seven or eight years, and they no longer understand one another. And that is when they start to say: "Humph . . . ! This guy thinks he is so cool!"

Here again Margarita's and Robustiano's voices seem to be present in Martín's account; he is acutely aware of how many Mexican nationals living in Mexico dislike these emigrants who brag that they are now living in the United States and who always talk in English. Therefore, teaching their children the Spanish language is not only a way to maintain communication with their family, but also a way to avoid the usual Mexican criticism about Mexican immigrants severing their relationships with their relatives living in Mexico—becoming Pochos. As we can see, the imaginary "dialogue" with Mexican nationals seems to always be present in these interviewees, and—not by chance—they use very similar metaphors to point out the distance many Mexican immigrants (but not they themselves, of course) want to establish between them and the Mexican nationals who stayed at home: "*Se le subieron los humos a la cabeza,*" "*Se le subió la* [sic] *azúcar,*" and so on—expressions that refer to excessive pride and/or "putting on airs."

However, Martín and Patricia have no other choice than to acknowledge that *some* Mexican immigrants have changed after their journey to the United States and use that journey to brag in front of their old Mexican neighbors. They describe this behavior in very critical ways, though, showing total disapproval and, implicitly, arguing that they do not behave in that manner.

> **Martín:** Well, it's true that there are some people that are very boastful, that come, cross over, get their immigration papers, and then start bragging and demanding. All they want to do is get a job at Levi's, buy a car, and then go cruising through the neighborhood where they used to live, have a few beers, and let everyone see them cruising in their car. They buy a nice stereo, then cross back over the bridge, and next Sunday they are over there again.

Again, it seems almost as if Martín knew Robustiano and Margarita and that they were discussing these issues at length. Nevertheless, despite all their efforts to prove they are still loyal to Mexico and have not changed their customs, they have changed somewhat and, after living for a while in the United States, they criticize Juarenses for some of the behavior they do not like anymore. Here the malleability of the process of identity construction on the border appears in its full expression: these interviewees do not have any problem in alternatively putting themselves in different ethnic and national positions, to account for attitudes and behaviors they regard as belonging to "others." Namely, after having made a tremendous effort to "convince" the Mexican nationals they are not Americans, Mexican Americans, or Pochos, Martín and Patricia do not have any problem saying that, regarding some customs, they already behave "like" Americans or Pochos, where the "others" are Juarenses, that is, themselves in the past. Hence, when Martín and Patricia have to make sense of the supposed "dirtiness of Juarenses," they do it taking symbolically the position of those "others" they were criticizing before, namely, Anglos and Pochos.

> **Martín:** Of the million people living in Juárez, if one drops a piece of paper and then picks it up, he would be the only one.
> **Angela:** So you think that over there, they would think that is a weird behavior?
> **Martín:** Yes! They would say: "Look at this dummy who is picking up litter, he's crazy, this guy." [laughs]

What Martín is doing in this testimony is to fictionally construct the clean person who dares to pick up a piece of paper in Juárez (the fool, the crazy one) as a *deviant* one, and he imaginarily places himself in that anomalous position.

> **Martín:** The same people from the neighborhood, those who gather on the corner, and if they are one of those beer drinkers, they act like this: "This is great . . . and they throw the empty cans on the roof" [laughs]. And if one picks it up, and puts it in the trash bag, they say: "Hey, don't be a snob, you're acting like a Pocho . . . *gabacho sangrón!* [snob American] . . . Leave it there, so what! . . ."

We can see how Martín continues his imaginary dialogue with Mexican nationals living in Mexico, but in this particular case he does not defend himself against some Mexicans' argument that he has become a Pocho. Instead he defends what he believes, to the common sense of some Juarenses, is Mexican American ("*pareces pocho*") or, still worse, Anglo ("¡*gabacho sangrón!*") behavior: to take proper care of your trash. In this way he fully acknowledges that he has somehow departed from what is supposed to be a "Mexican way of behaving." Consequently, regardless of his beliefs about "being changed so little," and his desire not to be confused with a Pocho, Martín also acknowledges he is, somehow, a Pocho himself, at least in relation to dirtiness and cleanliness.

The deployment of his brief fictitious narrative did not necessarily require a national system of classification (" ¡*gabacho sangrón* . . . !") or a national/ethnic one ("*pareces pocho* . . ."). He could have pointed to "personal characteristics" to define that kind of behavior. He could have talked about "some people in Juárez who do not look after their environment"; or better still, he could have used some Juarenses' argument to explain why their city looks so dirty: "Because of economic reasons we do not have a good garbage disposal system." Defining himself as a "proud" Mexican who lived most of his life in Juárez, such statements would not have been strange. Nevertheless, he not only jumped rapidly to the national and ethnic systems of classification, but also engaged again in his fictional (and seemingly endless) dialogue with Mexican nationals ("And if *one* picks it up . . ."), construing himself in the process as the fictional "crazy" and "foolish," "Pocho" or "Gabacho" who takes care of the environment (the "proper" thing to do). Meanwhile, Juarenses would be the "real" crazy and foolish ones who do not understand how important it is to look after the place where they live.

Here again the social categories that are relevant in classifying people on the border (regional, ethnic, racial, and national) are used to "explain" attitudes and behavior of "others," allowing almost no room for differences inside those categories ("of the million people living in Juárez, if one drops a piece of paper and then picks it up, he would be the only one"). In this manner, "dirtiness" and "carelessness" are not *personal* characteristics but *social* traits belonging to particular social groups. It is not coincidental that the groups that bear these "disgraceful" features are those whom the speaker considers, regarding *that* particular behavior, the "other." This shows how Mexican immigrants select from contradictory categories to make sense of different behaviors.

"The differences between Mexicans and Mexican Americans are due to the country of residence, and are not related to the persons themselves"

The complexity of the process of identity construction in a nationally mixed setting also became apparent in our interviews with Alex and Alicia.[7] These interviewees advanced a discourse that, even as it constituted Mexican nationals as the "others," made a sharp distinction between the country and the people who live (or used to live) in it. Mexican nationals act differently in Mexico than they do in the United States, these interviewees argue; thus the problem is not Mexicans but the country itself. Therefore, in the polyphony that is an inescapable feature of the process of identity construction on the border, some poor Mexican American and Mexican immigrant residents of El Paso sharply distinguish the country they live in (and themselves) from what happens daily in Juárez, in an attempt to construct a "we" that symbolically brings them nearer to the "common American" and moves them farther from the "common Mexican." That is, by locating the differences between Mexicans and Mexican Americans in the country of residence, instead of in the persons themselves, these interviewees are able to avoid denigrating friends and family who still live "*al otro lado*." Once this is accomplished, they can construct an identity that refers to categories of national difference — Mexico and the United States as sovereign nations — to mediate their highly stigmatized place in the American ethnic and racial classification system.

This was what happened in our interview with Alex and Alicia, where blame about Juárez' disgraceful state was always displaced from the people to a generic if vaguely specified Mexico that encompasses everything — government, country, "culture," and so on — except Mexicans themselves.

Pablo: What do you think is the cause of the difference in tidiness?
Alicia: The government doesn't provide money for cleaning. Here, if you are in your car, and throw out a piece of paper, you get a ticket! There, you throw out an entire bag . . . and they don't say a word.
Pablo: And why do you think that happens? How would you explain that people do that?
Alicia: Because they are used to it! I bet you that if right now you go out to drink a soda you wouldn't throw the cup out in the street! You go to Juárez: What's the problem? Let's throw it. Everybody does it!

This interviewee clearly differentiates between people and culture, as if people that in other circumstances would be "clean," are "dirty" due to inescapable social pressure ("Because they are used to it!" "Everybody does it") for which they have no personal responsibility. In order to reinforce her argument, this interviewee provides a short story from her personal experience:

Alicia: Because I have watched my cousin Miguel, who lives in Juárez. When he comes here, he doesn't litter. When he goes there . . . strangely enough: he litters! And he is the same person, only an hour has gone by.

Pablo: How would you explain that?
Alicia: They are used to it over there!

Here, the argument is followed to its logical conclusion. If the cause of "improper" behavior is not in the Mexican people, but in the country's customs (understood as independent from the people who enact them daily), then a mere geographical movement can produce incredible results. By the simple action of crossing a hundred-meter border, an irresponsible slob starts to behave with dignity. For these interviewees, this explanation — or one similar in logic — is in some sense overdetermined. On the one hand, these interviewees neither use the Chicano discourse nor appear to be comfortable explaining the poverty they share with Mexicans nationals by referring to the situation of exploitation in which they both live. On the other hand, they cannot constitute Mexican nationals *tout court* as the stigmatized other who provides them with relative dignity, because their loved ones still live in Mexico. Accordingly, through the process of separating the culture of Mexico from Mexico's inhabitants and blaming the former for the whole situation, these interviewees create an internally coherent response to a situation that would otherwise be unbearable.[8]

Once the logic of separating the good Mexicans from the bad Mexico is firmly established, everything that is not valued, and against which a meaningful identity is constructed, can be attributed to Mexico. Thus, an entire arsenal of negative words were employed to describe everyday life in Juárez: backwardness, disorder, dirt, deterioration, violence, carelessness, corruption, and lawlessness. Consequently, these interviewees went to great lengths to identify all the photographs that depicted poverty with Juárez. The solution used by Alex and Alicia was ultimately simple — all those photographs showing dirt, disorder, and carelessness were located, as if by definition, on the Mexican side, and all photographs showing cleanliness, organization, and care were located, almost without discussion, on the American side.

Alicia: No, I say it is Juárez!
Pablo: And why?
Alicia: The light cables.
Alex: The wires . . . and . . . I can't find anything . . . clean!! It's everything run down!

Pablo: And this one, why did you choose this one to represent El Paso?
Alex: Because it is much cleaner!

Besides dirt, disorder was the other characteristic these interviewees laboriously searched for to decide, "without any doubt," that a particular photograph had been taken in Juárez and not in El Paso.

> **Pablo:** And this photograph, why would this be Juárez?
> **Alicia:** Well, for the same reason! How the houses are built, the highways . . . it's all the same! . . . the same as in the first one. It's all a mess! . . . All untidy, . . . or the houses are built anyway they can. [She refers to photo 13, shown in Chapter 3.]

Here these interviewees easily identified the photograph as depicting Juárez, as it conformed to all the criteria they used to distinguish it from El Paso: disorder, dirt, and disorganization. However, this particular photo had not been taken in Juárez but in El Paso; and not only in El Paso, but from the vantage point of their own backyard! They were talking about the photograph of the trailer, which many interviewees working with the thematic plot "all poverty is Mexican" systematically confused. Here, the need to locate poverty without dignity in Mexico was so intense that they could not recognize a scene they view daily: a decrepit house behind their own.

The need to see "bad" poverty as foreign to their daily lives is so profound that, when advised of their mistake, they reinforce rather than modify the essential logic of their initial argument, much like Joel and Ramón did before:

> **Alicia:** Well, here the photo looks like Juárez! To me it looks like Juárez!
> **Alex:** Yes, there are parts in El Paso that look like Juárez!
> **Alicia:** Where I live looks like Juárez, so! Once we cross Paisano Avenue, it's El Paso!
> **Alex:** Yes . . . because . . . that's [the photo] where we live!

They do not change their argument to claim that poverty *is* the same in both countries; rather, they continue to insist that the ugliest poverty is a Mexican phenomenon, but add that parts of the United States still *resemble* Mexico. The visual metaphor is crucial here. They do not say that parts of El Paso *are* like Juárez—thus bringing to bear the profound sense of immutability implied by the verb *to be* (*ser*) in Spanish. Rather, they maintain that El Paso's poor areas only *look like* Mexico—you can see them differently and in so doing transform them—or they *appear* to be Mexico—but they could appear differently. Their true essence is American, although from the outside they may seem to be Mexican.

In the context of arguments that people are weak, but culture is powerful, they assert the "infection" of parts of El Paso by elements of Mexican culture that have somehow slipped over the border. Here, the argument implies that people can live "like Mexico" or "like the United States," without being within the legal borders of the country in question. If this is the case, then there is no contradiction in claiming, as these interviewees did, that Juárez extends a bit into the United States. The logic here is similar to that employed by some Mexican interviewees quoted in Chapter 2, who distinguished themselves from Mexicans of other classes by implying that they were "like Americans." They felt that the United States was somehow present in those Mexican neighborhoods that already had telephones, gas, running water, and so on, because the inhabitants had to "*endrogarse*" (as do the Americans) in order to pay for these "luxuries."

Since these types of interviewees could not locate *all* poverty in Juárez, and since they had no choice other than to accept that poverty also exists in the United States (including their own . . .), they began to differentiate *degrees* of poverty.

> **Pablo:** So, there is no need to go to Juárez to find poverty, there is also poverty in El Paso . . .
> **Alicia:** But, not in many places! If you look over here, where are you going to find a place like this? You have to go to Juárez. [She refers to photo 9, of a very poor neighborhood in Juárez, shown in Chapter 3.]
> **Alex:** And yes, there are in El Paso, but . . . you have to look for them!
> **Alicia:** And in Juárez, they are all right there, after you just cross the bridge!!

While Mexican poverty "is everywhere," and is "highly visible," American poverty can be found only in a few parts of the city, and then only with difficulty, because it is "rare," and "less prominent." After being confronted with poverty (literally) in their own backyard, they began to separate that poverty from *extreme poverty*. The first one — normal poverty — can be found on both sides of the border; the second — extreme poverty — only on the Mexican side. Their home, themselves, may "look like Juárez," but it (and they) *are not* Juárez. They are poor people, but not extremely poor people.

> **Alex:** We have crossed and . . . we notice the difference! . . . Here, it is run down, but not as run down as over there!!

We have to remember here that all these claims about the difference between "extreme" poverty (the Mexican one) and "common" poverty (the American — their own — one) are being made by a couple living in

"America," one of the poorest colonias in El Paso, which, at the time of the interview, lacked running water and sewage.

Mexican Immigrants Who Do Not Use the "all poverty is Mexican" Thematic Plot

Three years after we conducted the set of interviews with Alex and Alicia, we had the opportunity to interview a group of female activists that were deeply involved in the process of bringing water and sewage to "America."[9] However, these interviewees, being in fact poorer than Alex and Alicia, did not use the "all poverty is Mexican national" thematic plot to organize their identities (in either its individual or its cultural stance). On the contrary, they consistently stressed that poverty exists on both sides of the border. They also recognized that sometimes their own poverty (above all when they did not have running water and sewage) was worse than Mexican poverty. Thus, although they live in the same colonia where Alex and Alicia live, they construct their material living conditions in very different ways, using alternative plots to make sense of something that, from an external point of view, would be considered the same social environment. When the "material" conditions of the colonia improved due to the presence of running water and sewage, these women—who did not use the "all poverty is Mexican" narrative theme—still did not have any problem comparing their own poverty with Mexican poverty.

> **Leticia:** Here, in this picture [photo 13] . . . imagine you can also see "America" here.
> **Pablo:** Why?
> **Leticia:** Because we also have unpaved roads, although there are more trees here. Here we have water, but yes, that's how it is . . . it looks like . . . this colonia has a lots of things in common with Mexico, a lot, a great deal.
> **Sukis:** Because before it was like that [like the photograph of a poor colonia in Juárez], before they set the pavement and all . . .
> **Leticia:** No! And it is, it still is . . .
> **Pablo:** And why do you think "America" looks like parts of Mexico?
> **Rosario:** Because . . . we still have a lot of poverty. We are in the U.S., but Mexico and the U.S. are the same thing . . . sometimes the U.S. is worse . . . like us, who have lived so long without water, they were better off than us, those who live in the colonias in the outskirts of Juárez had water and we don't, they were better off than us.

Even with the worst photographs of poverty—those that almost without exception had been located by other interviewees in Mexico—these women comment that something similar can be found in El Paso. Thus, in regard to a shot of a Juárez outhouse, these interviewees say that such bathrooms are not uncommon in their own colonia:

Leticia: Look, there are also, in the States, things like the one [the outhouse] you see here . . . There are people here in "America" who still have them . . .

Rosario: . . . here there are people who still live the same way . . .

If poverty is very similar on both sides of the border and not necessarily "Mexican national," it is not surprising that when they looked at the photograph of the mobile home they did not have any problem, first, identifying the photo as having been taken on the American side of the border, and, second, rapidly discovering that this shot portrayed a house in their own neighborhood.

Leticia: Like here, look . . . you can imagine we are looking at certain parts of "America" . . . a little trailer, and since it is a trailer house . . . one doesn't see many of these in Mexico . . .

Rosario: The picture seems to have been taken here, in "America." It looks like over there, where they have all that trash, where there is . . . What's its name? Here, . . . look . . . [laughs]. Yes, it is "America." It is "America," isn't it?

Sukis: Yes, it looks like . . . this is the arroyo . . .

Rosario: I suddenly remembered that place! Where I said to my husband, "No, man, we are worse than in Mexico! Look over there, nothing but trash." That was the house I showed him. I remembered because I have always thought that that area is the ugliest one in the colonia, all the trash they have makes me think. . . . It's Solorzano's house, it's their house, when it was Solorzano's house, which the wind tore down . . . [laughs] it's Solorzano's . . .

I want to make a comparison between Alex and Alicia, on the one hand, and Leticia, Rosario, and Sukis, on the other, to show the degree to which the narrative plot "orders" the photographs and the "reality" that those photographs represent. First, however, I must introduce some contextual data regarding the picture.

For one thing, the photo had been taken just one month before the interview with Alex and Alicia, when "America" still lacked running water and sewage—something it had in common with many poor Mexican colonias. Moreover, the shot was taken from Alex and Alicia's own backyard. Nevertheless, without hesitation these interviewees located the photograph in Juárez. Their need to locate all poverty on the Mexican side of the border was so intense that Alex and Alicia (following pari passu the thematic plot that "all poverty is Mexican national") could not

PHOTO 16

Outhouse in Juárez.

recognize a scene that was completely familiar to them: a run-down house located only a few yards from their own.[10]

The interview with Leticia, Rosario, and Sukis, by contrast, was conducted three years after we took the photograph of the mobile home, by which time "America" had those basic utilities that would clearly differentiate it from the extreme poverty of some poor Mexican colonias, and by which time the run-down house had disappeared from the scene. However, these interviewees did not have any problem in identifying the photo with "America," basically because their narrative plot did not "ask" that such a photograph should be located in Juárez. Of course these interviewees, like Alex and Alicia, used various linguistic devices to stress that, finally, their poverty was not exactly the same as Mexican poverty. Like Alex and Alicia, they avoided using the verb *ser* [to be, in a permanent sense], using instead a verb like *ver* [to see] ("Hágase de cuenta que *ve* aquí también 'América' . . ."), *estar* [to be, in a temporary sense] ("Así *estamos* aquí, en cierta forma aquí sí es . . ."), or *tener* [to have] (". . . *tiene* mucho de México 'América' . . . esta colonia, *tiene* mucho de México, mucho, bastante . . .") — each of which conveys a sense of impermanence and appearance as opposed to an immutable reality. Nonetheless, they could accept both that there is poverty everywhere and that sometimes American poverty is worse than Mexican poverty.

Who, though, is the "other" for these interviewees? Or, to put it differently, what axes do these women use to construct a meaningful identity? Our interviewees deployed different strategies. They pointed out that their *past* was similar to the *current* poverty as portrayed in the Juárez photographs. Hence, they claimed that *before* the installation of running water and sewage, poverty on both sides of the border was similar, but not right now, at least for them, who had struggled for many years to bring those utilities to the colonia.

And the issue of "before and after" introduces us to one of the most important explanations these women use to mark the difference they feel distinguishes poverty on each side of the border: if they already have running water and sewage, it is because the American government helps its population more than the Mexican government does.

> **Rosario:** Here one does not die of hunger, right? It's because there are food stamps. But let's assume they take the food stamps away . . . It's Mexico, another Mexico!
> **Leticia:** I don't agree with what she says . . . about us being the same as in Mexico. For me, in Mexico in the first place, people have no help . . .

none! Here, instead, there are many governmental programs. They are going to take the food stamps away but new programs are going to come out, one way or another people are going to survive, more than in Mexico . . . there is going to be a way in which the government will help people anyway, and in Mexico people get nothing from the government . . . there they have to steal to survive. Here, they don't have to steal, here, the one that steals does it . . . for no reason at all . . . because he's a lazy bones, doesn't work . . .

Consequently, one explanation of the persistence of poverty in Mexico versus the supposedly provisional character of poverty in the United States is American governmental assistance, which makes temporary something that in Mexico is permanent: poverty. Therefore, most people who are poor in the United States, considering all the government assistance available, are poor because they have just started out on their own (young Mexican American couples) or because they are new immigrants from Mexico. According to our interviewees, both having enough time to settle and being able to count on assistance from the American government will lead to a better situation—something that won't happen in Mexico because there is no assistance from their government. And those Americans who do not improve their situation remain poor only because of some kind of personality defect (basically laziness).

But sometimes this thematic plot ("American poverty is provisional due to governmental assistance") does not work, because they know of cases where people were living in poverty for many years. That was precisely what happened with the inhabitants of the mobile home. Here is where Leticia and Rosario offered different explanations for such "unusual" circumstances.

> **Leticia:** Do you know why they have their house like that? Their house was burnt down . . . and then the arroyo eats up everything, . . . there were even some people over there whose wall of dirt, of rock, of concrete blocks was taken away, so, why spend money? That's why they have so much trash . . . they put all that out there after their house burnt down . . .

Leticia attempts a kind of "catastrophe" logic to explain why, at least in the case of the mobile home's family, the "American poverty is provisional due to governmental assistance" plot does not work: she says that the people living in the mobile home in such deplorable conditions for so many years (and despite *all* the governmental assistance available) did so out of necessity, due to a catastrophe that hit them harshly. If Leticia (the leader of "America") attempts a "catastrophe" explanation to account for something that should not be there, that is, permanent American poverty in spite of government assistance, Rosario is less kind with her neighbors, and step by step delineates her own "other."

> **Rosario:** I think those houses are built (in my opinion, OK?) by those who don't have papers, the undocumented, who say: "No, why should I try so much to have a good house, if maybe I finally cannot *arreglar* and they send me back to Mexico . . ."

According to Rosario, those who impoverish her colonia basically are the undocumented immigrants who do not want to improve their conditions due to the contingency of their legal status. She also says that undocumented immigrants are basically lazy people who instead of working hard in Juárez at maquiladoras, where "there are plenty of jobs available . . . there is a lot of work in Juárez, the maquilas are empty . . . ," prefer to cross to the United States illegally because "they want (oh, with your permission) a shitload of dollars!"

When I point out that maybe the people want to come to the United States despite the availability of jobs in Juárez' maquiladora industry because of the salary differential, Rosario deepens her criticism toward the "illegal" immigrants, addressing an issue that was also important for many of our other low-income interviewees in El Paso; that is, how the availability of cheap Mexican labor depresses salaries in the city.

> **Pablo:** But they pay too little.
> **Rosario:** But we have to accommodate ourselves to where we live . . . how is one going to come to the U.S. being an illegal? One has to accept what one is going through in one's own homeland, one's own country, where one is living.
> **Pablo:** But the border is so close, and people look at it and say, mmmh . . . I'm going to go and earn some dollars.
> **Rosario:** But who is suffering? Those who are legally in the States! Because the undocumented with twenty dollars a day, fifteen, he makes it, right?

Rosario, an immigrant herself, claims that people do not have to venture beyond their situation (as she did many years ago); rather, they should adjust to it because such is their destiny. Thus she is denying the "others" what she did before, that is, to migrate to the United States to improve their economic situation. Once more, Leticia has a very different approach to the same issue.

Leticia: It's hard but one does think in that way sometimes, right? That the salaries sometimes do go down because of that, because of the workers. But it's not that the salary goes down, the salary here is the same and doesn't go down, . . . the one who lowers it is the employer . . .

As we can see, Leticia deflects the guilt from the undocumented themselves to the contractors who take advantage of the huge supply of cheap labor existent at the border. Leticia also draws a parallel between the situation of Mexican workers on the border and the American Civil War.

Leticia: I went to school and I took history, and they told us to make comparisons about what the Civil War meant to us. So, I compared it to El Paso and Juárez . . . in this way, for example, in the Civil War there was the North and the South, and Juárez the same, North and South . . . the slaves in the war were freed and what they wanted was to get out of the situation they'd lived in, and so they wanted to go North to earn more money because there was everything there; just like Juaritos, right? People come here from Juárez, because they just want to earn dollars, it's better here, but those from here, we do not want them . . . because they come to earn our salary; in the same way, during the war, those from the North thought that the Southerners would come to earn their money, their jobs. Another similarity is that during the Civil War, the one who had relatives in the North had more possibilities of getting a job. It's the same thing that is happening between Juárez and El Paso; the one who has relatives here finds a job faster. That's how, more or less, I compared it.

Leticia thus "explains" why the immigrants want to cross the border and to work (legally or illegally) in the United States. They do so because they want to escape the "slavery" they undergo in Mexico, and to take advantage of the opportunities that are available on the north side of the river. In the same statement she acknowledges that such a move creates resentments among those who already live on the American side, because they believe the newcomers are going to take away their jobs. Accordingly, while Leticia is always looking for some kind of argument to avoid stigmatizing the illegals *tout court* (in this case, justifying illegal immigration using the metaphor of them being like Black slaves), Rosario does not have any problem constructing her "other," the illegal crosser, in very bold terms. Therefore, it is not surprising that Rosario supports the anti-immigrant stance that characterizes American politics lately, while Leticia does not:

Rosario: I'm telling you! Now many illegal immigrants complain that the government wants to take their children out of school. I say that is OK . . . I also suffered a lot in Mexico, as a child I suffered a lot, but I say it is not fair to take away our children's benefits to give them to those who are not . . . legally here in the U.S. . . . Our kids are getting less and less supplies and services and I do not think that is fair, either! The problem is that before there were fewer people, right now *there is no room* for more people here . . .

Rosario's *"ya no cabemos . . ."* is a very dramatic way of addressing her anti-illegal immigrant stance. Of course Sukis and Leticia do not agree with her, and base their explanation of the prevalent anti-immigrant stance in the United States on the racist attitude they know many Americans have toward Mexicans *in general*, not only toward illegal Mexicans.

Sukis: The anger has always been the same . . . Americans think they are superior to any race.
Leticia: And this does not only happen at the border, because this boy has just arrived from Washington, and there there's a lot of discrimination, toward us, who are legal. I mean, we are going to really feel that discrimination, like those from Juaritos are feeling it, our discriminatory attitude toward them, we are going to feel it when we go toward the interior of the U.S.

Once more, Leticia finds a different (and kinder) avenue to understand the "other," in this case putting herself in the other's shoes and pointing out that many Americans (Anglos, in this usage) do to Mexicans in general (including herself, Rosario, and Sukis, finally) what some legal Mexicans living on the border (i.e., they themselves) do to illegal ones.

Middle-Class Mexican Immigrants and the "all poverty is Mexican" Plot

As we can see, being poor and a Mexican immigrant is very difficult in a city where the plot "all poverty is Mexican" is so pervasive. But we found very similar testimonies in middle-class settings, too. In the interviews we conducted with two lower-middle-class families in El Paso (the Pérez and Antunes) [11] and one middle-middle one (the Armendariz family), [12] we found a similar approach. However, they were also using some of the arguments that many of our Mexican American interviewees advanced, regardless of their time of immigration. It is thus not surprising that these interviewees, not without contradictions, used the "all poverty is Mexican national" thematic plot more often than our poor immigrants.

In this sense, these interviewees very consistently tended to locate the poor photographs on the Mexican side of the border.

Beatriz: Well, I chose these houses because how can people live in houses so . . . They do not even have a roof! I think it is Juárez. [She mistakenly locates photo 13, shown in Chapter 3, in Juárez.]

Catalina: I chose this one because when it rains so much the streets look like this, plenty of mud. And this one could be Juárez or here . . . I do not know. It seems to be over there near Juárez outskirts . . . the Juárez "colonias." Because of the streets, the mud, what the water carries away: trash, boxes . . . [She describes photo 8, shown in Chapter 3.]
Carlos: Yes, it's Juárez.

Humberto: There are very poor neighborhoods here, in El Paso. But the houses are not like these. This one *is* from El Paso, it's the irrigation canal. But then, these paper and wood houses, they are . . . and then this one with the puddles and the unpaved street and all, it's also Juárez. All of these . . . yes, all four photographs are from Juárez. [Humberto correctly locates in Juárez photos 8 and 9, but incorrectly locates photos 6 and 13 in Juárez, too.]
Angela: And you, ma'am?
Marta: Well, these are from over here, where the irrigation canal crosses, right? Toward Ysleta. This one as well, from El Paso, because there are hardly any trailer homes in Juárez. They are like this [photo 9] over there. But, these three are from Juárez.
Humberto: They have a trailer house!
Angela: Yes, she was the only one that discovered the photograph was taken in El Paso . . .
Humberto: Because of the trailer house . . .
Marta: Yes, because in Juárez there hardly are any trailer houses . . .

Except for Marta, who "discovered" the trailer house in the shot and for that reason put the photo in El Paso, all the other interviewees tended to locate all poverty on the Mexican side of the border. Ivette and Encarnación also were inclined to put all the pictures of poverty on the Mexican side of the border. Their sense of separation regarding those kinds of situations was such that there was no way they could imagine themselves living in those conditions, even if they were actually poor like the people depicted in the photograph.

Ivette: This picture, I locate in Juárez, the *vecindarios* . . . they're just in really bad living conditions.

Encarnación: It's in bad conditions, but even worse are the conditions of these people [showing photo 13, of the trailer house, which she believes was taken in Juárez] . . .

Ivette: Just to imagine, to even think of living in those conditions . . . I don't know. Even if I think, see myself, ever as a poor person, I would . . . I cannot imagine having kids living in these conditions. I don't think they would be living in this environment, how can you think of school or trying to progress when, maybe, what you want to do is feed yourself or . . .

Pablo: Do you think it is possible to get this kind of photograph in El Paso, or only in Juárez?

Ivette: Juárez, definitely! I don't think you can see a situation like this in El Paso.

Encarnación: How can the mothers and the fathers of these children who live here think about sending them to school if what they want is to survive? To eat . . . They eat in the dumps, I have seen it. They fight for food, for shoes, for everything.

Encarnación's image of people eating food at the dump and struggling to get used clothes is a very powerful one. They do not live, but survive. Ivette and Encarnación also reached another extreme when, following an argument some Mexican Americans used before, they considered as the epitome of Mexican poverty . . . the trailer house that, as we already know, was taken in El Paso and not in Juárez.

Ivette: This one is poverty in Mexico. The last time one of my operators told me how she's living . . . this is how I imagine this girl living. And they work and she was supporting her sister, her kid, and her father . . . And this is how I imagine her living.

Pablo: And you both put those photos in Juárez?

Ivette: Definitely. I put them in Juárez.

Pablo: And these are the kind of conditions people from maquilas are living in?

Ivette: Yes, I think so, definitely. I see people from maquiladoras living in such conditions.

Pablo: Could you imagine some of those photographs in El Paso, or it is impossible?

Ivette: Yeah. I wouldn't think definitely not in El Paso.

And here again, as with Leticia and Rosario, the explanation of why supposedly there is no such poverty in El Paso is that the American government helps, something the Mexican government does not.

Encarnación: In Mexico, since there are no government programs like in the U.S., then there is more of this [the poverty shown in the photo of the mobile home taken . . . in El Paso!]
Ivette: Yeah. I don't see it here [photo 13] because of all the programs the government has. So that's why I don't think people here get to that level because there're programs to help them here.

Pablo: Why do you think it's impossible to see a picture like this here in El Paso?
Elena: Because here the government helps everyone.
Elisa: I'm not so sure, there is also a lot of poverty here.
Elena: But do you know why there is poverty here? Because there is no communication. If I had known there was help here through the food stamps, and all those things, well . . . I think it would have been a little bit more easy going, not to limit oneself in some consumptions. But since we did not know . . .
Adriana: A lack of education of the public from the government.

Just as Leticia pointed out before, the narrative goes that if there still is poverty in El Paso, it is because people do not use in full *all* the assistance that the American government brings to its inhabitants.

And, when they do not have any other choice but to admit that extreme poverty still exists in the United States ("¡ *Tienen un trailer house*"!), they use the subplot that "all poverty relates to undocumented Mexican nationals — I am a legal one" (the plot used by Rosario, above). People living under those conditions must be undocumented immigrants.

Angela: Do you think something like that would exist in El Paso?
Marta: Well maybe over there, where the city is growing . . . yes.
Angela: And what sort of people would live there?
Marta: Well, the vast majority would be Hispanics, who come as immigrants, without papers, . . . Mexicans.

But to complicate matters further, these middle-class interviewees not only use some of the common plots that other Mexican immigrants living in poverty utilized to make sense of their identity, but they also mix into their narratives a thematic plot that, in some sense, is very similar to that used by Alfredo (see Chapter 3). I am referring here to the construction of an idealized Juárez of the past to which they can relate proudly, because, supposedly, that Juárez did not have the problems that afflict the Juárez of the present. And, not surprisingly, the before and after coincide with their own time of immigration.

Humberto: For us, it is much more quiet to live here than in Juárez . . . it is much better.

Marta: There have *always* been crooks in Juárez, there have always been of all sorts of people everywhere. But Juárez, because of the earthquake in Mexico City, a lot of people came from over there, from Central Mexico, and a lot of robberies started, and a lot of those things. And Juárez was overpopulated.

Humberto: Many came to Juárez, but they came empty handed and now they fight to find work or don't want to work where they are paid little. That's when there starts to be a lot of delinquents, because they start to steal, they mug people and all that. Lately, even in Avenida Juárez, they mug you even in downtown! There is no security anymore. And before, one could go at two, three in the morning anywhere in Juárez, and you were safe. And now, no, they even mug you downtown in broad daylight.

Marta: The neighborhood in which we used to live was very calm and we were fine and all. There were no robberies, but because of the earthquake and the maquilas, it is ugly now. It is no longer like when we lived there.

Encarnación: This photo is the bus station, where unfortunately come the people who didn't make it in their states, in their cities, those who are scum. They say that in the border there are bad people. No! The problem is that the people who come here are those who were thrown out from their towns, their cities.

Pablo: Then the people you think are living in those conditions are coming from elsewhere in Mexico?

PHOTO 17

164 Ciudad Juárez' bus station.

Encarnación: It isn't the natives . . .

Ivette: They come from the interior . . .

Encarnación: It's the poor people from over there, or the criminals who are fleeing, too. Not all, right? But the people who flee their cities, their states, are the ones who come to the borders.

And because these interviewees are still working with some of the classification systems, metaphors, and narratives they brought with them from Mexico, it is not by chance that the before and after in their relationship to Juárez is related to the supposed "invasion" Juárez has undergone from those "undesirable people" (Marta's crooks, Humberto's delinquents, Encarnación's criminals and scum) coming from the South. As we can see, these middle-class Mexican immigrant interviewees constantly mix the different organizing elements that were used by many Anglos, Mexican Americans, and Mexican nationals in their process of identity construction, using metaphors, categories, and narratives that combine, in very complex ways, the different commonsense cultural elements available on the border.

Introduction

Thus far I have been interested in showing the mechanisms of identity construction in a very special setting like the border, where different countries, economies, cultures, religions, and ethnicities come together. Because my interest has been in *mechanisms*, I relied on an ethnographic technique; that is, I traded extension in my knowledge of reality for profundity in its analysis. In other words, I know a lot about the ways *some* people narrate their identities to make sense of themselves and others on the border, but I do not know *how many* people use the mechanisms I have described so far. Of course, discourse analysis about commonsense narratives is of great help in knowing that the discourse you are analyzing is not just individual, but social, shared by many people, because common sense, by definition, is collective, never individual. But still you do not know *how many* people share that particular version of common sense.

However, from time to time reality comes to the aid of fiction, and something happens in society that confirms that the types of commonsense discourses the researcher has gathered in his sample (254 interviews constitutes a large sample for an ethnographic study, but still not enough to generalize) are very widespread in the community. Fortunately, this is what happened in my research when "Operation Blockade" was launched in September 1993. In the following pages, I want to show the reaction of many Juarenses and El Pasoans (Anglos, Mexican Americans, and African Americans alike) to Operation Blockade. In this way, I will present *other* types of data, that were not generated by me, and that still support my interpretation of the basic plots that make up many people's identities on the border.

El Pasoans' Support of Operation Blockade

On Sunday morning, September 19, 1993, El Paso and Ciudad Juárez woke up to a new border patrol strategy to deter illegal immigration into the United States. A surprise border patrol action — "Operation Blockade" — placed four hundred agents and dozens of government vehicles and helicopters on the twenty-mile stretch of

Chapter 5

**OPERATION BLOCKADE, OR WHEN
PRIVATE NARRATIVES WENT PUBLIC**

border dividing El Paso from Ciudad Juárez. This strategy ended decades of laissez-faire attitudes held by the border patrol toward undocumented people, an attitude that had fed a utopian image of El Paso and Juárez as a model of brotherhood along the border. This image was so strong that I had problems convincing people outside the area that there was a profound resentment underlying the relationships between many Juarenses and El Pasoans (both Anglos and Mexican Americans alike). As a matter of fact, some local people were also unaware of the amount of resentment underlying the supposedly "smooth relationship between sister cities." As Salvador Balcorta, director of South El Paso's La Fe Clinic, stressed, however: "The thing we have to overcome now is the hatred . . . For the longest time we have blinded ourselves to the feelings that may be out there" (*El Paso Times*, October 3, 1993).[1]

As Howard, Carrillo, and Peregrino (1994, p. 6) point out: "The hostility and pent-up frustration that had been unleashed by the blockade was astonishing. These feelings had obviously been submerged by the official rhetoric of oneness, by the unspoken assumption that Mexicans and Mexican Americans would naturally sympathize with each other . . . that blood was thicker than the water flowing in a river with two names."

At first there were thumbs-up signs, passing cars with their headlights on and green ribbons (the color of the border patrol) tied to their antennas, people honking their car horns, and the like. Then, neighbors near the border brought coffee and doughnuts to the border patrol agents parked facing the river, within sight of each other and would-be crossers. Immediately many El Pasoans started calling radio programs, sending letters to the local newspapers, and painting their walls supporting the blockade. What some people had thought was something impossible to achieve, to unite El Paso behind a common goal, suddenly happened. For years, politicians and business and religious leaders had desperately sought some issue that would bring El Pasoans together. Then, in only one movement, border patrol agents lined up along the river were able to get what leaders could not. Different polls showed overwhelming public support for the strategy (80 percent to 95 percent, depending on the source).[2] As one El Pasoan wrote:

> If Border Patrol Chief Reyes didn't do anything else, he got the silent majority in El Paso coming out in the open to express their gratitude for what should have been done years ago . . . even the local newspapers were surprised, I am sure, that there is a silent majority here in El Paso. Maybe now, there is a chance for Unite El Paso.[3]

What happened? I think that the nationwide anti-immigrant wave was responsible for some of the support the operation received. In addition, however, the border patrol was doing physically what — as we have seen throughout the book — many El Pasoans (both Anglo and Mexican American) had been doing symbolically already: separating themselves from Mexican nationals in order to construct a valued narrative identity of people living in the United States.[4]

The feeling of many people in El Paso was described by some journalists as "euphoria": "[as if it were] the best time of our lives. That was the feeling I sensed in El Paso this week as we rallied around our Border Patrol" (John Laird, *El Paso Times*, September 26, 1993). Supposedly the blockade would solve all the social problems of the city, because behind them, of course, many people saw the shadow of the "illegal aliens"—that is, one of the most prominent "Mexicans" of the "all poverty and social problems are Mexican" thematic plot. What were those problems? The chief of the border patrol, Silvestre Reyes, argued that one of the most important reasons for the blockade was to answer a community demand to clear the city of beggars, auto thieves, burglars, welfare cheats, and "transvestite prostitutes." The opinion of city officials and El Pasoans' phone calls to the media and the letters to the newspapers thoroughly supported that demand. For instance, El Paso's mayor, Larry Francis, not only was delighted about the possible outcomes of the blockade, but also used the operation to complain to the federal government about the expensive cost the city was paying to provide services for the undocumented: $30 million per year, according to his account.

> Francis said he expects El Paso Police Department reports to show a "dramatic" decline in crime next week. And he said reports from health clinics and other agencies also should show drastic changes. "The impact on social services and crime—arrests, car thefts, burglaries— . . . Thomason Hospital and schools, it all could have a significant (positive) impact on our budget" (*El Paso Times*, September 25, 1993)

Following Francis' excitement, many El Pasoans supported the blockade because they believed that all the beggars and almost all the criminals were Mexicans:

> More than 130 people called the *El Paso Times* Wednesday to express opinions on the Border Patrol's "Operation Blockade." By a 10-to-1 ratio, callers supported the Patrol's action . . . A sampling of responses:

John Fernandez—"This is the only way we can deter some of the crime and some of the illegals coming into our country."

Robert Muñoz—"I think this is the greatest thing that has happened. I live in an area where there is a lot of illegal traffic and since Sunday I have felt safer about my house."

Ralph Woodbridge—"I'm getting sick and tired of my city being viewed as the city of beggars and panhandlers on every corner." (El Paso Times, September 23, 1993)

Forty-four people called the *El Paso Times* . . . a sampling of how El Pasoans said the operation was affecting them:

Estela Mata—"I feel safe."

Ernest Alvillar—"I feel much more secure in that I don't have to worry about some illegal alien breaking into my home."

Rock Ontiveros—"It has affected me in that I don't have to shoo away window washers and seventy-year-old ladies with two-year-old babies begging for money. And I'd like to enjoy an evening at home and not worry if my truck will be there in the morning."

Art Provencio—"For one you don't have people jumping on your car at intersections smearing up your windshield. And I'm sure that crime and car theft has drastically dropped." (El Paso Times, September 24, 1993)

Keeping undocumented immigrants from entering El Paso would benefit the city economically in the long run, according to most of the 132 people who called the *El Paso Times* with opinions . . . A sampling of responses:

Fred Fulton—"It will be better for El Paso because there will be less thefts."

Patty Olivas—"I think the crime rate and auto thefts will go down dramatically."

Michael Bradley—"I think that since the blockade has started, the number of stolen vehicles has gone down. I think that over a long period of time that might mean our insurance rates will drop."

Terry Williams—"I believe the long-term impact will be favorable. We'll have reduced crime, reduced cost of deporting those illegals that are caught, reduced welfare costs, and fewer instances of instant citizens that are born at our expense in our hospitals."

Julia Lopez—"I think the long-term economic impact will be favorable. In fact, my husband and I talked about it and even if our taxes had to go up, it would be worth it. It would be worth it to get all this crime and illegals out from our city." (El Paso Times, September 28, 1993)

Operation Hold the Line[5] has made it possible for me to go to the grocery store with more peace of mind. Before there were loads of beggars daily, some only looking for an easy house to burglarize. It happened three times in my block. All I have to say is thank you, Mr. Silvestre Reyes. (P. Lopez, *El Paso Times*, March 20, 1994)

We're not seeing people being shot or stabbed or robbed. It's different for the better [after the blockade], because now we don't worry about having to look behind and worry about these undocumented immigrants committing crime. (Freddy Morales, director of Chihuahuita Community Recreation Center, *El Paso Times*, March 20, 1994)

As we saw in previous chapters, a very common complaint against Mexican immigrants among my interviewees was that the "illegal aliens" take advantage of the American welfare system that is supported by "us, poor taxpayers." That complaint was very prominent in several letters to the editor that appeared several months before the blockade:

Everybody dislikes Jay Armes[6] because he says it like it is . . . I just wish people would stop being so sensitive. I'm a Mexican-American and yes, every time I see Mexican aliens with their food stamps eating steak while all I can afford is hamburger, I tell them: "Damn wetbacks, why don't you get a job instead of living off us poor taxpayers?" This is a free country, and I can say what I want. And like Armes said, if they don't like it, they can go where they came from. (Juan Perez, *El Paso Times*, March 17, 1993)

We agree 100 percent with California Gov. Pete Wilson. It's time to do something, like not give U.S. citizenship to the children of undocumented immigrants. It just might deter these people from perpetually crossing the border. Undocumented aliens think the red carpet is rolled out for them, which, in a way it is, by the U.S. government. They get free housing, medical care, education and Social Security, while those U.S. citizens who deserve it go without because of the red tape. Certainly, LULAC and a whole bunch of brown-nosed U.S. citizens will come to their defense. And those who do most likely are married to a person from a different country. (Diego Figueroa and Santiago Pellot, *El Paso Times*, September 16, 1993)

If those were the complaints, it is not surprising that many people saw in the blockade the ultimate solution to those abuses:

The long-term effect [of the blockade] is beneficial because they won't be taking advantage of the welfare system or our schools or any other freebies that are offered to them. Our taxes will go down and we'll save money. (Carmen Jimenez, *El Paso Times*, September 27, 1993)

[Due to the blockade] we'll see things like Thomason emergency room a lot less packed and we'll also notice slower days at the welfare department. These will be two large financial impacts on El Paso. (Maria Medina, *El Paso Times*, September 27, 1993)

I would be happy to pay more taxes so that the blockade will continue permanently . . . Thomason Hospital is used to care for illegals. They come to have their babies, who are immediately eligible for benefits such as the WIC [Women, Infants, and Children Program]. Our schools are overburdened by undocumented children. Most of them do not want to speak or will not speak English. Our cars are being stolen and our homes burglarized. Thanks to our Border Patrol for doing a great job. Keep it up. (Julie Del Palacio, *El Paso Times*, September 30, 1993)

I was so angry to see our supposed neighbors to the south burning the U.S. flag we citizens are so proud of. What makes the protesters think they are so special that we want them here in our border cities? All they do is take advantage of privileges that only we American citizens should have. They invade our schools, jobs, food stamps offices and welfare. That's why they're mad at the Border Patrol guarding the border . . . Why don't they stay in their country? We don't need such people in America or El Paso. Let's back our Border Patrol and speak up for our country and our flag. (Mrs. M. Arciniaga, *El Paso Herald-Post*, September 30, 1993)

Americans are tired of undocumented aliens coming to the United States and getting aid in the form of food stamps, welfare and health care. In addition to all that, Americans furnish interpreters for the convenience of undocumented aliens. Even after years of living in the U.S., many legal and illegal immigrants make no effort to learn English. Americans are tired of it all. (I. J. Ryan, *El Paso Times*, January 13, 1994)

The thematic plot pointing out that Mexican undocumented workers were the cause of the high unemployment in El Paso was not absent, either:

Now the United States will build more maquiladoras in Mexico so that people in Mexico that do not have the trade skills can work at the maquiladoras. On the other hand, Americans that use food stamps will now not have excuses as to why they are unemployed. Now lazy people can get to work and not complain about being unemployed. (Marcela Ruiz, *El Paso Times*, September 23, 1993)

[After the blockade] the economy should be looking good because the unemployment in El Paso will go down because more people will be able to get jobs that these Mexican illegals have been getting. (Mary Arroyos, *El Paso Times*, September 27, 1993)

The border blockade has had many positive effects . . . A substantial part of the jobs along the Juárez–El Paso border are taken by people from Mexico. This increases the city's unemployment. These jobs could stabilize some El Pasoans' lives and help improve their living conditions. (*El Paso Times*, November 21, 1993)

And the supposedly complicity of Mexican illegal aliens with drug trafficking was also mentioned:

That is a grateful "thank you" from a taxpayer to the Border Patrol. It has been a long time coming, but the cost of the blockade has aided a big drop in everything from food stamps to handouts, stolen cars, stolen property and, I'm sure, drug trafficking. Also, a drop in transvestites and prostitutes that spread disease. There is now more safety on our streets. Please tell me how anyone can be against the Border Patrol's action. (Ruth Flynn, *El Paso Times*, September 27, 1993)

El Paso sector Border Patrol Chief Silvestre Reyes appeared Friday on Jeff Limberg's radio talk show . . . Only one caller—Robert—protested the blockade. Two subsequent callers caused me to worry. The first said that Robert opposed the blockade because Robert's cocaine dealer obviously had been delayed and thus Robert could not snort a few lines. The second said Robert ought to stick his opinions where the sun does not shine. (John Laird, *El Paso Times*, September 26, 1993)

Other people had less dramatic claims about the disgraces Mexicans supposedly brought to El Paso, but they still were very happy about the outcomes of Operation Blockade:

I have been relieved of seeing so many rude young men selling anything from tortillas to garlic. They are a nuisance, passing by in droves at all hours of the day and night. They roused all the dogs in the neighborhood and made life miserable for me. (Epifania Clarke, *El Paso Times*, March 20, 1994)

Some other people, trying to smooth somehow the "anti-Mexican" sentiment, not only made incredible mistakes, but also showed that the "anti-Mexican" stance was, in some cases, a broader "anti-Hispanic" one:

> It doesn't take a lot of intelligence to see that illegal immigration is not a good thing. It is not just Mexican nationals that come over our Southern borders, it is also Chinese, South Americans, Arabs, Europeans, Puerto Ricans, etc. (Betty E. Coleman, *El Paso Times*, January 20, 1994)

Of course, Puerto Ricans, American citizens by birth, felt insulted, and they answered Coleman's letter immediately.

> This is in response to a Jan. 20 letter, "Keep Our Border Closed." I would like to remind this letter writer that . . . Puerto Ricans have enjoyed United States citizenship since 1917 . . . Puerto Ricans are not illegal immigrants. They have been legally here nearly a century. I advise this writer to visit a public library and review the American History. (José Torres, *El Paso Times*, January 27, 1994)

> We, the members of the Civic-Cultural Organization of Puerto Ricans in El Paso . . . want to refute the contents of Betty Coleman's letter, in which she portrays Puerto Ricans as *illegal aliens* . . . Puerto Ricans are United States citizens . . . and therefore are entitled to enter the United States from the North, South, East, or West just as any other citizen of this country. (Lydia Diaz, *El Paso Times*, January 28, 1994)

> This is in response to Betty E. Coleman's letter "Keep Our Borders Closed." I do agree with her and I am very happy with the excellent work that the Border Patrol is doing . . . But how dare she call the Puerto Ricans illegal immigrants. I am an American citizen since birth, sixty-seven years ago . . . So I advise Betty E. Coleman that she have her facts straight before writing to a newspaper. (Juana Colon de Rodriguez, *El Paso Times*, January 28, 1994)

Nevertheless, and showing the complicated relationship between "facts" and narratives (i.e., that straightforward facts do not necessarily have the power to change the way one perceives the "others," above all when such perception is basic to the construction of a particular narrative identity), Betty Coleman answered her critics by saying that even if Puerto Ricans are not "illegal aliens," they still take advantage of law-abiding American citizens:

> To all the intelligent, erudite and sweet people who pointed out my mistake . . . I would like to say thank you for pointing out the error. I am also

aware that Puerto Rico is a commonwealth . . . The citizens of Puerto Rico do not pay federal taxes although they receive welfare checks from the U.S. government. I also know that they recently conducted an election to determine whether they would accept statehood, self-government or remain a protectorate, and they voted to remain a protectorate. Who wouldn't when you do not have to pay income taxes as a protectorate? (Betty E. Coleman, *El Paso Times*, January 31, 1994)

Hence, Ms. Coleman recognized her original mistake only to go on to denigrate Puerto Ricans even more than she had in her original remarks!

If the blockade rallied El Pasoans around the banner of anti-immigration, it also brought to fruition the sweetest dream of many politicians: it elicited people's willingness to pay more taxes:

A total of 235 readers called the *El Paso Times* reader call-in line to respond to the question: Would you be willing to pay higher taxes to make the border blockade permanent? All but twenty-five of the callers said they support the blockade and the vast majority of them want to see it continue, even if it means higher taxes. Some responses:

A. Velasquez—"I support the border blockade 100 percent. I'd rather pay extra taxes for border protection than have to pay taxes for free medical care for a bunch of illegals."

John C. Renegar—"I would be willing to pay higher taxes. It is so good to see El Paso back in the United States of America."

Tony Lespata—"I would favor increased taxes, but only if it went toward the maintenance of the border to keep the illegals out. If it were diverted to any other source then I would not support it."

Judy Natividad—"There may not be a need for higher taxes. We will save tax dollars by not having to support undocumented 'residents' with their food stamps, medical care and their children's schooling." (*El Paso Times*, September 25, 1993)

And the feeling of safety some El Pasoans experienced after the blockade seems to have changed some well-entrenched domestic habits in the city:

The *El Paso Times* asked readers if they employ a maid . . . who has been unable to get to work because of the blockade and, if so, how that has affected them. The calls were anonymous. Here's a sampling of responses:

• "My maid has not been able to make it across and, surprisingly, I have done very well without her. I was reading in the paper that the maids were saying we lazy Americans were sending our husbands to work with wrinkled clothes. I am ironing my husband's shirt with no problem and I don't need the maid back even if the blockade is over."

• "We do have a maid who has not come for the last two weeks. But that's all right, we are all just pitching in and it is worth it for the safety that our children are feeling now in the streets of El Paso." (*El Paso Times*, October 1, 1993)

Many of the comments people made during the months following the launching of Operation Blockade followed the same line of thought as the narrative identities we had collected a year earlier in our fieldwork. Some of the letters to the newspapers repeated, almost word for word, the comments some of our interviewees had made to us a year or so before:

My mother was born in San Lorenzo, Chih. She faced long lines and waited the necessary time (in Ciudad Juárez) before she was granted her resident alien passport . . . She worked [here] cleaning apartments for minimum wage . . . Since her entry in 1951, she has obeyed the laws, paid taxes and saw that her six children get a proper education. That's Hispanic pride . . . Juarenses should think long and hard before setting our flag on fire. This blockade is not about pitting U.S. workers against Mexicans. It's about separating the hardworking, honest, law abiding resident from the law breakers. (Maria Luisa Moore, *El Paso Times*, October 10, 1993)

The story Ms. Moore tells is very similar to Alfredo's narrative about the old, good Mexico as opposed to the new, degraded one (Chapter 3). Here again morals, values, and "true" Mexicanness (in this case "Hispanidad") are the trophy this writer ascribes to herself and her family but denies to contemporary Mexicans, who are not willing to wait and work hard as her mother had, to become good American citizens of Mexican descent, proud of their "real" Mexican heritage, that of the Mexico of the past.

Another writer made the same claim as many of our interviewees on both sides of the border: the illegals are not Mexican citizens, but people from Central and South America:

The Border Patrol must be aware that not all illegal aliens trying to cross the border are of Mexican descent. In fact, Juárez has been swarmed recently by immigrants from Central and South America, whose final destination is the United States. Yet, this fact is ignored when statistics are presented reflecting the positive effects of the blockade. As interpreted, these results create a stereotype that all Mexicans coming across the border are responsible for crime in El Paso. (Ricardo A. Compean, *El Paso Times*, November 12, 1993)

This letter echoes Estela's attempt (analyzed in Chapter 4) to prove that beggars in El Paso were from Central America and not from Juárez. But the people who wrote letters supporting the blockade were not the only ones addressing some issues we had heard in our fieldwork a year earlier; some of the letter writers who opposed the blockade were also picking up familiar narrative elements:

> The recent Border Blockade has once again proven the lack of heritage pride among Hispanics in the United States. I've noticed that the majority of El Pasoans approve 100 percent of the blockade and believe this will help in reducing crime and violence in El Paso. I wonder how many of these same El Pasoans are in this country thanks to their parents or grandparents coming here illegally? (Luis P. Gallegos, *El Paso Times*, September 29, 1993)

> It is incredible to read the amount of letters sent to the editor of this paper by "Mexican-Americans" who are pro-blockade. I, a first generation American born to Mexican parents, am ashamed to read how these so-called Mexican-Americans can take time to write a letter expressing how they are so much in favor of this blockade and how keeping "illegals" out of El Paso has made their lives so much better. Do these "Chicanos" or Mexican-Americans not realize that somewhere along their family tree someone from Mexico migrated to the United States in order for them to be here in the first place? It never fails that the Hispanics who complain about the "illegals" are usually the ones who lack an education, destroy the English language (not to mention the Spanish language), and keep the welfare program going in this country. Why not educate ourselves about who we are and where we come from. There's nothing worse than a "want-to-be." (Victor Ayala, Jr., *El Paso Times*, October 31, 1993)

As we can see, some of the same issues addressed by Norma and her friends in Chapter 4 are also present in these two letters. More specifically, Gallegos' reference to the "lack of heritage" (central to the "ethnic" division performed by Norma to separate the "good/proud" Mexicans from the "bad/malinchistas" Mexicans) and Ayala's reference to Mexican Americans being the ones who "keep the welfare program going in this country" and his comment that "there's nothing worse than a 'want-to-be.'" Of course I am not claiming that the *entire* process of identity construction is the same in both cases, because a letter is not enough to make that claim. But I do claim that some *elements* are common to the narratives of the letter writers and the narratives of Norma and her friends.

El Pasoans' Opposition to Operation Blockade

These last letters show also that not all El Pasoans supported the blockade or used Mexicans as scapegoats for all the foibles of the city. A few writers and citizens braved the tide of public sentiment to challenge Operation Blockade, and some writers expressed their opposition through letters to the newspaper:

> Since this horrendous blockade was erected, I have developed a sadness in heart that I cannot explain . . . If Joe [Olvera] was angry at his own people, I am furious and ashamed at some of them. I am an American of Mexican descent. Most of the time I am proud of my people, but not now. (Mary L. Hutchins, *El Paso Times*, October 3, 1993)

> Operation Blockade has promoted intolerance in El Paso. As a longtime El Paso resident, I have never heard as bigoted of comments as I have in the last few weeks. This is especially distressing when stations such as KLAQ use public airwaves to impose racism. We Chicanos must shoulder some of the responsibility for this recent rise in race baiting . . . Supporting Operation Blockade gives license to bigots who poison the tolerant culture El Pasoans take pride in . . . Our neighbors are welcome here. Bigots and those who promote a police state for brown people aren't. (Juan Sybert-Coronado, *El Paso Times*, October 15, 1993)

> The Border Blockade—the letters and comments about it—has shattered the illusion that El Paso is a model of bicultural and bilingual harmony . . . Now we have seen the extent of hatred, bigotry, fear and ignorance that prevails . . . The Border Patrol is not the problem. They are doing their job. The problem is that the vast majority in this country are xenophobic . . . (Raymond Williams, *El Paso Times*, October 23, 1993)

> The recent border blockade has seen a dismal and gloomy phenomenon take place in our city . . . what is really perplexing is the wave of hate, racism and bigotry that this action has started. There have been countless detestable remarks made by otherwise respectable citizens against Mexicans. Antagonist contests are even being promoted by a local second-rate, outdated rock radio station. (Ignacio Garcia, *El Paso Times*, October 24, 1993)

If the people quoted above were deeply hurt by the reaction of most El Pasoans toward the blockade, other letter writers preferred the route of humor to express their opposition to the blockade:

Strictly from a cost-benefit analysis, instead of a manned blockade by the Border Patrol, we should build a tall, solid wall along the border, like the famous wall of China or the former Berlin wall . . . We can build it even cheaper and more cost effective by employing foreign labor, like we did with the bracero program . . . This way we don't have to pay Social Security, unemployment or workers compensation. The wall should be Bhutanese style to match the University. Maybe it can become a tourist attraction. In two hundred years or whatever time it takes us to find a solution to the illegal immigrant problem, we can break the wall down and sell its pieces all over the world as the final triumph of open borders and the good-faith effort to engage in free trade. I can see it. This wall put El Paso on the world map—the Great Wall of El Paso. (Bruno G. Romero, *El Paso Times*, October 12, 1993)

Beware you pro-blockade El Pasoans, for you might find yourselves under the curse of certain Aztec deities. Look what is happening in California to Gov. Pete Wilson . . . California burned because the followers of Huehueteotl (The God of Fire) were being offended. Tlaloc (The God of Rain) wasn't helping either. Come the month of March, you pro-blockade El Pasoans might yourselves be blown by an evil sorcerer all the way to the nuclear waste dump in Sierra Blanca. (Ernesto Ortega, *El Paso Times*, November 11, 1993)

Some of the people who opposed the blockade suffered hate mail, obscene calls, and vandalism to their homes as a result. And when they participated in panel discussions about the issue, they usually were harshly criticized for opposing the blockade. An *El Paso Times* account of one of these meetings is a good example:

Several hundred people, countering attacks on the Border Patrol by human rights and immigration activists, gave a rousing show of support Wednesday for Operation Blockade . . . Adrian Armijo, an El Paso insurance agent, asked Reyes, "How does it feel to be admired by racists, bigots and rednecks?" The Border Patrol chief replied, to applause: "If you're putting 95 percent of the people in El Paso in those categories, I think they would be offended." (*El Paso Times*, October 14, 1993)

One of the most prominent public figures who dared to oppose the blockade was El Paso's Bishop Raymundo Peña.

The Roman Catholic bishops of Juárez, El Paso and Las Cruces called Thursday for a temporary end to the border blockade. The bishops said a blockade moratorium of up to a year would give the U.S. government time to study possible relaxation of immigration law . . . [Bishop] Peña said the blockade should be shut down long enough "for due consideration to be given to . . . a viable plan for the easing of controls in our immigration policy . . . The easing of controls will enable us to begin to create the El Paso–Juárez metroplex of which we have spoken about for so long." (*El Paso Times*, October 15, 1993)

After his comments, the Letters to the Editor section of El Paso's newspapers were inundated by angry answers to his position:

Now is the time for Bishop Peña to call it quits . . . He has embarrassed me as a Catholic for the last time. Did he really think he was speaking for the church when he called for the Border Patrol to look the other way when they saw undocumented immigrants breaking the laws of the United States? . . . Have they [the bishops] looked the other way so many years with pedophile priests that they are now willing to suggest a U.S. government agency do likewise? Well, enough already. Peña should apologize to the people of El Paso, to the American people, to the U.S. Border Patrol for suggesting they disregard their oaths of office. The church should stay out of politics. (J. P. Renegar, *El Paso Times*, January 1, 1994)

Catholic Bishop Raymundo Peña does not speak for all Catholics. Peña should open his eyes and look around. Charity begins at home. Until the Catholic Church begins to pay taxes, priests and bishops should say nothing about what the U.S. government does or does not do. (Rene Marquez, *El Paso Times*, January 11, 1994)

The support Mexican Americans showed for the operation was so overwhelming that it changed the discourse of one of the most important Chicano advocates of the city, journalist Joe Olvera. In his weekly column, a month after the blockade started, he wrote one of his most passionate articles ever:

It saddens me the way things are going between El Pasoans and Juarenses. I don't think we're ever going to be friends again. Not that we've ever been really close friends, you know. Our attitude toward Juarenses has always been holier than thou. We, in El Paso, have always lorded it over Juarenses. Even those of us who are of Mexican descent have found it embarrassing that our people in Mexico can't seem to get their acts together. We cringe when we see our people begging on El Paso streets, some of us even lie when we're asked about our own ancestry . . . When I was growing up . . . we were ashamed to be Mexicans . . . we loved Mexican culture, mariachis, tortillas and *frijoles*, but sometimes we hated our own people . . . "We're more

American than some Americans," we say proudly. "We have nothing in common with those illegal aliens who only come here to take our jobs" . . . we're such good Americans that we rail against our own brothers and sisters . . . "Sure, my ancestors came over illegally, but they came to work, not to take the food from other children's mouths. They didn't go on welfare or food stamps." Come on, raza, don't turn against your own people. (*El Paso Times*, October 24, 1993)

In December of 1993, the Border Rights Coalition undertook a survey of residents in an El Paso neighborhood that the media continually portrayed as strongly supporting the blockade: Chihuahuita. This neighborhood is situated adjacent to the border and the "Puente Negro"—the black bridge—not only a popular crossing for the undocumented, but also the headquarters of a dreadful gang that preyed upon crossers on both sides of the border. Of 113 dwelling units visited, a total of 72 respondents were interviewed. As Howard, Carrillo, and Peregrino (1994, p. 7) comment:[7]

A majority of respondents did support the blockade and said that they feel safer now. However, just as the Coalition suspected, there was more diversity of opinion than had been previously reported. Approximately one third of the people interviewed said their sense of personal safety had not changed and that property crimes had remained the same. Surprisingly, men reported feeling safer since the blockade (81 percent) than did women (53 percent). Older residents of the community were slightly more supportive of the blockade than newer residents. One fourth of all residents reported that they had not perceived any change in crime since the blockade.

If this was the reaction of most El Pasoans to Operation Blockade, what happened in Juárez?

Juarenses' Reaction to Operation Blockade

As Howard, Carrillo, and Peregrino (1994, p. 1) point out:

Initial public reaction to "Operation Blockade" on the Mexican side of the border ranged from outrage to smugness that the strategy was only temporary, would never work, and that the people from Mexico could outwit the Border Patrol, as they had done since the 1920s, when the agency was established. Alberto Jimenez, a Juarense interviewed by the *El Paso Times*, was quoted as saying: "We're in no hurry. Let's see who has more patience" (September 21, 1993). There were initial protests, parades, rock-throwing, flag-burning and bridge-blocking incidents.

The initial counterblockade of the international bridges was a spontaneous action from the undocumented immigrants themselves. People screaming, "We want work!" halted traffic for a couple of hours. Subsequent actions were implemented by the CDP (Comité de Defensa Popular). This organization was responsible for the public events — burning the U.S. flags and displaying Uncle Sam piñatas while yelling, "Burn gringo, burn! Let all Yankees die!" — that so infuriated some of the letter writers quoted above. The CDP's main argument was expressed in a letter addressed to the American consul in Ciudad Juárez and later published by *El Fronterizo*:

> We regard Operation Blockade as . . . responding to an attitude among American government officials with sick, twisted mentalities, attempting to justify themselves in a coarse manner, based on the naming of our countrymen as "illegals," a label sprung on them because of their migrant status. From this label they [government officials] arrive at the conclusion that they are criminals and they deserve to be treated as such. (*El Fronterizo*, September 25, 1993)

What we can see in this letter are narrative elements very similar to those found in the interviews we conducted with Héctor and his family (already analyzed in Chapters 1, 2, and forthcoming in Chapter 6). In those interviews Héctor implied that a major barrier to real friendship between Ciudad Juárez and El Paso is the behavior of the American officials (border patrol and custom agents), who do not recognize what, according to his experience, is quite obvious to anyone who lives in these cities, that is, that they are "brothers." And the distance between a narrated story and a lived one collapses in Héctor's case, because he actually sued and won a public apology from the border patrol after he was incarcerated while defending some compatriots against what he thought was unfair treatment.

The CDP also initiated a campaign at Juárez maquiladoras asking American employees to leave the country, and asking managers to improve salaries to the level of the factories on the U.S. side of the border. By late September, and only two weeks after the blockade was implemented, much of the initial and violent opposition to the blockade coming from the undocumented themselves or from CDP was gone. As we will see below, many Juarenses did not sympathize with the situation of the undocumented workers. Nevertheless a different kind of opposition started; by that time, Juarenses already had discovered the prejudiced ways (well exemplified by the letters to the editor quoted above) in which many El Pasoans justified the blockade. Accordingly, different political and business groups in Juárez asked Juarenses to stop spending money in El Paso. The Juárez offices of the National Chamber of Commerce and the Chamber of Industry joined the city's Institutional Revolutionary Party (PRI), radio disc jockeys, and populist political parties in asking Mexican shoppers to boycott El Paso. The head of the Juárez office of CANACINTRA [Cámara Nacional de Comercio e Industria de la Transformación] was quoted in the *El Paso Times*: "We are asking people to find local alternatives to purchases in El Paso so they will not be humiliated by United States authorities at the border crossing" (*El Paso Times*, September 29, 1993). And further: ". . . Mexicans are tired of being considered thieves in El Paso" (*El Paso Times*, October 1, 1993).

Juarenses' outrage was also expressed in letters to newspapers and editorials:

> We go there [to the U.S.] to work, not to steal, or to contaminate their environment with our "stench," as some of our countrymen who are already "legal" say; and perhaps they have forgotten that they were once just as "illegal" as we are—they and all their relatives as well. (*El Diario de Juárez*, September 25, 1993)

As happened on the American side of the border, some letters to Juárez' newspapers closely resembled what we had found in our interviews one year before. In the letter quoted above we can find the basic structure of the script used by many of our interviewees analyzed in Chapter 2, well summarized by the characterization of Mexican Americans as "Pochos." I am referring here to Don Librado's argument that Mexican Americans like Mexico but not Mexicans; Concepción, Edelmira, and Nivia's experience of being discriminated against by border patrol, customs agents, and housewives of Mexican descent, as well as their sense of being considered inferior by their own relatives who are now "*arreglados*" and live on the other side; and so forth.

> Operation Blockade is far from being a mere police device, the product of the decision of a country well-disposed to have its laws respected and to defend its sovereignty . . . On the contrary . . . it constitutes an unmistakable gesture in regard to the value that is accorded to Mexico and its citizens in the U.S. . . . it has succeeded in reopening the old racial wounds and [rekindling] xenophobia on both sides of the rio Bravo [the name Mexicans use for the Rio Grande] . . . the time has come for Juarenses to defend our dignity and to redefine our role in the context of intercity relations . . . no one has the right to treat us like unwelcome guests or unwanted outsiders . . . We are not

claiming any privileges, or affirming that we have the right to violate the laws of a foreign country; but neither do we have to accept being called criminals, thieves or beggars. (*El Diario de Juárez*, September 25, 1993)

We don't like each other. Not because of voluntary feelings; rather because of historic reasons. They are our race. They've left for economic reasons. They've left their house. I'm not talking about all Mexican Americans, only about those who lead the struggle against Mexicans. (Lic. Héctor González Mocken, president of the Juárez municipal committee of the PRI).[8]

In these two letters we also find issues very similar to those addressed by Agustín and Rafa in Chapter 2 regarding American xenophobia, or Librado's argument that the Mexicans who left Mexico were the ones who could not make it economically in Mexico.

What the most important political and business groups in Juárez wanted was a commercial boycott of El Paso, an operation called "Operación Respeto" or "Operación Dignidad." Such a campaign would have required people to consume Mexican products instead of American ones; several slogans accompanied the impetus: "*Consuma lo mexicano*" [Consume Mexican products]; "*Si quieres ser respetado, quédate en Juárez*" [If you want to be respected, stay in Juárez].

However, regardless of all the support coming from the most important political parties and representatives of the chamber of commerce and the business community, the campaign was a total failure: not only did many Juarenses not stop shopping in El Paso, but also they expressed their disapproval toward the measure. The *El Paso Times* reported: "Dora Martínez, a Juárez secretary, said Tuesday she has no plans to stop shopping in El Paso regardless of the Juárez chamber's request. 'I don't think it's fair for the people who come to buy groceries or clothes,' Martinez said after grocery shopping at Furr's near Bassett Center" (*El Paso Times*, September 29, 1993). This kind of attitude shows how important it was for some Juarenses to keep their relationships with the other side running smoothly, as well as their lack of sympathy for the plight of the undocumented. Consequently, the problem of the undocumented people did not elicit widespread support among Juarenses; in fact, some of them publicly expressed their criticism against the former for blocking the bridges as a protest.

"The protesters are probably the ones that cross illegally and for them to ask others not to cross is wrong," Georgina Salas of Juárez said. "They are protesting in vain. If they want to cross, they should get their paperwork and cross legally." (*El Paso Times*, September 22, 1993)[9]

Juarense Maria Luisa Piñeda, who has a shopping visa to enter El Paso, said Friday that the United States has a right to its border. "And I had to go through a lot of trouble to get my visa. They (Juarenses without visas) should get in line like everyone else," Piñeda said. "Some people like the easy things." (*El Paso Times*, September 25, 1993)

Also, some Juárez newspapers voiced the same kind of criticism against the undocumented:

The needy and unprepared class of our city are the ones who cross the border, in a crouching and covert way, to seek their daily bread; it is precisely because of their lack of criteria, capability and culture that, within their ignorance, they do the most implausible things in order to cross to the other side; they don't resort to legal means, and there are many consequences of their actions at this time, including the economic disruption of our area. For what purpose?[10] (Rafael Taracena Franco, *El Fronterizo*, September 30, 1993)

As noted, the initial "euphoria" on the American side of the border and the way many El Pasoans addressed the blockade were in agreement with our account of the way in which many El Pasoans construct their identities. The same was true on the other side of the border: the public reaction to Operation Blockade was in line with the ways in which our interviewees constructed their identities. We have to remember here that for many native Juarenses, the undocumented workers (often equated with Southern Mexican immigrants in our interviews) were the "others"; Juarenses constructed their identities as those "*arreglados*" who can cross the border without legal problems.

Thus, after several months, the initial protest died down in Juárez. Meanwhile, the undocumented workers tried various ways of circumventing the blockade. First, they tried using fake visas for crossing. According to Ken Pasquarelle, deputy district director for the Immigration and Naturalization Service (INS) in El Paso, "False document use went up from twelve a day [before the blockade] to a peak of over one hundred a day [after the blockade]" (*El Paso Times*, March 20, 1994, p. 11A). False document use then began a steady decline, and after a while it averaged twenty a day. Document violations range from using another person's border crossing card to using forged documents. INS officials cannot say whether demand for legal border crossing cards increased after the blockade. The El Paso office can handle about two hundred applications a day, and applications were already at that level when the blockade began. It is, however, possible that some undocumented workers were crossing legally but working illegally.

Second, they tried to circumvent the blockade by entering El Paso from Fabens or Canutillo. Therefore, after the initial, dramatic plunge in the number of arrests of undocumented immigrants, the figures began to edge back up. Illegal crossers were going around the edges of the twenty-mile blockade zone, especially near Sunland Park. "We've created more of a market for the illegal smugglers (of immigrants), who now charge about eighty to one hundred dollars each, where they charged about five dollars before," border patrol chief Silvestre Reyes said (*El Paso Times*, March 20, 1994). To solve the problem, Reyes proposed building a 10-foot-high, 1.3-mile-long steel wall near Sunland Park.

Some of the undocumented workers who for some reason could not cross have found work in Juárez. It seems that a rapidly expanding Juárez economy was able to absorb a good number of the displaced workers, largely through jobs at maquiladoras. "'In the first two months of this year alone we had a 7 percent growth (in jobs),' Mayor Francisco Villarreal said" (*El Paso Times*, March 20, 1994, p. 11A).

Discourses versus Facts:
What Happened After Operation Blockade

Thus far I have focused on the various public discourses about the blockade: how people made sense of a situation that suddenly brought to the surface the way many people construct identity on the border. But what are the "facts" about the consequences of the blockade? The sheer numbers for the first year after the blockade tell us that there was an important decrease (20 percent to 30 percent) in some crimes (robbery, burglary, and auto theft), a negligible decrease (less than 10 percent) in other types of crimes (rape, assault, and larceny), and an increase (13 percent) in homicides. In general, the overall rate of crime reported in El Paso dropped 9.6 percent in the first four full months of the operation compared with a year earlier. Police credited the blockade for the decrease in auto thefts, but drops in other categories were attributed to other causes (*El Paso Times*, March 20, 1994, p. 10A). For instance, an El Paso police spokesman, Sergeant Bill Pfeil, stressed: "Most people are focusing on the fact that they [the undocumented] are perpetrators . . . That's not always the case. They're not a plague or a pestilence to the people of El Paso." He also commented that undocumented immigrants are often the victims of crime, and that that could be why some categories, especially robberies, were down (p. 10A). On the other hand, El Paso had been experiencing a steady decline in crime since 1990, three years *before* the blockade was implemented; thus, it is not clear how much of the decrease in crime was part of a long-term trend and how much might have been a product of the blockade. Accordingly, the total number of reported crimes (murder, rape, aggravated assault, robbery, burglary, larceny/theft, and auto theft) was around 58,000 in 1990, roughly 49,000 in 1991–1992, and 47,000 in 1993, an impressive 19 percent decrease *before* the blockade started in full. By 1996 the total number of crimes was very similar to its level before the blockade: 45,000 (*El Paso Times*, February 19, 1997, p. 1A).[11] Written in July 1994 and using a very sophisticated statistical analysis of crime data, *Illegal Mexican Migration and the United States/Mexico Border: The Effects of Operation Hold the Line on El Paso/Juárez*, presented by Frank Bean et al. at the U.S. Commission on Immigration Reform, concluded that (p. 93)

[s]erious crime does appear to have declined since the Operation began. However, not enough time has elapsed to be able to tell if the reductions in serious crime are due mostly to the Operation curtailing illegals who commit crimes or to the redeployment of El Paso police so that serious crimes among noncrossers are being deterred. Downward trends predate the onset of the Operation, and earlier years have experienced similarly comprehensive and sharp downturns in crime rates (1990–1991 in particular). The trends may have as much to do with local law enforcement and other factors in the community that may have gone unnoticed until the Border Patrol's Operation drew attention to such issues.

The other "fact" that is brought forth to "prove" the success of the operation is debatable. According to the border patrol, arrests of undocumented immigrants in El Paso dropped 73 percent in the first five full months of the operation, compared with a year earlier (*El Paso Times*, March 20, 1994, 10A). What this impressive statistic does not address is how many undocumented are not caught because almost all the border patrol manpower is located at the border points and not searching for illegal immigrants in the El Paso streets, as they did before.

More importantly, some other statistics contradict El Pasoans' widely held assumptions. Before the blockade, many people believed that the county-owned Thomason Hospital and El Paso's bus system were heavily used by undocumented immigrants. But officials from the two agencies reported that demand for their services actually *increased* in the months following the blockade (*El Paso Times*, March 20, 1994,

10A). The same can be said about another myth: unemployment. It did not decrease after the blockade; on the contrary, it increased more than two percentage points: in March 1993 it was 9.3 percent compared to 11.5 percent one year later (*El Paso Times*, May 22, 1994, p. 3E). And the beggars did not disappear, although the blockade somehow had the effect of allowing a distinction between the good beggars and the bad ones:

> I have been reading over and over again that ever since the beginning of the Border Patrol blockade, there are no longer any panhandlers in El Paso. That's odd. On a daily basis, I still see the same old scary-looking, weird-acting, bunch under the freeways. You know, the ones with the blue buckets and with the signs (in English) that read, "Will work (they won't) for food." Well? (Luis R. Rodriguez, *El Paso Times*, October 5, 1993)

> Believe it or not, there are still plenty of beggars in our city, despite Operation Blockade . . . Based on our reaction to the blockade, I'd say we have determined as a community just who is qualified to beg and who isn't . . . Now we have shown that beggars with signs reading "Will Work For Food" and a host of other messages are more tolerable than those who don't speak or write English. Actually, our response to beggars has come down to whether they are here legally or not. (Moises Bujanda, *El Paso Herald-Post*, October 1, 1993)

The sign a beggar held in his hand at a very busy intersection one morning in October 1993 was very expressive of the situation Bujanda described in his article. The sign read: "Hire a Vet, not a Wet."

Nevertheless, as Howard, Carrillo, and Peregrino note, the more-than-dubious results of the operation did not change the "euphoric" climate of the city about the border patrol strategy:

> The fact that the anticipated outcomes failed to materialize in El Paso has not dampened enthusiasm, nor been cause for the public or the media to re-examine the Border Patrol's policy. Car theft was initially reduced, but has inched up to former levels. Serious crime was never affected. Births at Thomason were not reduced. In fact, they have continued to increase . . . Vietnam veterans have replaced Mexican beggars at popular intersections. El Paso is still one of the poorest counties in the United States. Hatred and intolerance are still common in the letters to the editor section of the local newspapers. (1994, p. 8)

The problem is that data (used as a metaphor for facts) are not going to change the narrative identities of people who are totally impermeable to facts. Some individuals, while not acknowledging the narrative character of their own identities, "accuse" facts of having a narrative structure, that is, of being discursively malleable. For these people, facts can be manipulated, but the basic plot behind their own narrative identities cannot.

If this were not so, how could we understand the following letter, in which the writer did not believe Thomason Hospital data showing that deliveries were not down after the blockade, but up?

> *Thomason stubborn.* Yea! To the Border Patrol—they spent our tax dollars well. Boo! To Thomason Hospital—they won't admit that the newborn count is half that of pre-Blockade times. They want to keep spending our tax dollars until we become like California—broke. (Norman G. Fisher, Jr., *El Paso Times*, October 11, 1993)

We have to remember that one of the most common claims about undocumented workers in El Paso is that they frequently go to Thomason Hospital (the county's public hospital) to give birth so that their children will enjoy American citizenship. Mr. Fisher, wedded as he was to his narrative identity, simply did not believe the hospital's data, released two weeks after Operation Blockade began, which showed, "surprisingly," that deliveries had not decreased at all after the blockade; in fact, they had actually increased. Did people like Mr. Fisher change their attitudes about undocumented immigrants after learning that "data coming from reality" contradicted their claims? We do not think so, and Mr. Fisher's reaction seems to have been widespread. That is, I think that for people whose identity plots absolutely required the presence of the despised "undocumented worker," it was more vital to deny "reality" than to change their scripts.[12]

The question we have to ask ourselves is, what do people like Ralph Woodbridge, who was "sick and tired of my city being viewed as the city of beggars and panhandlers," think about "the Mexicans" after more than four years of blockade—now that the Mexicans are gone but the beggars are still there? Or those like Patty Olivas, who was sure the crime rate was going to go down dramatically and who must face the fact that its reduction is not as significant as she thought it would be? Or Michael Bradley, who was so sure that his auto insurance rates would go down because auto theft was going to disappear after the blockade? Or Terry Williams, who thought that the delivery rate at Thomason Hospital would go down—and instead it went up? Or Mary Arroyos and Marcela Ruiz, who thought that "those Mexican illegals" were depriving Americans of jobs—yet El Paso unemployment rates are higher than before the blockade? Or Carmen Jimenez and Maria Medina, who hoped that their taxes would go down because there were not going to be more "illegal aliens" taking advantage of the welfare system and free schools —yet there was no change in the number of welfare recipients after the blockade? Betty Coleman, as we saw above, did not change her plot even after it was pointed out that Puerto Ricans were American citizens by birth; she merely reinforced her racist statement toward them. Is it likely that these other letter writers would change their narrative identities simply because the "facts" do not fit into their discourses?

The problem, again, is that the relationship between "facts" and narratives is a very complex one, and the possibility of "accommodating" new, or "unexpected," or "contradictory" facts to one's narrative identity seems to depend more on how flexible one's plot is than on how forceful the facts are. In this sense, if people's negative images about the "others" can be changed at all, it will not be by opposing their narrative identities with "facts," but rather by confronting them with the "narrative character-ness" of their identities. That was precisely what I did in a pilot dialogical social science experiment I conducted in the region between 1995 and 1996. The analysis of that exercise is the topic of the next chapter.

Introduction

When I decided to use the discussion of photographs as a methodology instead of surveys, I also decided I would engage my interviewees in a dialogue instead of relying on a researcher's monologue. For two different but related reasons, I designed my research in such a way that returning to the people I interviewed was a must. First, I wanted to challenge the prevailing monological way of doing social science. Until the late 1970s, in many ethnographic accounts only the researcher's voice attempted to make sense of people's lived experiences. The people who lived those experiences were denied their own voices, except as "illustrations" of the researcher's descriptions. In the 1980s a dialogical approach gained momentum, in which it was proposed that all voices should have similar weight in the process of constructing knowledge. Many prominent researchers have written about the importance of dialogic anthropology in understanding how people construct meaning (R. Rosaldo 1989; Marcus and Fisher 1986; Rabinow 1985; Tedlock 1983; Tyler 1986), but not many anthropologists have carried those ideas into the field (but see Tobin and Davidson 1990; Campbell et al. 1993). Accordingly, I agree with Tobin and Davidson (p. 272), who state: "This research approach was designed to empower informants by replacing traditional ethnographic authority with polyvocality, and to de-center the text from its authors by shifting the power of reflexivity from the meta-discourse of the ethnographer to the understandings of [the interviewees] . . ."

However, I am aware that a commitment to dialogism does not necessarily guarantee its realization. As Tyler asserts,

> Dialogue rendered as text . . . is no longer dialogue, but a text masquerading as a dialogue, a mere monologue about a dialogue since the informant's appearances in the dialogue are at best mediated through the ethnographer's dominant authorial role. While it is laudable to include the native, his position is not thereby improved, for his words are still only instruments of the ethnographer's will. (quoted in Marcus and Cushman, 1982, p. 44)

Notwithstanding Tyler's criticism, and being totally aware that the final product, this book, does have an author, I believe that a dialogi-

Chapter 6

DIALOGICAL SOCIAL SCIENCE AND THE POSSIBILITY OF NARRATING BETTER STORIES

cal approach still allows some of the author's power to be shared with the interviewees. Second, reinterviewing my interviewees would provide the opportunity to open a discussion about their images concerning the "others." Like everybody else, Mexicans, Anglos, African Americans, and Chicanos manipulate reality in order to make sense of themselves and "others." People always have a certain amount of room to "play" with reality in order to fashion a more or less coherent narrative identity. But if "data" and discourse are both narrative devices, they nonetheless create material effects. People live and die under the sway of partial, erroneous, malevolent, or biased "data" and discourses. The particular problem in the relationship between "reality" and narrative identities is whether, and to what extent, people are willing to change their plots if they learn that some of the "data coming from reality" do not fit the script they have developed to make sense of themselves and "others." Of course, there are no easy answers to these questions. I wanted to try to engage people in a discussion about the narrative character of their identities, surmising that self-reflective exchange might result in more flexible narratives. Rosenwald (1992, p. 276) states:

> In order to achieve a satisfactory understanding of themselves, individuals must at the very least evolve a conception of those features of culture that narrow their vision . . . an individual's or group's emergence from culturally typical perplexities depends on an understanding of the mystifying structures they have surmounted. The later accounts of their social existence should not only remedy the inadequacies of the earlier ones but also help them (and us) to understand why those defects were necessary.

Consequently, my attempt was to dialogically engage my interviewees in a discussion of how their own narratives functioned as those "necessary defective" cultural artifacts that biased their visions about themselves and the "others." The El Paso–Ciudad Juárez area seems to me a likely place to conduct such an experiment because the level of racial and regional animosity is there, but not to the palpable degree that exists in other areas where well-developed social movements (Ku Klux Klan, Skin Heads, diverse religious fundamentalisms, etc.) are very active. Therefore, using a dialogic methodology, I decided to ask people to think about how their identities have a narrative character. In this way I introduced them to the idea that, if we are all storytellers, we are also characters in the stories of others. We may usually be the "good guys" in our own scripts, but we frequently end up as "bad guys" in other people's stories. Of course, people generally believe that they have excellent "reasons" and "data" for describing themselves and other characters the way they do, and for constructing identities accordingly. For this reason, I intended to explore with my interviewees some of the intricacies involved in the games that Anglos, Mexicans, African Americans, Mexican Americans, and Chicanos play on the border, where each side weighs itself and the "other" on a moral basis to prove who is better. My hope was that engagement in negotiating scripts about themselves and "others" would allay their need to portray the "other" so negatively. Ergo, this is the partiality, the kind of commitment I want to be accountable for in my research. As Bhavnani and Haraway point out:

> What kind of partiality, what kind of commitment, engagement, what way of life are you *for*, in your knowledge-production factors? This question insists on accountability. A kind of relentless situating as part of objectivity, so that objectivity is not maintaining the boundaries of the knower intact vis-à-vis what is studied, but is the opposite—is opening up the boundaries of the knower to a kind of accountability for positioning in all knowledge production. Call that "strong objectivity." It is an attempt to intervene in what's going to count as science . . . Standpoint is crafted out of struggle, out of engagement, and then becomes a powerful possibility for fueling a different kind of knowledge in the world . . . standpoint theory becomes a way of producing—of materializing—the world differently. (p. 36–37)

Narratives versus Facts, or How the Discussion of Biased Perception Helps in the Process of Flexibilizing People's Narrative Plots

The mechanism of the reinterviews was the following: I started the interview with a basic speech explaining that I was returning to the people we had interviewed to share with them the results of the research. In that initial talk I addressed the two main reasons for my coming back to reinterview them. First, I wanted to give them the opportunity to review my own narrative about them, to, with good luck, negotiate a middle-of-the-road narrative between theirs and mine. Second, I wanted to offer them my idea that, perhaps, in trying to understand their testimonies in terms of the narratives I believed were behind their sayings, we could understand better not only the narratives of the "others," but also the narrative character of our own definitions of reality.

In this sense, I was striving to go beyond the usual scope of dialogical anthropology. I not only offered my analysis of their narratives to elicit their criticisms about it in the search for a negotiation of meaning between the researcher's and the interviewees' points of view, but also, and more importantly, I actively pursued their negotiation of meaning with other interviewees with the same negotiating goal in mind. Hence, in the process of reinterviewing people we were dealing, all the time, with three different narratives seeking common ground on which to negotiate meaning: theirs, mine, and those narratives of the "others" that I brought up constantly to show them how other people constructed very different accounts of reality, using, basically, the same "data" (the photos I showed all my interviewees in the different meetings we had).

After my initial speech, we started a discussion of their own plots following a transcript of the interviews. The first and foremost common reaction was surprise: most of my interviewees did not know they were using those plots in the first place. But after they were confronted with their own arguments during the interviews, it became quite obvious that they were using, again and again, a basic plot to sort out and comment on the photographs I showed them.

The second reaction in most cases was shame. They could not believe they were so stereotypical in their views of "others." In most cases the third reaction was to ask me what could be done to avoid repeating these kinds of stereotypes. Here most of the interviews developed into discussions of the need to avoid the use of categories to address other people, because categories establish hierarchies and, not by chance, many people want to place themselves in the "best" category.

The last reaction was to acknowledge how difficult it is to change the way we construct the "others," but also how important it was for them to participate in an experiment like this one, where they learned that something can be done to stop this process wherein everyone seems to stereotype the "others" in order to achieve a valued identity. If this was the general context of many reinterviews, there were variations that are worth analysis.

The Mexican Side

"Easy" Reinterviews versus "Uneasy" Ones

On the Mexican side of the border there were interviews that could be described as "ideal" in terms of the purpose of my pilot research: the interviewees rapidly discovered their plots, criticized themselves, started laughing about the absurdity of the emplotment of their arguments, and used what they had discovered about themselves to plan a different approach to their lives.

One such interview was the one I conducted with the militants of the leftist party in Juárez (analyzed in Chapter 1). In that meeting the anti-Southern Mexican stance was prominent and I confronted Julián with that plot in the reinterview:

> **Pablo:** How many people from the South do you need in Juárez . . . so that the argument that all the social problems and poverty are from the South holds up?
> **Julián:** Let's say . . . five hundred thousand people.
> **Pablo:** We're talking about 40 percent of Juárez' population.
> **Julián:** Yes, probably.
> **Pablo:** Only 14 percent of Juárez' population is from Southern Mexico. The majority of Juárez' immigration is from the state of Chihuahua.
> **Julián:** I hardly believe it . . . Wow!

Obviously this census "data" cannot be incorporated into Julián's plot without major changes in it, because his 40 percent is quite distant from the 14 percent of Southern immigrants living in Juárez in 1990. Accordingly, instead of "fighting" my data (as we will see other interviewees did), Julián accepted as valid the information I gave him and started a very interesting process of self-reflection about his narrative identity:

> **Julián:** This hour that we have been together has made me see many things differently! Among others things, how I see myself. It was important to learn how we make mistakes that are fundamental, that often keep us from doing the *right things*, in spite of the fact that we *have the intentions* to do them. That thing about the regionalism, the categorizing of social processes and events . . . for example, poverty, that situation, right? It limits us, closes us in, right? And it's so important *that we function with it all our lives.* Now that I see it properly, I know why we don't have a Proposition 187 here in Juárez [he refers to California's Proposition 187]. Purely and simply because we don't even need it! [laughs]
> **Pablo:** Yes, it functions de facto.
> **Julián:** If we continue like this, we'll prevent other maquiladoras from coming to Juárez, not because we don't want them to exploit Mexicans, but just so that people from Zacatecas don't come to Juárez [laughs].

The process of self-reflection Julián started also related to his political experience; he rapidly discovered how his own political practice was colored by the anti-Southern plot so prominent in Juárez, to the point of undermining the chances of being successful in his political activities. As the exchange quoted below exemplifies, for Julián regionalism can be at times stronger than political affiliation to identify who is the "other."

> **Julián:** We have a system of categorization . . . [very] divisive. If someone from the PTA [Julián's party] comes from Yucatán: "You're from Yucatán! You're not in the PTA!" That's your substance [your regional origin], the rest is . . . variations . . .
>
> **Pablo:** Exactly, the theme is the *substance*! The idea of essence, "essentially, you are . . ." And perhaps that man behaves 90 percent of the time like a Juarense, but because 10 percent of the time he behaves according to this image I have of Yucatecos . . . "Oh, I knew he was from Yucatán! Deep down, he was Yucateco!"
>
> **Julián:** [laughs] Yes, yes . . . deep down! yes . . . "You finally revealed yourself! . . . Ninety percent of the time you were trying to fool me, but finally it came out, the Yucateco in you!"

On the other hand, the discovery of the basic plot behind most of his comments about Southern Mexicans in general, and Chilangos in particular, induced Julián to profoundly reevaluate the goals of his political agenda. He realized that power is, basically, a multilayered relationship:

> **Julián:** Now I'll even work with more clarity for the city. Because until now we have been focusing all our efforts and our interpretation on the fact that the relationship between the federal government and the city has to change, and that centralized government has to be transformed into a real federal system. Mexico, Mexico City, the federal government, etc., etc., etc. We're looking at these two points but we don't see that the state government in Chihuahua is also operating in a centralistic manner in relation to the city. And we were missing it!
>
> **Pablo:** And the city I am pretty sure is working in a centralistic manner regarding the neighborhoods.
>
> **Julián:** Exactly! And probably the neighborhoods in relation to the families, and the father in relation to the mother, and the mother regarding the children and . . . !

Perhaps Julián's ideology as a leftist predisposed him to agree with an articulation of egalitarian values such as those I was proposing to him in the reinterview process.[1] If this is so, at least part of the explanation of his quite flexible plot comes from that ideology. However, there are plenty of examples of highly inflexible plots held by leftists not only in Mexico but all over the world. Therefore, the only thing I can say is that, for some complex reason (of which his ideology is only a part), the flexibility of his plot allowed him to rapidly (and with a very highly developed reflexivity) accept my argument about the narrative character of his identity and to expand his understanding of himself as a person and as a political militant.

The reinterview I conducted with the Figueroa family (a family whose discourse I analyzed in Chapters 1 and 2) followed a very different pattern. In the original interview, the plot that "all poverty and social problems are caused by the Southern Mexican immigrants" was prominent, and a good portion of the reinterview was used by Héctor (the former law enforcement officer) to challenge my data about the real amount of Southern immigration in Juárez. This interview is a good example of Polkinghorne's (1988) idea that people try to maintain their plots even if doing so requires denying new evidence. In this case it must be said, though, that many Juarenses believe—with some justification, given the highly politicized way in which bureaucracy works in Mexico—that the census office consistently undercounts the population of their city to help Ciudad Chihuahua politically. Thus Héctor was (and I am sure still is!) totally convinced that the number of Southern Mexican immigrants is much higher than my figure of 14 percent, and we debated the validity of our respective sources extensively, the Instituto Nacional de Estadística, Geografía e Informática (INEGI) national census in my case, a municipal account in his. According to INEGI figures, in 1990 Juárez' population was 789,522; by 1995, it had increased to 1,011,786. Héctor's figure of 1,700,000 inhabitants is well beyond both, and the proportion of people he asserted were not from the state of Chihuahua (40 percent) is also a little bit higher than what the 1990 census claims: 34 percent. However, Héctor's use of the statistical data distorts reality, because what he was doing was equating straightforwardly all immigration to Juárez with *immigration from the despised South*, a move that, we will see, is essential to maintaining his plot. The point I want to stress here is that in order to support his argument, Héctor lumped together *any* immigration to Juárez (from North, South, or Central Mexico) with immigration from the South, when most of that immigration (*for any census, his included*) is from the North.

Héctor: But I don't know if it's worth anything, we see here in Juárez that . . . it's overrun with extremely needy people! Only to mention to you what happens here, in our house, during the day . . . twenty to twenty-five people come asking for help. And for instance . . . the person who came today asking for help and water . . . was from Durango . . . He was already very hungry . . . and he's from Durango . . .

I can imagine the laughter of my readers who know Mexican geography: to name Durango as the "personal experience that supports my claim that most immigrants in Juárez are from the South" is the epitome of Juarenses' regionalism. Durango is the state that borders Chihuahua to the south, that is, a Northern Mexican state by any account. This testimony makes Héctor a good example of those Juarenses who claim that almost anyone who is not Juarense is from Southern Mexico (and those from this expanded version of Southern Mexico are the cause of all problems Juárez has). The identification of Durango as Southern is of course technically correct, because there *is* no Mexican state or city to the north of Juárez. From a symbolic point of view, this idea of "Southern" is overdetermined by the anti-Southerner stance that we have seen throughout the book in the narratives of many Juarenses.

When Héctor brought out another personal experience to support his claim that "all immigrants are from Southern Mexico," his definition of "South" was again "anything south of Juárez." In the maquiladora where his son worked, he said, "all the workers were from the South" — by which, again, he meant Durango and Torreón. The latter is the capital city of Coahuila, another Northern state that borders the United States. The Figueroa family, with Héctor leading, steadfastly resisted any data that did not conform to their basic narrative: not only are most immigrants in Juárez from Southern Mexico but, more importantly, those immigrants are the unique cause of Juárez' problems. Therefore, after I recited an array of information I had about the northern nature of most immigration arriving to Juárez, Héctor dismissed my data without hesitation:

Héctor: Well, you know what? All your information is wrong. We Juarenses know people from Chihuahua, it's unmistakable! Just as a person from Sinaloa is unmistakable, and one from Sonora . . . those people are unmistakable. But if you get on a bus, right away you'll get . . . for every ten Juarenses, the rest of the bus is full of outsiders . . . of people who come from outside Juárez.

Here again Héctor marks a sharp division between "us" (those from Juárez and Chihuahua) and "them, those from Southern Mexico," who in his example are the people from Sonora (the other U.S.–Mexico border state to the west) and Sinaloa (still another Northern Mexican state bordering Chihuahua to the southwest). And in this reinterview, in which I constantly tried to show the narrative character of their construction of the Southern Mexican as the stigmatized "other" (the same argument that totally convinced Julián and many others of the force of their anti-Southern plot), "those from Southern Mexico" were nevertheless consistently portrayed as the "bad guys":

Héctor: No one is safe here, and it's definitely because of the overpopulation that exists in Juárez! And you see it every day! In the crime section of the newspaper, right? It says . . . the person who committed the crime came from such-and-such a place, right? And sometimes it also says, "He was running away from such city or state, and came to hide in Juárez. Once here, he went back to drinking and he again did his . . . bad action, and for that bad action was caught, and his criminal past became known."

By this point, it had become quite obvious that the strategy that I had used successfully with other interviewees — introducing new data and discussing the idea of narrativity — was not working with the Figueroa family. Then, I attempted another route — claiming that what they were doing with the Southern Mexicans (namely, to categorize them as criminals in toto) was exactly what people from Mexico City or from El Paso usually did in relation to them, to Juarenses. And it seems that my change of strategy worked, because from this point of the interview on, both Verónica and Héctor not only deepened their reflections about their approach to Southern Mexicans and Chilangos, but also reworked and reframed their previous (and extremely harsh) anti-Southern Mexican stance:

Héctor: What I commented on when you came the first time, was that every city has its problem, and that Juárez *already has* its own by itself, right? Problems that already exist, but that have been *aggravated*, combined with the overpopulation that exists. And it's mostly people from outside Juárez. That's what I mentioned in that interview.

Of course that was not what Héctor really said in the first interview . . . (see Chapter 1). But now, after being confronted with the fact that there was not much difference between his narrative construction of the despised Southern Mexican and what some Chilangos and El Pasoans narratively constructed about Juarenses like himself, Héctor started recognizing that, in any case, what the immigrants from Southern Mexico did was to aggravate some problems Juárez *already had* previous to their arrival. Having done that, Héctor and Verónica went still a step further and started debating with me about the scope of my proposal and how important a change in the way we address the others can be in the relationships among people on the border and elsewhere.

> **Héctor:** What you want is for people not to use that expression . . . Southerners . . . That is to say, your proposition is that this experiment will serve to construct better relations, or make for a better perspective . . . and it would be ideal, it's the ideal, in order to live better, it's the best concept of your fellow human being. But you know very well that people generalize . . . I see your proposition as very noble. That that expression, "Southerner," should change, but the word is widely used . . . ingrained. It would be ideal, the dream of all human beings, that any human being be dignified.

Thus the strategy of drawing a parallel between their anti-Southern narrative and the El Pasoan anti-Mexican narrative was much more effective than the strategy of offering data that contradicted their narrative plot. For one thing, Héctor had a couple of "pending issues" with people from the other side of the border. At one point of the interview Héctor commented that "for a long time now I haven't liked to go to El Paso," and the reason for that reluctance to go was that he felt "humiliated, violated" by the ostentatious display of power by American authorities. Their attitude, Héctor felt, implied that all Juarenses are suspected of being drug dealers or smugglers or illegals—an especially insulting attitude considering that a great portion of El Paso's commerce depends on the expenditures of Juarenses. He himself had sued some custom agents once because they had harassed him at the bridge when he inquired why they were mistreating some Mexicans. As part of the settlement for the trial, Héctor demanded not only the firing of the agents, but also a public apology from the INS.

It was only when these interviewees realized they were emplotting people from Southern Mexico basically in the same way that the customs agents had emplotted Héctor that he and Verónica finally discovered the narrative character of their construction of the despised "other" from Southern Mexico.

> **Héctor:** It' true, I can see, it's obvious that there really needs to be another expression for referring to the people who come from Southern Mexico. But as I told you earlier, it's so widespread here that the people no longer see it, no longer see it! But it's so true that, for example, the Americans [here we are talking about the El Paso authorities], the police . . . for them, a criminal is a Juarense, and he's Juarense, and Juarense, and there is no

way to convince them otherwise! It's the same thing that happens here. For the immigration or customs agents, all Mexicans or all Juarenses are drug addicts, are drug dealers, because as soon as they start that operation, so . . . so idiotic, I definitely see it as a wrong thing to do. Well, God help us, because it's true. Yes, I agree, it is necessary for this to change, because it causes more and more and more harm every time! And everything goes downhill . . . And we hope that this study will bring some benefit.

The other reinterviews I did in Juárez can be located somewhere in between the two I have analyzed so far. For instance, in the one I had with the Buendías,[2] a gender division appeared that was absent in other interviews. In this family the females rapidly discovered their plots, were ashamed of them, and looked forward to ways to avoid stereotyping the "other," while the father was more reluctant, avoiding any serious involvement in what was being discussed, and participating only in the final part of it to stress his skepticism that something could be done regarding the well-entrenched plots we use to negatively construct the "other." Therefore, Diana and her mother early in the interview discovered how they were using the category "Chilango" in their narrative identities:

Diana: It's true, because sometimes, people just look at some people with the . . . let's say the characteristics that we've been told they have. And that's how it is . . . "she's a Chilanga" and nothing else, that's it . . . you already know that . . .

At the same time, Cristóbal believed that nothing could be done to change people's categorization processes.

Cristóbal: I don't think that it will change!

The Struggle to Try to Get Rid of the Plots That Construct the "others" Negatively

In the interview we conducted with Aurelio and Flor, the anti-Southern and anti-Chilango stances were prominent in Flor, while Aurelio (himself an immigrant from Southern Mexico) contradicted his wife's harsh criticism against Southerners but shared with her the anti-Chilango stance. Aurelio and Flor are upper-middle-class professionals in their forties. Flor is a native Juarense and Aurelio came from Guadalajara when he was six years old. In the reinterview they accepted (like many of my interviewees in Juárez) without too much resistance my data showing that the anti-Southern position was unsubstantiated in factual terms (confirming Aurelio's position in the first interview):

Pablo: Do you know how many people from Southern Mexico there are in Juárez according to statistics?
Flor: No, I have no idea.
Pablo: Fourteen percent.
Flor: From the South?! That's all? It's very little. I always had the idea, and not from any statistics, that it was . . . listen, I was born here, and if Juárez ended at Borunda Park, and the maquiladora industry came in, Juárez grew at a rate very . . . so, I thought it was people from outside!
Pablo: It is people from outside, but not people from Southern Mexico.
Flor: Oh, OK. [laughs] Oh now I remember what I said in the interview [laughs] . . . No, I always . . . all my life . . . I always had that idea.
Pablo: No, no, most people do have that idea. What happens is that we use the plots without thinking about the origins . . . of the plot. Like when you said in the interview: ". . . people from Chihuahua aren't so screwed up, people from Southern Mexico would be more screwed up." It couldn't be Chihuahua . . .
Flor: No, no, Chihuahua nooo! . . . [being sarcastic about herself] [laughs]

They also rapidly discovered their plots and, being ashamed of them, tried to figure out how to change them. I discuss this last example of my interviews in Juárez less for its content (basically the same as other re-interviews in Juárez and El Paso) than for the "struggle" these interviewees underwent trying to get out of a very stereotypical way of understanding their identities and into another one where the "other" could appear in his/her own light, beyond the categories and plots we usually use to deal with him/her. Thus, very early in the interview this couple discovered their plots, but also from the beginning they advanced their doubts that something could be done to change them:

Flor: But to change this idea, it's very, very difficult! Because right away you identify people: "What's-his-name is from . . ." [laughs] . . . and you say: "No, it's that I'm from Chihuahua, no, no way!" [laughs] I mean, somehow it would be very difficult for the simple fact that it's . . . like a culture! You learn it so young that, then, how do you change it?

The problem seemed so insurmountable that Aurelio brought his own experience, as an immigrant from Southern Mexico with many years of residence in Juárez, to illustrate how many settled Southern immigrants *also* show a well-developed anti-Southern Mexican stance:

Aurelio: And for those of us who are already here, even though we aren't from Juárez . . . when we're settled here in the city, we always think about . . . "They're Southerners, right? They're Southerners."

Nevertheless, Flor and Aurelio were quite willing to change how they related to their plots, from being stuck with only one plot and one character to confront any situation, to the possibility of modifying both plots and characters to see reality from another point of view, the point of view of the "other."

Flor: I'm very drastic about everything [laughs], that's the truth, and it's not easy to change my ideas. But, OK, it's very important to know the plots I was using so far, and hopefully if . . . perhaps I won't change my idea, but I'll see other points of view in another way, right? And that's very good!

However, regardless of this willingness, Flor and Aurelio found it difficult to address the "other" without using the usual categories and plots they have developed over the years:

Flor: People from Chihuahua don't really accept people from Juárez! Someone from the capital of Chihuahua doesn't accept people from Juárez because of, well, this was the city of vice. It gets to the point, and this maybe is a widely used plot . . .

Everyone: [laughs]

Flor: But it gets to the point that the men who come from Chihuahua, over there they were at home by ten at night, but they get here, and they become dissolute and they don't go home in two, three days! I swear to you! Perhaps it's just one of my plots, but . . .

Flor was totally aware that what she was saying about Chihuahuenses "maybe is a widely used plot . . . ," but she was not willing to discard her claim just because it was a plot. Obviously, she needed something else to change her story line that Chihuahuenses are hypocritical and anti-Juarense. The proposals I make at the end of this chapter may help in such situations, where people who are quick to understand the narrative character of their identities are less willing to change the plots that are so powerful in the construction of their identities. The situation repeated itself when Flor referred to Chilangos:

Pablo: I'm not saying that regional influences don't exist, but the error is in applying them to everyone from that region! For example the Chilangos: half of the Chilangos aren't from Mexico City, they're from other parts of Mexico, so it can't be that all the Chilangos behave the same way.

Flor: Oh, but when one of them has been living there for two years . . . by that time he or she already acts like a Chilango!

Everyone: [laughs]

Pablo: But not all of them, it can't be that all of them . . .

Flor: . . . all the ones that I know [laughs], when they come from over there, and it's quite, it's quite obvious that . . . !

To my dismay, and *after* all the discussion we had already had about categorization and stereotyping and her discovery of her plot about Southerners, Flor nevertheless returned to personal experience to support her plot about Chilangos. A comparison of Flor's statement with Julián's shows how powerful regional logic is in the construction of cultural identities on the Mexican side of the border. In Flor's testimony, any Mexican is transformed into a Chilango (one of the "bad" categories in the Juarense regional taxonomy) if he/she lives for a couple of years in Mexico City. In Julián's testimony, a Southerner remains a Southerner his/her entire life no matter how many years he/she has been living in Juárez. As we can see, the power of the "bad" regional category (Chilango, Southerner, etc.) is so strong that it cannot be overcome by the power of the "good" regional category (Juárez). It seems that for many of my interviewees, it is almost impossible to move from the "bad" to the "good" regional category but it is very easy to slip from the "good" one to the "bad" one, when one abandons "paradise."

Aurelio's reaction, on the contrary, was quite different. Showing once more that his plot was much more flexible than his wife's, he rapidly qualified, in class terms, his previous anti-Chilango stance, dismantling the monolithic picture of the Chilangos he had offered in the first interview, and demonstrating how the reinterview process can be much more successful with people who already have some maneuvering room in their plots:

Aurelio: OK, but . . . the upper-class Chilango, OK, the upper-class, right? And the one with a certain amount of education is the one who behaves that way, like a *Chilango*! Because he's so prepotent! . . . because of his knowledge of culture, and the political relations that he could have, right? That's what makes him have such an attitude! . . .

As usual, when I encountered this kind of argument in my reinterviews, I tried to displace the discussion from a regional category to explain a particular behavior, to using another frame to make sense of that behavior. In this particular case I encouraged Flor and Aurelio to think in terms of "people with power" in general, from whatever Mexican region, instead of "Chilangos" in particular. After my intervention, both Aurelio and Flor consciously tried to change the categories of their plots while at the same time maintaining the basic argument of their story; that is, they changed the people to whom they were applying the particular combination of events that their plot puts together:

Aurelio: OK, the Chil . . . they come here . . . OK, those people come here [laughs] . . .

Flor: [laughs] . . . the stingy ones . . .

Aurelio: . . . and, and . . . so that everyone hears! So that everyone is listening! "Waiter, please!" Yelling! . . . "What's your best cut of meat?" But loud enough so that everyone hears them, right?

It is clear that Aurelio uses the euphemism "*esas personas*" [those people] and Flor shifts from Chilangos to "*tacaños*" [stingy ones] in order to avoid emplotting a particular behavior using the harsh regional system of classification they now recognize as being behind the process of stigmatization they systematically used in the past and want to avoid using in the future. Flor is highly aware of how rigid her plots are (remember her "I'm very drastic"), and she jokingly comments that she does not want to talk anymore—then she offers her personal experience to show once again how consistent the Chilangos are in their arrogant behavior.

Flor: I'm not going to talk anymore, Dr. Vila! [laughs] . . . No, it's true! Because, I'm telling you, this woman friend of ours . . . born here, had all her schooling here! But went to study in Mexico City, and then when she came back to Juárez, she had totally converted to a Chilanga. And then [laughs] she came back here, and she married a doctor who was born over there [Mexico City] and went to school there and everything, but came to Juárez to do his internship, and here they meet each other. OK. Well, her own husband says, "Ay! That's why people here don't like Chilangos!" Because the woman who is from here, she behaves like a Chilanga! And the doctor didn't behave that way, can you believe it? There's a typical case that not every Chilango behaves the same, but the woman who wasn't even from there, no way! [She behaves like a Chilanga]

Yet, to her surprise she discovered that her own argument was actually proving that Chilangos are not so consistent in the arrogant behavior many Juarenses impute to them, because the "real" Chilango of her story, the husband, not only does not behave like his wife (the "converted" Chilanga), but is also her first and most demanding critic.

The other reinterviews I conducted in Juárez followed, in one way or another, the patterns already discussed. For that reason, instead of repeating some arguments, I prefer to move to the other side of the border and show the complicated process of identity construction some El Pasoans underwent when confronted with the narrative character of their identities.

El Pasoans' Reaction to the Reinterview Process

Mexican Immigrants: The Recognition That Not All Poverty Is Mexican

El Pasoans' reactions to my reinterviews were very similar to what happened in Juárez; that is, I had interviewees who rapidly accepted their plots, realized how those story lines were behind their biased perception of the photographs, tried to figure out how that discovery could change how they related to the "others," and almost immediately started to use what they had learned in the experiment in their personal lives. At the other extreme, I had interviewees whose process of accepting their plots and what it entails to emplot the "others" was much more complicated.

A good example of the first kind of interviewee was the Armendariz family, whose interview I analyzed in Chapter 4. We have to remember that both Encarnación and Ivette considered the photograph of the mobile home as the epitome of poverty in Juárez, located all the photographs of poverty on the Mexican side of the border, and totally confused the cemeteries in a very consistent pattern that demonstrated the power of their plot that "all poverty is Mexican." Confronted with their perceptive mistakes, they could hardly believe it:

> **Encarnación:** This picture is in El Paso? [surprised]
> **Pablo:** Aha! You said in the interview: "This is what people want to leave behind in Juárez when they come to El Paso." Well, that photo is from El Paso. That photo was taken in "America."
> **Ivette:** . . . Wow.
> **Pablo:** You were looking at reality very focused on the plot that points out that "all poverty is Mexican." And do you know why the people who don't use that plot don't make a mistake on that photo? Because of the mobile home.
> **Encarnación:** Oh, because of the mobile home!
> **Pablo:** If you paid attention, there is a mobile home in the upper part of the photograph, and there are no mobile homes in Juárez.
> **Encarnación:** That's true! [laughs]

After she discovered how biased she was regarding the photographs, Ivette attempted to grasp the source of such a bias, that is, why the "all poverty is Mexican" plot was so ingrained in her that it completely blurred her vision. She pointed out that for her, a Mexican immigrant living in the United States, it is very difficult to justify all the sacrifices she and other immigrants like her went through when she finds in the United States what she supposedly had left behind in Mexico, that is, extreme poverty.

> **Ivette:** And what do you say to yourself, when you come from Mexico and you imagine that this [the extreme poverty depicted in photo 13, shown in Chapter 3] can't exist here. Why did you come to the U.S.?

From this point of the reinterview on, the discussion followed the same pattern that most of my interviews followed, that is, a debate about how we usually emplot people into categories that do not allow them to be anything different from what the category establishes. Encarnación reframed a very important experience in her life along the lines of the discussion we were having, and tried to learn from her re-emplotted story.

> **Encarnación:** To me particularly, after this interview, I'm going to be more . . . more fair, more observant.
> **Ivette:** We never know what a person has to offer us, before . . . before you prejudge 'em . . . maybe they could offer us a lot and teach us a lot.
> **Encarnación:** Any person can teach us something, because they have a different way of thinking. We don't learn anything from the person that's just like us. I knew a person that if you would see him . . . ugly, shaggy, *martajado* [pockmarked]! His hands paralyzed, due to an accident . . . he came to the bar we have . . . drunk and crude and I ran him off! One day some people came, a couple, and told me: "Hasn't Alberto been here?" "Alberto who? . . . . A crude kind of person . . . ?" "No, he's a very cultured person! He's the kind of person with whom you can talk about everything! He's very intelligent! He speaks very agreeably." "Him . . . ?" OK, . . . so when he came back and I saw him . . . so ugly, so surly, so horribly ugly! I started to test him out, to throw him bait to see . . . we've had such a beautiful friendship for five or six years, that never in my life has a person impressed me so much, and been so interesting and has given so much to my daughters and me, and it was he! . . . But as I told you, if someone hadn't told me that he was such a wonderful person, or like you, if you hadn't told me that about the . . . cemetery, I wouldn't change my mind . . . And now people go by to my bar and I'm on the defensive just like I was

before, and I never remember what happened to me with that person . . . but after this interview, I think this has helped me a lot in my life, a lot!

As we can see, Encarnación was able to rethink a very important event in her life and to foresee changes in the way she would approach people in the future; that is, she would allow people to transcend categories she usually used to "understand" their behavior.

In the reinterview I had with Joel, Ramón, and their friends (whose testimonies I discussed in Chapter 3), besides following the usual pattern of shock, shame, and the willingness to change, something different occurred, something that shows the importance in any dialogic research endeavor of offering yourself (the usually "invisible" persona of the researcher) as an "object" to be scrutinized by the "others." Thus, in most of the reinterviews I discussed my own struggle against my stereotypical ways of categorizing people as an example of the difficulties of pursuing a change in the way we emplot ourselves and "others." In some of those reinterviews, when the circumstances of the discussion allowed it, I also offered for their scrutiny (and laughter) the absurd ways I had emplotted myself in the past in order to avoid being classified in one of the "bad" categories of the Argentine regional system of classification, "*porteño*." In this reinterview, Ramón was encouraged by my presentation to tell us something he had not told us before, that is, how he manipulated reality in order to avoid being identified as a "Juarense."

> **Ramón:** When they ask me where are you from. I'm not from Juárez. Because I hear a lot of bad things from Juárez. And I say: "I'm not from Juárez. I was born in Juárez but I'm from Torreón." [Ramón was born in Juárez but raised in Torreón]
> **Everyone:** [laughs]
> **Pablo:** And you're not lying, you're not lying.
> **Ramón:** No. If they ask me where I am from, I'm from Torreón. Because bad guys don't come from Torreón.
> **Everyone:** [laughs]
> **Ramón:** The bad guys come from Juárez.
> **Pablo:** But when we discover this mechanism . . . I think you have to laugh about it, instead of being so serious. And that way, we are more flexible in understanding reality from the point of view of the other, no?
> **Mary:** That's true . . . And only we can make a change like this. I think that's the main thing you gotta get out of this whole thing. This whole interview, this whole experience, you know, to learn all of that, and just do something about it, in our lives. Right, Ramón? [laughs]

Mike: Now, we're not gonna talk bad about the Mexicans.
Everyone: [laughs]

Chicanos and the Difficult Process of Accepting
Anglos as the "other" beyond Categorization

In my initial interview with Armando, Serafín, and their family, which I analyzed originally in Chapter 3, the participants wanted to stress the differences that they perceived separate the United States from Mexico using the trope of "First World versus Third World." Most of them identified themselves as "Chicanos" and emphasized the importance of their process of migration to the United States in improving their lives. In this sense, for them it was very difficult to understand the behavior of those Mexican immigrants that only wanted to work in the United States for a while and to return to Mexico as soon as possible. Another characteristic of this group of hard-core Chicanos was the very negative image they had of Anglos. I did not analyze this characteristic in Chapter 3 for lack of space, but it is very similar to César's narrative, discussed in that chapter.

Accordingly, it is not surprising that this group was very reluctant to accept my point that we have to treat people apart from the categories we use to classify them in order to allow people to transcend the category. Because they had framed their experience in the United States in terms of the discrimination they have suffered at the hands of Anglos, their reaction was quite understandable. Hence, when I commented that they, somehow, were doing with Anglos what the latter were doing with Mexicans, Serafín defended their actions with, "We are doing it because they started it!" That began a discussion about what is "fiction" and what is "real" in Anglos' behavior, wherein my interviewees were trying to prove to me that what I considered "stereotypes" about Anglos were "real" characteristics of that ethnic population: that they behave in a domineering manner, they are demanding, and—as Serafín said in the first interview to "prove" how arrogant all the Americans are—"no matter that if they are bums, they know very well that they have more rights, they feel that they have more rights." These characteristics, according to Serafín, applied to anyone who was not Mexican or Black. Consequently, after I read their comments from the first interview to them, Irene and Serafín simply reiterated that Anglos *are* like that.

Pablo: . . . I imagine that not all Anglos are like that!
Irene: Yes they are like that . . .

Everyone: [roars of laughter]

Pablo: Are they like that . . . ?

Gabriela: That's what I was going to tell you . . .

Serafín: Don't tell me they really aren't like that . . . ?

Gabriela: . . . even though you try not to think about those things, you come across situations where you think: "Not all Anglos are like that, why put them all in that category." But something happens and you confirm that all Anglos are like that.

On the other hand, Gabriela, who is finishing her degree in social work at UTEP, tried another explanation as to why minorities like themselves or African Americans tend to discriminate against Anglos. According to her, the real reason is that they have been discriminated against and that is the only behavior they know.

Gabriela: I think that what happens to us . . . is that we learn a lot from this culture, from the majority culture, from the ruling majority, where the pattern of categorizing everyone is very strong here, all races are categorized under this pattern. So we learn that and I listen to Serafín and when I listen to him, or people who think that way . . . what I hear is an Anglo-Saxon, who thinks that way! . . . Once my brother and I were talking about that, right? So I asked him, why do the Chicanos instead of uniting with the Blacks . . . ?

Serafín: Jesus! Oh, come on! [laughs]

Gabriela: . . . or with the minorities, with the ethnic minorities that are suffering the same kind of oppression that we are . . . why are we against each other, why are we against each other? . . . So one thing my brother told me, is that the only thing that they have known is oppression, so it's like a child who has been abused since very young, right? . . . That the only thing he knows is that he was abused and that he will continue to abuse others. And I said to my brother: "Why don't we unite, right, why does he discriminate against us and vice versa?" And he says: "Because he . . . he learned that, he learned to be discriminated against, so he doesn't know anything else but to discriminate . . ."

Whereas Gabriela was looking for alternative explanations as to why some Mexican Americans discriminate against Anglos and African Americans, Armando did not believe anything could be done to stop racism anyway, at least under a capitalist system. And if this was so, he could not understand why I was asking them to withdraw their animosity against Anglos, when Anglos use their racism to advance economically.

Serafín: I don't give a shit what you are, if you are, if you are stable economically and you have the bucks and you have a business, they'll respect you. If not, you're a piece of shit.

Armando: Well, I think they'll . . . I think they'll think you're a piece of shit anyway. They disrespect you as a person. They still wouldn't want you to marry their sister. You know, I think everybody is . . . There's not one person anywhere that can say, "I'm not racist and I'm not prejudiced." Because . . . in a capitalist, profit mode of economic environment where we have to pick from a pool of people, who is going to come out ahead . . . There's an old saying, "Shit rolls downhill." And the problem with that is that, who picks the shit first are the people that are in power, that are white and all of that, that enjoy the economic benefits. And as you try to move up the scale, your shit starts rolling downhill to whoever the bottom guy is . . .

Pablo: My question is, can we stop that kind of process or is it impossible to stop?

Armando: I don't think you can stop it. I don't think you can stop it unless you stop the basis of this whole society in a civil war.

Gabriela: It'll stop when . . . we're the . . .

Irene: . . . when we're on the top! [laughs] . . . It will stop when we're on the top. [laughs] I'm another racist.

Armando: Yeah, you kick the shit and it rolls down the hill, right? It's gonna stop when the shit doesn't hit us on the face. We're going up the hill like that, man. And it's gonna stop when we get to the top of the hill.[3]

In Armando's account, what Chicanos like him are doing (that is, discriminating against Anglos) is nothing more than adjusting their behavior to the necessities of competition in a very fierce capitalist society, the United States. According to Armando, racism against Anglos is a kind of necessary evil in a society where Chicanos did not start the process, but have to succeed under its premises. Other members of the family were not in agreement with Armando, and were more inclined not only to recognize their own racism against Anglos, but also to accept my point that something can be done to break the cycle of racism.

Gabriela: I see a lot of reality in what Armando says, because it is economics, the economy, as they say, "Money makes the dog dance," right . . . but everybody here knows me, I've always been very idealistic, and I see that there's always hope . . . someone has to break that cycle, or some of us have to analyze ourselves and see what kind of people we really are, the naked truth, then we can say, based on our pasts, and envisioning the future to . . . to create a better present. I think that it can be done . . .

Serafín: Excuse me, but this is the first step, that you make the effort to come here, you know, to listen to us, or whatever, to understand you . . . I don't know what I'm doing here! You all are asking me my opinion, I'm giving it to you, right? Because . . . that's, that's a step . . . ! I'm not getting any money out of this! . . . This is a start. This is the beginning!

From this point on the discussion developed around a confrontation between "idealism" (Irene and Gabriela's) and "pragmatism" (Armando's), with Serafín moving back and forth from one position to the other—between the possibility of diminishing racism or stressing it in order to "compete" in an economic system that, essentially, is a racist and a classist one.[4]

Armando: What are you gonna give me to change? Besides a beautiful world where the tulips grow and the air smells fresh and all that kind of stuff?

Gabriela: To change people, to join together, Armando.

Armando: I'm only here for about eighty-five years. God willing. And am I gonna waste my time . . . ?

Irene: If we couldn't do it and we have such a little bit of time left, then we've got to show our generation of our children to stop it, and hopefully down the line . . .

Serafín: Isn't that right? It's a step. They'll go on, the little ones will continue.

Armando: Why don't we show them what's really out on the table? Why don't we show them how really prejudiced we are? Why don't we show them what we really are and maybe later then they can change it? Because that way they won't be like us. Because I think we're hypocritical. I think we want to be idealist and want to be all of that, but I don't think we've really come out and said, "Hey, I'm this way and I judge people like this, because of their skin." Because when you talk to somebody you don't say, "Oh, he's not Black, he's a person." What it does mean? He's not Black? He *is* Black. And therefore you're gonna treat him like he's Black. And if he's white, that person is white and you treat him like a white person. Then we also have to understand the racism of white America. When they see me, they're gonna see me as Mexican, and I want them to see me like that!

As we can see, Armando wants to stress his Mexicanness, not to minimize it, but he wants to emphasize how proud he is about his ancestry, not to mix it into a new version of the melting pot. And this is so because, being a Chicano, he is fully aware of how the melting pot ideology did not work in the United States for those who were people of color, how it worked only for those who were "the same," that is, white people from Europe.

> **Armando:** I find it as offensive for someone to say, "You're not like a Mexican, you don't even talk, you don't even look like a Mexican." That, I find that as offensive . . . [Armando is phenotypically a white person].
> **Irene:** What does that feel like? [This is a joke, because Irene is dark-skinned] *O te dicen*, "I like you because you're not the same as some of them." Ay, I hate that.
> **Armando:** People tell me constantly! "You know what? I thought your wife was white." All the time! Do you believe that? And when Chris came to work the first time I thought, "No, and what's up with this white girl?" Like that. And then, "Oh, her last name is Ibañez. She's not all that bad. She married a Mexican. She's half bad." [laughs] Yeah, that to me is as offensive as someone . . . you know, "Hey, you Spic," or whatever. So you're trained to know, hey, if someone meets you and puts in the hand, you know, I can guarantee you that's what they're thinking about you. But you can . . . *ay guey*! You gotta be a hypocrite, that's what it all comes down to. If a white guy is coming up to you and you see him and you smile at him, "Hey, how are you doing? How are you? How the hell are you?" And he leaves, and you say to yourself, *"Pinche güero culero"* [fag, white son of a bitch or damn white asshole]. [laughs] That's the first thing that comes to your mind. You gotta be . . . Hicoprick! [laughs] Hypocrite to go up that scale, to go up the hill and not get shit on you. That's what you gotta be. Hypocrite. You see some . . . *"Hey, quihubole. ¿Cómo estás?"* [Hey, what's up? How are you?] And in between your teeth you hate him . . .

In the following, his symbolic framing of the confrontation with Anglos as a gunfight shows the fierce character of the ethnic confrontation he believes characterizes the relationships between Chicanos and Anglos on the border.

> **Armando:** But for me it's like being in a situation where, an American, a white person, has a gun, fully loaded, and I have one too. And I'm thinking, OK, if I take the bullets out maybe he'll take his bullets out too . . . so it's a game where he has the power or he has the advantage of firing first, right? . . . But the minute he takes the bullets out, he falls . . . !

In the longest of all my reinterviews (three hours of very heated discussion between the "idealists" and a "pragmatist"), Armando, the "pragmatist" repeated, again and again, that racism is inherent in any capitalist society, that if we are successful in overcoming racism in terms of race and ethnicity, it is going to be reproduced in relation to whatever people can use to mark differences (". . . if we eliminate everything else . . . it's just left-handed, you know, something like that!"). The only way to solve racial problems, according to Armando, is to destroy the capitalist system (". . . so to break a cycle like this, you have to break an entire economic system . . ."), and any other proposal amounts to compromise with the system (". . . we already know that we can't break the economic system, so we have to go another way . . . that's easier . . ."). At the same time, from a "pragmatist" point of view, if everything around racism is economic, it makes a lot of sense to do what Armando has decided to do, that is, to orient all his economic transactions toward people of his own ethnic group.

> **Armando:** I have made a commitment . . . a conscious choice that I've decided to make. It's wrong, because the white person is this or whatever. It's wrong but that's a choice that I've decided to make: if you need a real estate agent, I'll pick the one that's a Mexican. If there's a salesperson or whatever, I'll pick the one that's a Mexican. So little by little . . . doesn't make it right.
> **Serafín:** But we're biting their asses!

Nevertheless, Armando's "doesn't make it right" shows that he recognizes that "reverse racism" perhaps is not the best solution to overcome a racism.

> **Armando:** Even though I've made a conscious choice to do that, I'm not very comfortable with it, because . . .
> **Irene:** Yeah, because you feel bad.
> **Armando:** 'Cause . . . maybe the more actions you have, the more reactions you're gonna get. So as a group, the more actions and blah, blah, blah that we send out and signals that we send out to white America . . . they are going to react the same way we do . . . That's a personal problem *that I have* . . . that you lean and you've made a conscious choice to do that. But you know it's wrong! . . . You know it's wrong, you got two qualified people . . .
> **Irene:** You've got two qualified people . . . and he's a stinker and he's a stinker but he's a Mexican stinker. So I'm gonna choose him, because anyway this guy is gonna be even worse on me, because he's a white stinker.
> **Armando:** It's a hard struggle . . . because we're doing it . . . so often. Once we become a general manager or a facilities manager or a partner in a law firm, do we want somebody, a white man . . . going home and telling

his family, his white family: "I wasn't hired 'cause of this guy, that guy, that guy," and the kids are listening! And he's formulating hatred and all that so . . . even though we gave the job to a Mexican, and thought we were progressing in that way, we might be counterproductive . . . in that this guy's kid is gonna grow up maybe one day to be a lawyer, or a facilities manager . . .

When I finally retrieved from the first interview all the times Armando, notwithstanding his pro-Mexican attitude, was using consistently the "all poverty is Mexican" plot, like many Anglos do in El Paso (that is, making a synonym between poverty and Mexican), Armando did not have any other choice but to concede that perhaps the struggle to re-articulate plots by disconnecting some words from their hegemonic meaning is not so hopeless. Thus, he finally recognized that my point about the closure of meaning from the perspective of the hegemonic power made some sense (see Appendix).

Pablo: Going back to the synonymity between things and words, no? Remember when this woman Smith killed her children? What was the first thing she tried to convince people?
Armando: That it was a Black person.
Pablo: What was the first idea of many people about the Oklahoma bombing?
Saúl and Armando: Arabs.
Armando: I knew! I am so proud of that. I am so proud of that, because I told everyone. I told 'em, no it's not. No, it's not.
Pablo: My point is, if you cut those synonyms: Terrorism equals Arabs. Crime equals Blacks. Poverty equals Mexicans, change occurs.
Armando: Yeah, 'cause it's the way we communicate, it's the way we understand. It's the way we think. Communication is the . . . that's the way we do it. I think you're right. The colonias, you know, yeah. I never thought colonias meant poverty . . . until now! You know what? Until they mentioned colonias in the United States!
Irene: Yeah, that's what it is . . .
Armando: Because colonias over there . . .
Serafín: Because a colonia, isn't necessarily . . . The Anglos made that up because a colonia doesn't have to be . . . Arroyo Colorado, exactly, is a colonia I've seen on the west side, it's a west side colonia . . .
Pablo: Or for example: in one interview they told me about the problems they had had with plumbers that didn't come, that said, "Yes, I'll be there tomorrow," and showed up three days later. And do you know how those Anglo interviewees explained that? We have a word in English that's "pro-

crastination"; however, those Anglo interviewees, *who don't speak Spanish*, explained it as "mañanismo" [tomorrowism] . . . using again a Spanish word . . .

Irene: Oh! really . . .

Pablo: Sure! Because supposedly the only ones who do it are Mexicans . . .

Irene: Oh! Yes, yes, the Mexican . . .

As happened in other interviews, the final part of this interview involved a reframing of some of their previous experiences in light of our earlier extended discussion. For instance, Serafín recognized, with a lot of shame, how he so eagerly wanted to be accepted by some Anglo friends that in some cases he himself stigmatized Mexicans in order to "conquer" the friendship of Anglos.

Serafín: I gather with . . . businessmen who own companies . . . and more or less on my level . . . they're white guys and whatever . . . to fit into the group . . . to make, to make a group of friends, eeeh . . . you start talking about . . . about employees, and they start, "And this and that" . . . and I've done this! . . . I've told them, ". . . Oh, you know . . . Mr. Johnson, what do you think? Well, you know, shit, these damn Mexicans, you know. Yeah, you know, these fucking Mexicans, you know," *yo también* [me, too] . . . This is me . . . *Yo estoy hablando* [I'm talking] . . . ! "These Mexicans! Yeah, yeah, these Mexicans they don't wanna work." "God! Would you believe that Mike Ramirez wants two more dollars per hour? He's full of shit! I'll get me another one!" I am saying this . . . You know how I feel? I feel good, you know, because I feel part of this group! I've been accepted. Yeah! I look at these guys. They're all white, and I'm the only brown guy there, man. [laughs]

Armando: Yes, but that's an illusion, man, because although you feel accepted, they still wouldn't want you to marry their sister.

Serafín: I agree with that! I got no argument with that! I wouldn't want to marry their sister, anyway, in the first damn place!

Everyone: [laughs]

Armando: You should see the sister! [laughs]

Serafín: There's not a more beautiful woman than a Latina sister, in the whole world . . . ! [laughs]

Irene: Prejudice!

At the same time, Gabriela was able to reframe experiences with some other subject positions she occupies (in this particular case, being the mother of a child with Down's syndrome) in terms of the discussions we'd had during the reinterview.

Gabriela: A very interesting thing has happened to us with our son Sebastián . . . He has been the victim of discrimination . . . it's the same analogy! You know what I mean? Kids like Sebastián . . . They've been discriminated against because they're different, for being different, right? And the excuses are, "Oh, we don't have the teachers . . . we don't have the support . . . we don't have the special materials, we don't . . . ! So little by little we've taken away . . . let's see . . . we've taken away the issue about materials, we've taken away the excuse of no money. And now . . . now we've asked them: "You don't have the excuse that there's no money any longer, so what is it now?" . . . And they turn what the real problem is all about! It's that we don't want him because he's different . . . it's the same thing, it's the same thing as racism! . . .

Pablo: . . . yes, to say that all the children with that problem are the same. And it's not true, they are different . . .

Gabriela: That's what I was referring to is that it isn't just the economic system [referring to Armando's main hypothesis of racism] . . . what one points out . . . but the human aspect . . .

Armando: . . . and all the children aren't the same . . . they're not. The presumption that all the children are the same, when it's obvious that they're not! What's the . . .

Amador: That is why Gabriela made the comparison with racism, how do you think about certain people being the same . . .

Armando: Ah, oh . . . aha . . .

Amador: . . . all are the same, *todos son iguales*, when they are not . . . labeling . . . and the issue is what you do with that . . .

Pablo: Yes, Gabriela's right. The mechanism is very similar . . . I mean, attaching a label . . . and everybody that's there is the same . . .

Gabriela: They are all retarded, they are not going to learn . . . they end in a segregated class . . .

African Americans, Anglos, and the Process of Negotiating Scripts

In the reinterview with the group of African Americans discussed in Chapter 3, who very prominently used the plot that "all poverty is Mexican," the interviewees felt very uncomfortable being portrayed as stereotyping another minority group like Mexicans or Mexican Americans. Being African Americans and the object of Anglo prejudice, they believed they were "free" of prejudice themselves, and it came as a shock to discover their own negative perceptions of Mexicans and Mexican Americans. Nevertheless, they rapidly discovered their own biased conceptions when they could connect their own experience of discrimination to what they were doing to Mexicans.

After an initial attempt to prove to me that his "all poverty is Mexican" plot came from his lack of knowledge that there were such a thing as rich neighborhoods in Juárez, Miles suddenly realized that it was not by chance that he had never wanted to go to Juárez in more than two years living on the border. What for, if he already presupposed that all Juárez was poor?

Pablo: How many times did you go to Juárez in the two years you were here?

Miles: I've never been to Juárez.

Pablo: Why? This is the question . . . my point is that also you have to be willing to be exposed to certain things.

Miles: OK, I agree. But, you gotta have some reason, right?

Pablo: Yes but the reasons are related to your plot. If I have the presupposition that "all poverty is Mexican," why do I have to go to Juárez? If I have another presupposition, for instance, about different things, I am more willing to go to Juárez, and to discover Juárez, the Juárez that is behind or beyond the presupposition . . .

Miles: Yeah, that's right.

Teresa: Yeah, we do the same thing in America. Look what we do along our racial lines. Look how we had the ghettos. We know what kind of people live there because we have labeled those people. So we don't have to go there. I don't have to go there.

Pablo: No, why do I have to go to the ghetto? I know what the ghetto means.

Miles: Yeah, you bring up a good point . . . 'cause having grown up in the ghetto, when I mention I'm from a ghetto, they look and me and say, "Are you . . . ?"

Pablo: I won't go to the ghetto when I go to visit New York.

Miles: Yeah, yeah or you might die, people die in the ghetto, yeah. Point well taken.

Something similar happened with Bessie, who remembered and reframed an experience she had had with the border patrol, and suddenly discovered how prejudiced she was regarding illegal immigrants, and how she had taken for granted that all the illegals were Mexicans.

Pablo: Let me tell you another example. A year ago, the border patrol discovered that there was an amazing smuggling of Polish, people from Poland were crossing the border illegally at El Paso. They discovered that after six months of that, because the Polish were whites and blonde and they have learned to say "American" and they crossed. Because the border patrol was looking for Mexican illegals, not for blondes and whites! And they discovered it after six months.

Miles: That's amazing.

Pablo: My point, my point is that we have presuppositions, and we apply those presuppositions to reality. And the presupposition here is that Mexicans are poor and the presupposition was that Mexicans were the illegal crossers, not the . . .

Bessie: But it's true and I fell into that very same trap. I did this. We went across the border into New Mexico and you have to show your IDs coming even from here. And I thought this is so funny. And, so I was pretty flippant. I mean, I didn't smart off to the guy but I thought . . . and he asked for our IDs to prove we were American citizens and I laughed! Because I thought to myself and I had said to my husband, now do we look Hispanic to you?

Miles: How dare they?

Bessie: Yeah, I did the same thing! I did the same thing. And the guy says, "Hey, you could be from another country. Just because you don't look Hispanic." Now, wow, boy . . .

Of course, as happened with most of my interviews on both sides of the border, these interviewees did not necessarily accept my analysis of the first interviews without qualification. Expressing their positions with very good arguments, stressing how they understood Mexicans and Mexicans Americans because they also belonged to a minority group (Bessie: "We know how Mexican Americans feel"; Miles: "Having been exposed to that ourselves"), they rejected a couple of my interpretations about their testimonies in the previous interviews.[5] For instance, when I said that to me it sounded very weird that Miles stressed very frequently during that interview how clean Juárez appeared in the photographs, as if he expected Juárez (and Mexico) to be dirty by definition, Miles replied that that was not the case; on the contrary, he was allowing the photographs to go *against* his own presuppositions, not looking for aspects of the photos to use to confirm his biases. According to Miles, if he could do that, it was because of his own experience in the Black ghetto:

Miles: Having grown up in the ghetto, knowing that it could be clean. That was the other side that I was impressed with because we lived in the projects on concrete floors. But when you walked in there, the place was spotless. You could eat off of it. You know, so I, yeah, I was impressed by that, too. Hey, they're poor, there's poverty over there and they too can be clean. I know about that.

Miles also rejected my assertion that he equated Mexicans with manual jobs but not intellectual ones. He also said that I misunderstood his description of some old buses as a criticism regarding Mexican backwardness; in fact, he said, it was an appraisal of Juárez' more ecologically wise use of resources. In this way, the dialogic methodology allowed me to avoid misinterpreting what the interviewees had told me, allowing them to have a say in my interpretations.

Therefore, after having "negotiated" interpretations among ourselves, Miles made the following summary of the experience:

Miles: It's amazing to come back and have some more dialogue to see how, how everything kind of came out, you know? Especially with the plot. That certainly has been enlightening to me because . . . an example: we as a people, we don't smile a lot with each other. And, I go around trying to smile. When I see someone say, "Hi, how are you doing?" They go, "What do you want?" I go, "Damn." You know, this is me dealing with my people. And so, you know, you take that, you wonder, well, what plot is that person operating under when I say, "Hi, how're you doin' Bessie?" Bessie smiles back and that to me is a cordial agreement. So we drive on. The next person you go to, do the same thing. And they go, "Don't smile at me, man. I don't trust you. You're big, you're a big guy." I don't know. But the plot thing. That thing, that's gonna be lasting with me because that's gonna give me something to look for down the road.

In the reinterview I conducted with Bridget, Helen, and Arthur (group analyzed in Chapter 3), it became much clearer why Bridget fervently opposed the narrative theme "all poverty is Mexican," why Helen was more ambiguous about it, and why Arthur used it, but not very consistently (to the point of mislocating most of the poverty photographs, but correctly locating the cemetery). In this sense, they rapidly recognized that Helen and Arthur were more prone to use the trope "First World versus Third World" than Bridget, who, on the contrary, consistently searched for similarities instead of differences between Juárez and El Paso.

Pablo: Because you see similarities. [referring to Bridget] You are looking for similarities. And they [referring to Helen and Arthur] were looking for differences in the same photographs, not different photographs. Because your plot is different.

Bridget: I guess it's because . . .

Pablo: You are married to . . .

Bridget: I'm married to someone from there, I identify with him, you know?

Pablo: Yes, of course, you have to make sense of being married to one of them.

Bridget: One of them? [laughs]

Pablo: I am using the joke . . . Helen, you used that joke in the first interview.

Bridget: Yeah.

Pablo: Helen made a joke that you were married to one of . . .

Bridget: THEM.

At the same time, in the reinterview Bridget clarified a point that had struck me in the first interview: why she had opposed Arthur's use of the word "shame" to describe the photograph that portrayed the poor Mexican neighborhood of Anapra [photo 5, shown in Chapter 2], and proposing the word "pitiful" instead.

Pablo: With the photo of Anapra, taken from UTEP . . . you didn't agree with him that it was a shame, it was pitiful, no? I think it marks a difference, but I frankly cannot totally get it.

Bridget: Yeah, it implies . . . both imply sad, but . . . I mean, to me, piti . . . 'cause it's . . . it's not their fault.

Helen: I don't know, one shows empathy, I guess.

Arthur: Yeah.

Thus, in the process of reinterviewing them, I finally could make sense of a linguistic difference that I had not been able to get in the first interview, how Bridget's word "pitiful" was meant to address the human aspect of poverty in a more sympathetic way than Arthur's "shame."

In the same vein, these interviewees did not have any problem recognizing their different approaches regarding the photographs — how Bridget had not mistakenly located all the photos of poverty in Juárez, whereas Helen and Arthur had misplaced most of them.

Pablo: I think it's a good example of the different . . . Because you don't have exactly the same plot.

Arthur: I'm a hard-liner. [laughs]

Pablo: Yeah, but because of your stepmother [referring to Helen's stepmother, who is Mexican], you have a lot of influence of your stepmother. You're somehow in the middle. Using a lot of the, of the basic, what I call

Anglo stereotypes in relation to Mexico. But also you make, you discover subtleties, that it's not black and white. You put a lot of gray in the picture. [to Bridget] And you put a lot of white.

Arthur: And I put a lot of black. [laughs]

Yet, when I pointed out that according to my analysis of the first interview, Helen's "ultimate others" were the Mexican Indians who beg in El Paso, she did not accept my interpretation and claimed that she was very sympathetic toward the beggars, and that maybe her comments were coming out of shame for the things Anglos have done to Indians in the past — things that ultimately caused the Indians to have to beg in the present.

> **Helen:** When I see them, I kind of feel like we . . . we, not me personally maybe, but me as a race, you know, or me as whatever. We messed with them and, you know, and now that's where they're at today . . .

As we can see, and as happened in most of my reinterviews on both sides of the border, the process of going back to the people always involved a process of negotiation among narratives, with the interviewees accepting some of my points and rejecting others. This proved to be a fruitful process, giving me a better informed foundation for deciding which narratives I should discuss, both in this book and in *Border Identities*: "All social problems in Juárez are related to immigrants from Southern Mexico," "All poverty is Mexican," "Mexican Americans are abandoning some Catholic practices," and the like. The process of interacting with the interviewees in negotiating a shared sense of their narratives also made me think twice about the accuracy of some of my initial interpretation of their testimonies, and I changed the focus and course of my analysis accordingly.

Conclusion

I hope that this book has succeeded in showing how complex the process of identity construction is. What this book has attempted to prove is that the possibilities of identity construction are diverse, and not easily reduced or anchored in a master narrative about class, nation, region, ethnicity, religion, age, or gender. Accordingly, even the master narratives of race and ethnicity on the American side, or region on the Mexican side of the border, feature multiple variants that allow people to play with their identities to the point where the initial referent almost disappears. Hence, I think that we cannot talk anymore about "Anglo identity," "Mexican identity," "African American identity," "Chicano identity," or "Mexican American identity" as monolithic constructs; rather, we must begin to refer to the possible "Anglo," "Mexican," "African American," "Chicano," and "Mexican American" *identities*. In that way we will be more likely to recognize the complexity of the process of identity construction.

Needless to say, I am very happy about the results of this pioneer project in dialogic social science. I think that to confront people with their own plots really works, and this practice goes beyond the traditional Enlightenment idea that people stigmatize others simply because they really do not know them. Of course people construct a devalued other because they do not know the real other. The problem is that contact with the other is not going to change by itself the plots of people who have an important stake in preserving their narrative identities — identities which all too often depend precisely on a devalued "other." Consequently, the relationship between plots and "events" is not unproblematic, above all when some events may be such that the person's plot line cannot be adapted to include new information without producing huge alterations on it, or, still worse, without requiring its replacement by another story line. As I already mentioned, such a move is difficult, and many people resist it and prefer to maintain their past plots even if doing so requires distorting "facts" and events. Ergo, what I attempted to do was to dialogically ask people to articulate and bring to language and awareness the narratives they have developed to give meaning to their lives (Polkinghorne 1988). In this sense, my interviewees were able to examine and reflect on the themes they were using to organize their lives, and to interpret their own actions and the actions of others. In other words, I tried to help my interviewees to make better stories; according to Rosenwald (1992), a "better" story (1) is more comprehensive than the previous one; (2) recognizes that one's relation to the world and relationships with others and oneself are ambivalent and contradictory; (3) helps people to comprehend the earlier "defective" stories; and (4) is structurally more complex, more varied, and contrastive in the events and accompanying feelings portrayed, more interesting and three-dimensional. I think that in most of the cases discussed in this book, the new stories my interviewees started creating during the process of the reinterview can be catalogued as "better" stories. My bet is that through those "better" stories (but of course not *only* through those stories) people have more possibilities to construct fuller lives for themselves and the "others." As Rosenwald and Ochberg (1992, p. 2) comment:

> It is possible, though surely difficult, to enlarge the range of personal narrative. Individuals and communities may become aware of the political-cultural conditions that have led to the circumscription of discourse. If a critique of these conditions occurs widely, it may alter not only how individuals construe their own identities but also how they talk to one another and indirectly the social order itself.

For all these reasons I think that the method deserves a try, but next time I will introduce some changes. First of all, after a first reinterview like the ones I described above, I would arrange a meeting between interviewees who had constructed the "others" in antithetical ways. In this way I would promote a face-to-face discussion among people who would already have discovered the narrative character of their identities. Second, I will try to imagine some kind of community project these people could do together, in order to go deep into the understanding of the plot of the "other" when that plot organizes some kind of joint action or behavior. Finally, I think that a follow-up sometime after all this process is over is mandatory, in order to see if the changes in the way the interviewees understand themselves and the "others" have some lasting effects, or if they disappear as soon as the sociologist vanishes.

I do not have a naive approach to what I did and what I propose to do. Or to put it in another way, I think that despite the limitations of my sociological intervention it is still better than stopping this book at Chapter 5 and waiting for someone else to read the book and try to imagine a public policy that might mitigate the resentment that is so pervasive in the region. As Craig Calhoun argues in the context of feminist theory, it is sometimes useful to "risk essentialism":

> The point is to see that under certain circumstances—mainly identified as political but I think arguably also intellectual—self-critical claims to strong, basic and shared identity may be useful. At its simplest, the argument suggests that where a particular category of identity has been repressed, delegitimated or devalued in dominant discourses, a vital response may be to claim value for all those labeled by that category, thus implicitly invoking it in an essentialist way. (1994, p. 17)

Thus I am willing to "risk naivete" and to propose a dialogical attempt that I know is flawed and full of mistakes. However, I think that this chapter also shows how going back to the people interviewed allows them to deepen their understanding of their ethnic, racial, gender, religious, class, and national identities. I think that the reinterviews constitute the continuation of the conversation any social scientist is always looking for, in order to discuss ideas further and find much more complex and nuanced argument forming among the informants; to be a little more confident that the stories people told her/him initially were believable; and to "deepen" the encounter with the "other" that is implicit in any research situation.

As I indicated in the Introduction, I have separated the theoretical reflections from the empirical material in order to be accessible to different audiences. I agree with Douglas Foley (1990, p. 159) that it is very difficult "to write an engaging popular ethnography full of real people and events that [is] also full of dense, technical . . . theory jargon." For that reason, I have reserved discussion of the theoretical ideas I have developed during my six years of fieldwork on Ciudad Juárez–El Paso.

First, I address the importance of social categories and interpellations in the construction of social and cultural identities. Second, I discuss how tropes in general and metaphors in particular help in that construction. Third and finally, I talk about the central role narratives play in any process of identity construction.

Social Categories and Interpellations

Why do I consider the peculiar ways Southern Mexicans, Juarenses, Norteños, Fronterizos, Paseños, Mexican Americans, Chicanos, African Americans, Anglos, and so on, address themselves and "others" to be so important to the process of identity construction on the border? I do so because I agree with certain poststructuralists who suggest that experience lacks inherent essential meaning: "It may be given meaning in language through a range of discursive systems of meaning, which are often contradictory and constitute conflicting versions of social reality" (Weedon 1989, p. 34). Hence, I believe that experience is not something reflected by language. Insofar as it is a meaningful experience, it is constituted in language. If experience is discursively created, then there is an ongoing struggle among discourses to shape that experience, where the social recognition of truth is the strategic position to which most discourses aspire. To acquire the status of truth, discourses must discredit all alternative and oppositional versions of meaning and establish themselves as commonsensical. Here we meet Antonio Gramsci's shadow behind the poststructuralist approach. According to this approach, the relationships social actors participate in are multiple: relationships of production, race, ethnicity, nationality, sexuality, gender, family, religion, age, and so on. All these relationships have the potential of

CATEGORIES, INTERPELLATIONS, METAPHORS, AND NARRATIVES
A BRIEF THEORETICAL DISCUSSION

being, for the same individual, spaces of possible identities. In addition, each social position the individual occupies is the space of a struggle about the meaning of such a position.

I believe that social identity is based on an ongoing discursive struggle about the meanings that define social relationships and positions in society. The goal of this discursive struggle is for the particular labels at stake to enter the realm of common sense (Gramsci 1975, p. 1396), with the connotation proposed by the winners of the battle for meaning. This is so because uni-accentuality involves a practice of closure: namely, the establishment of an achieved system of equivalence between language and reality (Volosinov 1973, p. 23). The social construction of identity involves a struggle over the ways in which meaning gets "fixed." Nevertheless, this notion of closure is always a conditional stage in this kind of approach, because meanings that have been effectively coupled can also be uncoupled. Ergo, the political struggle over the meaning of a particular identity or subject position is never completely closed. The subjectivity of a given social agent, no matter how fixed it may appear, is always only precariously and provisionally fixed. In other words, social identity and subjectivity are always precarious, unstable, contradictory, and in process, and the individual is always the site of conflicting forms of subjectivity (Laclau and Mouffe 1985; Laclau 1991). Poststructuralism questions the idea of a unified, coherent subject, since a discursively produced self is experienced not as a single, completed identity but as multiple, incomplete, partial identities. As Pauline Rosenau (1992, p. 44) points out:

> Post-modern opposition to the subject is not entirely original. Two sources, Freud . . . and Nietzsche . . . are particularly important. . . . Nietzsche . . . disputed the validity of a "fixed, substantial, selfhood." . . . Freud also questioned the status of a coherent, integrated, unified, modern subject. He eliminated the self-conscious subject and substituted a decentered, fragmented, and heterogeneous subject who was often unaware of his/her unconscious.

Different poststructuralist authors such as Jacques Derrida (1978), Jean Baudrillard (1983), and Michel Foucault (1970) concur in this characterization of the postmodern subject. This idea of the multiple/fractured self is also central to some feminist thought, most noticeably in the works of Donna Haraway (1985), Mary Hawkesworth (1989), Gayatri Chakravorty Spivak (1988), Trinh T. Minh-ha (1990), and Judith Butler (1990). For instance, Haraway (p. 72) claims that "it has become difficult to name one's feminism by a single adjective . . . Identities seem contradictory, partial, and strategic." Haraway (p. 73) praises

Chela Sandoval's "model of political identity called 'oppositional consciousness' born of the skills for reading webs of power by those refused stable membership in the social categories of race, sex, or class. . . . Women of color . . . construct a kind of post-modernist identity out of otherness and difference." For Butler (1990, p. 3) it is very problematic to talk about "women" in general, "because gender intersects with racial, class, ethnic, sexual, and regional modalities of discursively constituted identities. As a result, it becomes impossible to separate out 'gender' from the political and cultural intersections in which it is invariably produced and maintained." For that reason Butler (p. 4) considers the singular notion of identity a "misnomer." In the same vein, Hawkesworth depicts the subject as an unstable self, a constellation of unconscious desires, fears, phobias, and conflicting linguistic, social, and political forces.

Those feminist authors who turn feminist criticism to the deconstruction of the homogeneous and unified images of the colonized subject, according to Patricia Clough (1994), argue that

> [w]hile colonization and de-colonization seem to urge the establishment of an identity and a homeplace, post-colonial critics instead reappropriate displacement: post-colonial criticism valorizes the hybrid rather than the unified subject-identity figured in the dominant fiction of Western discourse; it foregrounds the multicultural rather than the unified identity of the nation-state and it insists on locally articulated criticisms of the globalization of relations of power/knowledge. (p. 116)

Consequently, Minh-ha (1990, p. 157) points out that the question of identity is no longer "*who* am I?" but "*when, where, how* am I?": "There is no real me to return to, no whole self that synthesizes the woman, the woman of color and the writer; there are, instead, diverse recognitions of self through difference, and unfinished, contingent, arbitrary closures that make possible both politics and identity." Spivak (1988, p. 284) argues similarly that the claim for the identity of the subaltern subject favors antiessentialism, because the subaltern is not a unified subject-identity but an "identity-in-differential" in relation to the elite. As Stuart Hall comments (1996, pp. 4–5): "Above all, and directly contrary to the form in which they are constantly invoked, identities are constructed through, not outside, difference. This entails the radically disturbing recognition that it is only through the relation to the 'other,' the relation to what it is not, to precisely what it lacks, to what has been called its *constitutive outside* that the 'positive' meaning of any term — and thus its 'identity' — can be constructed."

Accordingly, I consider that the different subject positions that converge to form what appears as a unified and unique self are cultural constructions created by discourses, understanding "discourse" as the linguistic and nonlinguistic practices that carry and confer meaning in a field characterized by the play of power relationships (Laclau and Mouffe 1987). Of course, not all discourses carry the same weight, and therefore the problem of hegemony (Gramsci 1971, p. 161) appears. The construction of hegemony is, above all, the proposal to different actors in society of certain determined subject positions, where subject positions are defined in a way that is functional to the interests of the groups in power, and the acceptance by these actors, through a complex process of embracing, negotiating, and rejecting, of those subject positions (Mouffe 1985; Laclau and Mouffe 1985). Here is where classification systems and the struggle for hegemony converge with narrative identities (Vila 1997b).

In *The Order of Things*, Foucault (1970, p. xv), quoting Jorge Luis Borges, describes "a certain Chinese encyclopedia in which it is written that 'animals are divided into: a) belonging to the Emperor, b) embalmed, c) tame, d) suckling pigs, e) sirens, f) fabulous, g) stray dogs, h) included in the present classification, i) frenzied, j) innumerable, k) drawn with a very fine camel hair brush, l) etcetera, m) having just broken the water pitcher, n) that from a long way off looks like flies.'" The transparent absurdity of this classification system calls our attention to the arbitrary nature of such taxonomies. At the same time, it shows that the viability of a given system of classification depends neither on its "fit" with reality nor on its internal consistency, but rather on the field of forces within which the struggle over its meaning takes place. What Foucault basically asks us to think about is this: What kind of self-definitions does the organization of language allow us, and how does labeling effectively work to channel possible accounts of the self into forms acceptable to society? (Parker 1989, p. 61).

I think that our commonsense ideas about ourselves and the "others" are constantly using different classifications and labels: age, gender, race, ethnicity, place of birth, occupation, religion, class, and so on. All these classifications seem so fixed to us that we consider them part of the natural world. In everyday life we are immersed in classification systems whose credibility and connection with reality we never question. The very possibility of common sense is built upon this premise. If we believe, as Foucault does, that the knowledge that circulates in discourse is used in everyday interactions amid relations of submission and domination, then it becomes clear that classifications are not neutral identifications. On the contrary, they are loaded with meaning and with meaning linked to the construction of hegemony in a particular historical time and place.

Each label in our classification systems is loaded with "information" about the occupants of that position, information that we take for granted and that shapes our encounter with the "others." This is because social interaction always is, among other things, an interaction with the "other" as a particular category. Such categories produce subjects with various adjectives attached to them. On the one hand, the adjectives guide our encounter with "others." On the other hand, they predispose those subjects for further surveillance. As a result, it is impossible to know and interact with the "real" "other." We can only know the "others" through description, that is, through the narratives and classificatory systems that, being part of the battle for meaning, are available within a particular cultural context (Vila 1997b). It is through this complex construction of meaning that the names of the different social actors are being shaped and given content in the classificatory systems we use to "order" and comprehend the reality that surrounds us. We usually encounter in diverse cultural artifacts the different names we use to interpellate — or those we accept that "others" use to interpellate, or address us (Althusser 1971) [1] — names and connotations that refer to the different subject positions we occupy in society: family, job, class, age, gender, ethnicity, race, religion, and so on.

Here is where my approach differs from the Meadian (1934) account of the self, which also relies on the "other" as the source and guarantor for individual self-identity. My approach differs in that my "other" is historically constituted, while the Meadian one is not. Further, the "other" is totally embedded in the power struggle over meaning that lies behind social taxonomies — again, in a way the Meadian "other" is not. Hence, power becomes a central relational attribute of any inquiry directed toward understanding the identity construction process. As Parker (1989, p. 68) states: "We need . . . to ask how the self is implicated moment by moment, through the medium of discourse, in power."

What are the implications of all this for the U.S.–Mexico border? Mexicans and Americans belong to national societies whose classification systems share some aspects — both in terms of subject positions and their attributes. However, they differ greatly in other aspects that also impinge on the everyday attitudes and behaviors of their inhabitants. On the border, these similarities and differences meet, and the result is an unusually complex common sense, in which people are forced to move from one classification system to another, sometimes on a daily ba-

sis. Not only do people move from one system to another, but the proliferation of classification systems within which a single person can be
placed means that people constantly mix different systems of classification to make sense of the perceived "others" (Vila 1997b).

Throughout the book, I have tried to show how the different situational and contextual performances of the commonsense labels (such as
Sureños, Chilangos, Norteños, Juarenses, Juareños, Pochos, Fronterizos, Mexicans, Mexican Americans, Chicanos, Anglos, whites, African
Americans, and the like) work in the processes of identity construction
in the region.

Tropes and Identity

If in the previous section I wanted to show how important categories
are in the process of identity construction, in this one I want to prove
how important some metaphors are in that same process. My use of
tropes to understand identity follows a social science tradition in which
anthropologists such as Lévi-Strauss (1966), Fernández (1986, 1991),
Sapir (1977), Crocker (1977), Michelle Rosaldo (1972), Ortner (1973),
Turner (1974), and Quinn (1991), and linguists such as Jakobson and
Halle (1956), Lakoff and Johnson (1980a, 1980b), Johnson (1987),
and Lakoff (1987) have attempted to arrive at cultural meaning by analyzing tropes (especially metaphors). The importance of tropes in the
understanding of identity is linked to the selectivity process that is also
present (as we will see in the next section) in any narrative plot; as
Friedrich notes, "In terms of most language use most of the time, tropes
are the great and little prepatterns that variously channel, influence, and
determine how the speaker interrelates elements of language to each
other and interrelates language itself and the rest of the world" (1991,
p. 56). For that reason, as we will see below, tropes perform a very similar function regarding plots; that is, they organize experience in a meaningful way.

I suggest, following Burke (1966), that symbolic action (including
metaphoric predication) has the capacity to give identity, or, as Fernández puts it, "that is, a title — to persons, situations, or things otherwise
uncertainly conceived" (1991, p. 1). As we can see, metaphors are also
related to the use of categories to interpellate actors, as I described in
the previous section. On the other hand, metaphors in particular and
tropes in general are prominent in the narratives people use to understand themselves and "others." Many times tropes frame narratives and
bind the beginning of the narrative inextricably to its conclusion. In this

way tropes lend structural coherence to the narrative and suggest how the narrative is bounded, that is, where it begins and ends (Riessman 1993, p. 44). But in other circumstances, particular narrative plots "ask" for some tropes instead of others.

I use the terms "tropes" and "metaphors" following Fernández' proposition that reliance on metaphor to the exclusion of the other tropes is an obstacle to cultural understanding. I concur with him that "[t]he contribution of anthropology to metaphor theory . . . lies first in its insistence upon the role of culture in the formation of metaphoric models with which various people reason . . . and second in its concern to avoid overconcentration on metaphor as the uniquely interesting trope but rather to see metaphors in their natural context in dynamic relation to all the other tropes" (Fernández 1991, p. 10).

Accordingly, in this book I have analyzed certain tropes of sameness and difference that are used on the border; I did that by following the "polytropy" model developed by Paul Friedrich (1991). He identifies five classes of tropes or macrotropes: imagistic, modal, formal, contiguity based, and analogical. These "macrotropes are not exclusive to each other; on the contrary, every . . . conversation depends — at least implicitly — on the collaboration of all of them in a synergistic, simultaneous intertwining within every sentence and every line . . . All tropes also interact constantly with social situation, cultural values . . . and so forth" (pp. 23–24). What Friedrich wants to avoid with his polytropy theory is a common trap in linguistics: to automatically equate tropes or figures of language with the most obvious trope: metaphor. In this sense, if the "sister cities" trope I discussed in Chapter 2 is indeed a metaphor, then the trope I discussed in Chapter 3, "Third World vs. First World," is a contiguity trope, or, more precisely, an *inventory*.

Consequently, the "sister cities" is a simple metaphor, or, in Friedrich's terms, an "analogical trope." Like all the metaphors, this one does not include *all* logical and realistic similarities, but only those that are culturally appropriate and linked to the particular narrative identity of the speaker. If metaphor can be defined as a figure of speech in which one thing is likened to another by being spoken of as if it were the same (Goodman 1978), the "sister cities" metaphor likens cities to families and maps a particular kind of relationship — sisterhood — from the source domain of families to the target domain of cities.

If the "sister cities" trope is a metaphor that buttresses the construction of a Fronterizo identity on the Mexican side of the border, the "Third World vs. First World" is a contiguity trope, or, more precisely, an *inventory* that sustains exactly the opposite, that is, how different many Americans feel in relation to Mexicans. If contiguity tropes in general address contiguity in time, space, and other dimensions such as social and textual contexts, in the inventory in particular, "symbols of the same class are juxtaposed in a string. Yet, inventories involve not just syntactic juxtaposition, but the association of the referents in terms of space, time, function, and so forth" (Friedrich 1991, p. 35). Categories are, somehow, contiguity tropes too (taxonomies), because they also address issues of part–whole and whole–part relations — traditional synecdoche. Furthermore, the categories and inventory trope I am analyzing here (Third World vs. First World) also share the same identity potential, that is, to construct sameness but also difference.

Of course, I am not claiming that tropes are more important than categories and narratives for understanding the process of identity construction. My point is that all three are intertwined and that some of them can take precedence over the others in particular situations of identity construction. Sometimes people construct their identity purely in categorical terms, through the interpellations they assume for themselves and apply to others; other times they do so throughout a well-developed narrative, and still other times they rely on tropes. Most of the time, though, people use these linguistic devices (and many nonlinguistic ones, of course) all together in a complex intertwining of narratives, categories, and metaphors, where it is not always clear which one precedes the other, because all three devices have the same capacity of "ordering" reality, which is at the base of any process of identity construction.

In most of the interviews I conducted, people were presenting me a particular character throughout the interview process, differentiating themselves from the "others" using categories and metaphors because the character they were constructing "asked" for some coherence in the portraying of itself. That coherence was provided, most of the time, by the chief discourse or thematic narrative plot a particular interviewee decided to follow. Bruner (1987, p. 15) says that "eventually the culturally shaped cognitive and linguistic processes that guide the self-telling of life narratives achieve the power to structure perceptual experience." In the interviews, thematic structure was "asking" for categories and metaphors that would buttress its claims because, as I will show in the next section, the thematic plot is of crucial importance in the process of selecting the "real" that underlies any process of identity construction. In this selection process, categories and tropes are evaluated and used or discarded in accordance with their contribution to the particular narrative identity being constructed. For that reason I agree with Naomi

Quinn's observation that "recent theory in cognitive semantics has put a heavy explanatory burden on metaphor, positing that it structures and indeed constrains human understanding and reasoning" (1991, p. 56). According to Quinn (1991, p. 65), it is cultural understanding which underlies metaphoric language, and not vice versa:

> . . . metaphorical systems or productive metaphors typically do not structure understandings de novo. Rather, particular metaphors are selected by speakers, and are favored by these speakers, just because they provide satisfying mappings onto already existing cultural understandings—that is, because elements and relations between elements in the source domain make a good match with elements and relations among them in the cultural model. Selection of a particular metaphor for use in ordinary speech seems to depend upon its aptness for the conceptual task at hand . . .

In addition to cultural models in general, I would add that plots, in particular, are very important in the metaphor selection process. I believe that once an identity plot is well established (and of course categories and metaphors in turn help to compose any identity plot), metaphors are selected to conform to a point or to advance a particular identity claim related to a particular identity plot.

Narrative Identities

I believe that people make sense of themselves and "others" in purely categorical or metaphorical terms, and heavily use the available discursively connoted taxonomies to describe attitudes and behaviors. But they also construct stories or narratives to understand themselves and "others." I agree with several authors that point out that narrative is an epistemological category traditionally mistaken for a literary form. Paul Ricoeur (1984) contends, moreover, that narrative is one of the most important cognitive schemes human beings have. It presents to awareness a world in which timely human actions are linked together according to their effect on the attainment of human desires and goals. Therefore, narrative discourse is one of the most important systems of understanding that we use to make sense of reality, most particularly to make sense of time. As Polkinghorne (1988, p. 18) comments: "The narrative organizational scheme is of particular importance for understanding human activity. It is the scheme that displays purpose and direction in human affairs and makes individual human lives comprehensible as wholes. We conceive our own and other's behavior within the narrative framework, and through it recognize the effects our planned actions can have on desired goals." By inclusion in a narratively generated story, particular actions take on significance as having contributed to a complete episode, and the means by which specific events are made to cohere into a single narrative is the plot or story line.

> The recognition or construction of a plot employs the kind of reasoning that Charles Peirce called "abduction," the process of suggesting a hypothesis that can serve to explain some puzzling phenomenon. Abduction produces a conjecture that is tested by fitting it over the "facts." The conjecture may be adjusted to provide a fuller account of the givens. The reasoning used to construct a plot is similar to that used to develop a hypothesis. Both are interactive activities that take place between a conception that might explain or show a connection among the events and the resistance of the events to fit the construction. (Polkinghorne 1988, p. 19)

Emplotment is concerned with ordering the multiple realities that surround us, drawing out from the flow of events those issues that significantly contribute to the story being constructed. Of course, I do not pretend to defend the idea that people looking at photographs are always building complete narratives in the way literary theorists generally understand the term "narrative." On the contrary, most of the time my interviews consisted of chronicles, arguments, question-and-answer exchanges, and other forms of discourse. Nevertheless, in many circumstances people constructed either complete narratives, or truncated, unfinished ones, which still have the basic elements that compose a narrative (Vila 1997b). David Novitz writes:

> It is wrong, of course, to treat these ways of thinking about ourselves, these character sketches, as full-blown narratives. They clearly are not. They do, however, express an integral part of narrative. They are narrative structures, for they are the expression of the organizational principles around which detailed narratives can be constructed . . . they are dispositions to select, relate, and think of the events of one's life in specific ways. (1989, p. 64)

In this sense, if a full-blown narrative is absent in most of the testimonies I have presented in this book, the structure of narrative is nonetheless present. The characters my interviewees developed for themselves and "others," and the basic theme or nodal point that structured their plots (for instance, "Southern Mexicans are the main cause of Juárez' disgraceful state" or "all poverty is Mexican"), still guided the process of selection and thinking about events that was behind their understanding of reality.

Here is where narratives differ from discourses in general. First, narrative is a manner of speaking characterized by several exclusions and restrictive conditions (in the narrativizing discourse the events seem to tell themselves) that the more open form of discourse does not impose upon the speaker (White 1981). Second, narrative and narrativity are intimately linked with desire in a way that other forms of discourse are not: narrativity "makes the real into an object of desire, and does so by its imposition, upon events that are represented as real, of the formal coherency that stories possess . . . a formal coherency that we ourselves lack. . . . Insofar as historical stories can be completed, can be given narrative closure, can be shown to have had a *plot* all along, they give to reality the odor of the *ideal*" (White 1981, p. 20). Additionally, Hayden White (p. 23) believes that "the notion that sequences of real events possess the formal attributes of the stories we tell about imaginary events could only have its origin in wishes, daydreams, reveries." He is pointing out that the real world does not present itself to perception in well-made narratives with central subjects, proper beginnings, middles, endings, and a coherence that allows one "to see 'the end' in every beginning" (p. 23).

Finally, what distinguishes narrative from discourse in general is that "narration and narrativity [are] . . . the instruments by which the conflicting claims of the imaginary and the real are mediated, arbitrated, or resolved in a discourse" (White 1981, p. 4). Narrativity proposes a particular order of meaning that, according to Hayden White (p. 20), is always a moral one:

> The demand for closure in the historical story is a demand . . . for moral meaning, a demand that sequences of real events be assessed as to their significance as elements of a *moral* drama. . . . Where, in any account of reality, narrativity is present, we can be sure that morality or a moralizing impulse is present too. There is no other way that reality can be endowed with the kind of meaning that both displays itself in its consummation and withholds itself by its displacement to another story "waiting to be told" just beyond the confines of "the end."

For White (1981, p. 22) there is no other way of "concluding" an account of *real* events than to order them according to a "moralizing" ending, "for we cannot say, surely, that any sequence of real events actually comes to an end, that reality itself disappears, that events *of the order of the real* have ceased to happen." This moral stance of narrativity is crucial to understanding its relationship with identities, a characteristic of narrative that is not shared by other forms of discourse. As Charles Taylor (1989, p. 3) puts it: "Selfhood and the good, or in another way selfhood and morality, turn out to be inextricably intertwined themes." Accordingly, for this author, to know who I am is a species of knowing where I stand: "My identity is defined by the commitments and identifications which provide the frame or horizon within which I can try to determine from case to case what is good, or valuable, or what ought to be done, or what I endorse or oppose" (p. 27). If this is so, when some of my interviewees stated that they were Chicanos, Hispanics, or Mexican Americans, what they were saying by this was not just that they were strongly attached to this particular ethnic identity by chance but that this particular ethnic identity provided them the frames within which they could determine where they stood on questions of what is good, worthwhile, or of value.

While I am advancing these ideas about narratives and identities, I am aware that not all of those constructs are the products of the individual's own imagination. They may be borrowed from other sources, most obviously from popular culture. And here appears again Gramsci's hegemony, because sometimes they are not merely borrowed but actively imposed on us by others in order to preserve power.

Having clarified these points, I think it is worthwhile to go back to the issue of narratives being plagued by categories, but "[u]nlike the attempt to explain a single event by placing it in a specified category, narrativity precludes sense-making of a singular isolated phenomenon. Narrativity demands that we discern the meaning of any single event only in temporal and spatial relationship to other events" (Somers 1992, p. 601). This characteristic of narrativity is crucial to understanding why people use narratives to make sense of themselves and the "others," because if identity is relational and always in process, as I believe it is, there is no other way to fully understand it but through narrative. Making sense of my present situation always requires a narrative understanding of my life, a sense of what I have become that can only be given in a story. As Bhavnani and Haraway point out:

We repeatedly rehistoricize ourselves by telling a story; we relocate ourselves in the present historical moment by reconfiguring our identities relationally, understanding that identity is always a relational category and that there is no such thing as a subject who pre-exists the encounters that construct that subject. Identity is an effect of those encounters—identity is that set of effects which develop from the collision of histories. It is not an abstraction. It's an extraordinarily complex kind of sedimentation, and we rehistoricize our identities all the time through elaborate story-telling practices. . . . And those story telling practices themselves are ways of trying to interrogate, get at, the kinds of encounters, historical moments, the kinds of key moments of transition for us—both individually and collectively. (1994, p. 21)

As I project my life forward and endorse the existing direction or give it a new direction, I construct a future story (Taylor 1989, p. 48). Hence my self-understanding always has a temporal and narrative dimension in order to make sense of the complex combination of past, present, and future that is behind the process of identity construction. As David Novitz (1989, p. 61) puts it: ". . . narrative . . . is the only variety of discourse which selectively mentions real or imaginary events, orders them in a developmental or sequential way (the plot), so that the whole discourse (and the sequence of events which it mentions) eventually acquires a significance, usually a moral significance, from the way in which its parts are related to one another (closure)."

Therefore, what we have here is a peculiar weaving of narratives, categories, and metaphors as a means to understanding oneself and "others" (Vila 1997b). On the one hand, we need narratives to understand the sequential and relational character of our identities. On the other hand, we do not directly "encounter" our past and the "others." Instead, we do it through descriptions, that is, through the categories we use to depict them, and through the metaphors we use to "facilitate" the understanding of a difficult domain of reality through its "translation" to a familiar one. Reversing direction, however, we also tend to use narratives to support the connotations of the categories and metaphors we use, especially in a context of symbolic struggles. Stories are perhaps unnecessary to explain why I use the category "table" to describe a square piece of wood supported by four "legs." But surely a personal story is very helpful if I want to explain why I think that "Fronterizos are being Americanized," that "Anglos are materialistic and lack spirituality," that "Mexicans come to the United States to take advantage of the welfare system," that "Chicanos do not want to grow up," or to buttress my use of the sister cities metaphor. In racially and regionally conscious societies like the United States and Mexico, people tend to cite "evidence" to support their claims that "others" have negative properties and attitudes, or that "we" are better than "them." Narratives about ourselves and "others," then, are presented as "facts," because they are about events that we have personally witnessed or participated in.

What van Dijk (1993, p. 126) says about "minority stories" can be extended to stories in general in the border context:

> Whereas large parts of conversations about minorities are generalizations about ethnic minority groups or ethnic relations, personal stories provide concrete information, which is used as supporting "evidence" for a more general, argumentative conclusion. The weight of this evidence is epistemological . . . It suggests that the events told about are a reliable source of knowledge, because they represent a lived, personal experience. At the same time, it is suggested that the (negative) conclusion is not ethnically biased but supported by the facts.

We can thus propose that an important part of the connotation of human categories and metaphors is made by the sedimentation of multiple stories about ourselves and "others." There is yet another way that narratives, categories, and metaphors are related, and this overlap provides some clues to explain why some interpellations are accepted by some social actors, while others are rejected. The categories and metaphors we use to describe the reality that surrounds us, as well as the interpellations we accept as valid for addressing ourselves and "others," are in some way overdetermined by the different stories we tell about ourselves and "others" (Vila 1997b). Consequently, if on the one hand we "encounter" the "others" through categories, on the other hand the particular category I utilize to address a person is related to the particular narrative I use to depict myself and "others." The "character" I develop in my narrative about myself somehow overdetermines not only the interpellations (and their connotations) I use to address myself and "others" but also the metaphors I select to portray both of us; that is, non-narrative descriptions about myself and "others" are also in some ways narrative-laden. For example, if someone uses the acculturation-assimilation discourse as the main theme structuring his/her narrative identity (as Albert did; see Chapter 3), he will probably label himself as Hispanic or Mexican American (as Albert did) rather than as Chicano. On the other hand, those people whose narratives are structured around the very common theme "Mexican Americans are traitors to their own race" (e.g., Norma; see Chapter 4) usually refer to themselves as "Mexicanos," while the "others" (Mexican Americans in this case) are addressed as "*malinchistas*" [traitors].[2] Those interviewees who construct their characters as "modern Mexican nationals from the North," by contrast, extensively use the metaphor of "sister cities." Meanwhile, those American citizens whose character construction stresses that "all poverty is Mexican" prefer to use the "First World vs. Third World" trope.

Perhaps an example will clarify my point. In the interview I conducted with the group of middle-class professionals in Juárez (analyzed in Chapter 2), the theme that "Southerners are more Catholic than Fronterizos" was prominent. In that interview Grisel told me the following story:

Grisel: I witnessed a phenomenon when I lived in the Tarahumara Mountains . . . that I observed and it stirred my curiosity: it was the irreverence the Tarahumaras showed toward the church . . . the church was rather large, but the funniest thing was that it was empty; and in the year that I lived there [in the Tarahumara] the priest only came twice. And there were no religious images. Somebody had pasted a little stamp of a virgin on the wall, and the only saint they had, one day, so they say, a drunk came in and kicked it and broke it. Then there was a madman . . . Mr. Marcelino, who brought cow dung to the church [laughs]. He said that it was gold and that it was an offering for the virgin, but there wasn't even a virgin! There were no benches, and the windows were broken and without curtains . . . That's when I noticed that the people didn't have that fervor (except for some of the elderly people that I saw at funerals) . . . only the elderly knew how to pray, the very old; the middle-aged (we're talking thirty, forty years old) didn't know how to pray anymore, let alone the children. There wasn't that devotion that you see in the South, right? And something else that got my attention was, the second time that the priest came, to marry the village nurse, they gave me a camera to take some pictures. So I positioned myself in front of the altar (where the altar was supposed to be—there was only a wall, no altar) to take the pictures. But then I heard some hustle and bustle, even involving the bride, and I said to myself, "I can't be seeing what I'm seeing!" She turned around and looked at me and said that she was bored, then she gestured to me as if to say, "Enough of this!" and, "How much longer?" and that the priest was crazy. [laughs] At her own wedding! I just couldn't believe what was going on! And the priest talked and talked, but nobody paid attention to him . . . What I noticed was that this was a social gathering for all the people who hadn't seen each other for a long time (because there were people from all the surrounding huts), and everyone was "visiting" [carrying on conversations]. Look! The priest was talking and talking, and all the ladies were turned around talking to one another, about this, about that . . . that is, everyone was chatting among themselves! I just sat there and thought, "This would never happen in the South, no, never, never! In the South they have a permanent priest, and without a doubt they have gold and good images" . . . But over there in the Tarahumara Mountains they don't have anything! So this is quite different, and religion with the Tarahumara, it is for the sake of convenience, because it was the nuns who took care of educating the Tarahumaras, because there were hardly any schools for them . . .

This is a complete narrative with plot, characters, a beginning, a middle, and an ending, also including a moral stance about what is being told. In this narrative Grisel, a non-Catholic Fronteriza, strongly identifies with the Indians of the Tarahumara region (who are *norteños* themselves) and their lack of respect for the Catholic church. At the same time, she criticizes the Catholic fanaticism she believes is prevalent in Southern and Central Mexico. In this sense, Grisel has a very developed plot about her religious/Mexican identity that is attuned to the hegemonic "Southerners are more Catholic than Fronterizos" discourse — to be discussed in full in the chapter about religion in my *Border Identities* book. Grisel expresses this discourse with positive tones because she is not Catholic herself. This narrative can be analyzed using Labov's (1972, 1982) structural approach. In *Narrative Analysis*, Catherine Kohler Riessman describes this approach: "Narratives, [Labov] argues, have formal properties and each has a function. A 'fully formed' one includes six common elements: an abstract (summary of the substance of the narrative), orientation (time, place, situation, participants), complicating action (sequence of events), evaluation (significance and meaning of the action, attitude of the narrator), resolution (what finally happened), and coda (returns the perspective to the present" (p. 18).

My theoretical point here is that the non-narrative descriptions (interpellations and metaphors) about herself and "others" that Grisel gave me in that interview are also in some ways narrative-laden (Vila 1997b). In other words, when Grisel is talking in pure categorical or metaphorical terms about herself and the "others," she *still* has her Catholic/Mexican plot in mind, and she also is performing her "non-Catholic Fronterizo" character. Therefore, the plot Grisel uses to compose her story also organizes her other statements about Catholicism and the difference between Southerners and Fronterizos. When Grisel uses other non-narrative discursive devices to talk about the differences between Southern and Fronterizo Catholicism, she takes on the selective point of view of the kind of religious character she had already constructed for herself during the interview process.

Grisel: In Juárez there are fewer religious images and fewer churches; it's very different in the central part of Mexico . . . I think you have to look at our geographic situation as well . . . the influence that the Catholic church exercised over the Indians in Central Mexico, that had a lot to do with it.

Because the Tarahumara escaped the church's influence . . . the Tarahumara went to live in the mountains, and . . . look! There they are to this
day! And no matter what little town you go to from Puebla (no, don't say
Puebla because my mother says that they piss holy water there!) . . . uh . . .
in some towns in this our state you don't see the church's influence; and
in Central Mexico, the towns, no matter how poor or how tiny they might
be, they have their churches full of gold; and that is the big, big difference
in religious matters between Central and Northern Mexico . . .

Hence, Grisel's use of the categories "Indians" and "Central Mexico"
and her metaphor "in Puebla people piss holy water" were highly influenced by the kind of character Grisel was constructing during the interview process.

For all these reasons I disagree with Somers' (1992, p. 601) statement
that ". . . social actions should not be viewed as a result of categorizing
oneself ('I am forty years old; I should buy life insurance') but should
be seen in the context of a life-story with episodes ('I felt out of breath
last week; I really should start thinking about life insurance')." I disagree because the category "forty years old" was built, among other
things, out of several metaphors ("I am running out of fuel," for instance) and the sedimentation of many stories about forty-year-olds
(some of them who "felt out of breath" frequently), and those stories are
an inseparable part of the connotation of the category. For the same reason I disagree with Polkinghorne's point that "[t]he question of 'Who
am I?' is not answered simply by assigning a predicate to the subject
'I,' as in such phrases as 'I am an American,' 'I am a male,' and 'I am a
farmer'" (Polkinghorne 1988, p. 152). I think that the answer to that
question is contextual, and can be answered by assigning a predicate
to the subject, such as "I am American." But to answer that question in
categorical terms is nothing else than to bring into the answer all the
stories about being American in that particular situation that already
belong to the commonsense connotation of the category, and where
metaphors play a very important role (the "Americans are cold and dry"
metaphor discussed in Chapter 2 is a good example of this role).

Thus, we all carry narratives that help furnish us with ways of thinking about ourselves. Different people select different articulatory elements or "nodal points" to build their narratives, but regardless of such
diversity, people prefer to select and organize the events of their past
and to foresee their future in terms of these articulatory elements. This
is so because they inescapably need to arrest the flow of differences and
construct a center around which certain kinds of narratives can be con-

structed. Some of those articulatory elements, "nodal points," or themes are linked to public stories of private identities (such as "husband as breadwinner," "good father," "reliable worker," etc.). Others are public stories of social identities (such as stories of "union solidarity," "American social mobility," or, in the border context, stories about "the laziness of the Mexicans") (Somers 1992). Still, both types of themes are used in this constitutive back-and-forth relationship between narratives and identities:

> A good story presents a coherent plot. The narrative "now" must grow plausibly out of what has come before and point the way to what might reasonably come next. This literary criterion has implications for identity as well. For in telling their stories individuals make claims about the coherence of their lives. "This person I am today is who I have been years becoming." Further, what is included and omitted from the account renders plausible the anticipated future. (Rosenwald and Ochberg 1992, p. 9)

The issue of what is included or omitted from the account leads us to another crucial feature of narrative in the construction of identity: its selectivity. There is a kind of *evaluative criteria* in narratives that, according to Somers (1992, p. 602), "enables us to make qualitative and lexical distinctions among the infinite variety of events, experiences, characters, institutional promises, and social factors that impinge on our lives . . . in the face of a potentially limitless array of social experiences deriving from social contact with events, institutions, and people, the evaluative capacity of Emplotment demands and enables *selective appropriation* in constructing narratives." The plots we use to compose our stories determine the focus of our attention. The constant back and forth between narratives and identities (between living and telling) allows people to adjust stories to fit their own "identities" and, conversely, permits them to tailor "reality" to fit their stories.

Here is where narrative theory can overcome some of the limitations of approaches that rely on categories and interpellations alone to make sense of identity (Vila 1997b). In spite of the sophistication of the neo-Gramscian/neo-Althusserian theory of articulations and interpellations, this approach often cannot answer the question of why one interpellation is successful where another fails to address a subject. Very frequently researchers in this tradition end up using some kind of homological answer (such as, "that actor accepted that particular interpellation because it was structurally connected — or not connected — to him/her" — a very nondiscursive answer, as we can see); or, still worse, they use some kind of Cartesian remnant that lurks in the shadows trying to "center" an identity—which the theory supposedly had decentered in the first place. In a similar fashion, if on the one hand the theory of articulations and interpellations addresses the issue of the struggle over meaning and how different interpellations struggle to establish an equivalence between discourse and reality, on the other hand, it is not uncommon to find that to explain why one interpellation is more successful than another, this theory seems to resort to the idea of the hegemonic power of the successful interpellation, something that is, precisely, what it tried to explain at the beginning.

Therefore, if it can be argued (following both Althusser and Foucault) that individuals are constituted as subjects through the discursive formation, the theory of interpellation comes to a halt in terms of making sense of the particular processes by which subjectivities are constructed—that is, those processes that construct us as subjects that can be "spoken." In other words, the understanding of the process of identity construction does require not only that the subject be "hailed," but also that the subject invest in the position (Hall 1996, p. 6). The theory of interpellation as proposed by Althusser, or the similar Foucaultian notion of the subject as produced "as an effect" through and within discourse, accounts for the "hailing" or the construction of subject positions within discourses, but leaves unanswered why the subject invests in that particular version of a subject position and not in another one. As Stuart Hall points out (p. 12): ". . . there is no theorization of the psychic mechanism or interior processes by which these automatic 'interpellations' might be produced, or—more significantly—fail or be resisted or negotiated."

I believe that it is precisely here where narrative theory can help us to understand how interpellations function in the real life of concrete social actors and to explain why some interpellations (in our case, ethnic, racial, regional, gender, religious, and national interpellations) "hit" where others fail. Narrative theory can help through stating something that, at first glance, is tautological; that is, people seem to accept a particular interpellation (namely, a proposal of meaning linked to a particular social position) whenever that interpellation has meaning in relation to their construction of identity. This apparent tautology, however, hides a very intricate back-and-forth process between interpellations and plots, where both modify each other constantly. My idea is that social events are constructed as "experience" not only in relation to discourses that confer meaning on them in general, but also within plots that organize them coherently. Accordingly, it is precisely the plot of my narrative identity that guides the process of selectivity toward the "real" that is concomitant to every identity construction. In this selection of the "real" is also included the relationship that we have established between our plot and the multiple interpellations and tropes that culture in general — and the classificatory systems, in the case of interpellations in particular — offers us for identification. My point is that the multiple interpellations and tropes that surround us are somehow evaluated in relation to the plot of our narratives, in such a way that such evaluation triggers a complex process of negotiation between narratives, interpellations, and tropes, a process that can end in very different ways. On the one hand, that process may culminate in the plain acceptance of the interpellation or trope at stake, because it "adjusts" without major problems in the basic plot of my identity (e.g., when a Mexican American whose plot develops around the idea of discrimination "discovers" the Chicano interpellation or "*la raza*" trope). On the other hand, the process of negotiation between plots, interpellations, and tropes may end in a total rejection of the interpellation and metaphors at stake, because they do not fit in any way my narrative identity (e.g., those immigrants from Zacatecas who are interpellated as "Chilangos" or portrayed with the many negative metaphors Norteños use to describe Chilangos, by those Juarenses who use the plot asserting that "all those Mexicans who live south of Chihuahua are Chilangos"). Nonetheless, the most probable outcome of the negotiation process between plots, interpellations, and tropes is that each modifies the others, adjusting mutually here and there in the process of constructing a more or less coherent version of the self (Vila 1997b). As Polkinghorne (1988) writes:

> The life narrative is open-ended: future actions and occurrences will have to be incorporated into the present plot. One's past cannot be changed . . . However, the interpretation and significance of the [events of our past] can change if a different plot is used to configure them. Recent events may be such that the person's plot line cannot be adapted to include them. The life plot must then itself be altered or replaced. The rewriting of one's story involves a major life change—both in one's identity and in one's interpretation of the world—and is usually undertaken with difficulties. Such a change is resisted, and people try to maintain their past plots even if doing so requires distorting new evidence. (p. 182)

Of course, we still have to answer the question of why some people have particular plots instead of others, and to answer it discursively, without resorting to homological approaches or using hegemony to explain everything (all this is said recognizing how important social constraints and hegemonic discourses are to understanding the prevalence of some plots over others). Nevertheless, I consider that the complex relationships among *social identity, classificatory systems, interpellations, tropes, and narratives about myself and "others"* proposed here allows us to advance a bit in understanding the process of identity construction. At least we have a more concrete place to explore the complex relationship between structure and agency: in the plots that different social actors build to understand their identities. This offers us the opportunity to focus more on the commonsense contents that guide our everyday actions. In this book I have discussed how particular national, regional, ethnic, and racial thematic plots work as nodal points that "center" narratives on the border. The plots that are prevalent in Juárez—"All social problems are related to Southern Mexicans," "Juarenses have become Americanized," "Mexican Americans want to humiliate Mexican nationals," "Mexican Americans have become Americanized," "Americans are slaves of their consumerism"—as well as the plots characteristic of the American side of the border—"All poverty is Mexican," "All criminality is coming from Juárez," and so on—function as narrative themes around which many border inhabitants construct their "coherent" identities. In my forthcoming *Border Identities*, I analyze how class, gender, and religious plots—such as "Fronterizos are losing their Catholic traditions," "American women boss their husbands," "Catholic practices are very traditional in Mexico," "Mexican males are very machista," or "to advance economically you have to leave Juárez and move to El Paso," among others—organize the national, regional, ethnic, and racial identities of many border residents. These narrative plots determine how events are processed and what criteria will be used to prioritize events and render meaning to them. These particular themes selectively appropriate the happenings of the social world, arrange them in some order, and normatively evaluate these arrangements (Somers 1992, p. 602).

Therefore, I believe that people develop a sense of subjectivity, in part by thinking of themselves as the protagonists of stories (Bhavnani and Haraway 1994; Bruner 1987; Gergen and Gergen 1983; Kerby 1991; Novitz 1989; Polkinghorne 1988; Ricoeur 1992; Rorty 1990; Rosenwald 1992; Rosenwald and Ochberg 1992; Sarbin 1986; Sewell 1992; Somers 1992, 1994; Taylor 1989). In the texts of those stories, people narrate the episodes of their lives in order to make their world intelligible to themselves. Consequently, to narrate is to do more than merely describe events or actions. It is also to recount them, to organize them into plots, and to attribute to them a character or personage. In this sense, the character in a narrative is no different from his/her experiences (Reagan 1993). That is, the character of the narrative is not an entity distinct from his/her experiences. Instead, the narrative constructs the character's identity by constructing the story. Accordingly, what makes the character's identity is the story's identity (Ricoeur 1992, p. 147).

For these reasons, I have presented throughout the book different plots that people construct to achieve that understanding, treating those plots as texts. Yet, I do not wish to propose a "language imperialism" approach. I agree with Rosenwald and Ochberg (1992, p. 7) that "at its limit . . . this line of reasoning can be taken to support the notion that social life counts for nothing outside discourse. On this track the improvement of life can be accomplished if one tells a better story about it. But life is not merely talk . . . changes in narrative are significant to the extent that they stir up changes in how we live." "Life is not merely talk"; rather, changes in how we live are in themselves discourses, if we understand discourse à la Ernesto Laclau as those linguistic and non-linguistic *practices* that carry and confer meaning in a field characterized by the play of power relationships, or à la Haraway as *encounter*:

> There is no pre-discursive or pre-relational, using discursive as a kind of synonym for relational. One of the problems with using the word discursive is that the metaphor of language can end up carrying too much weight. I'm willing to let it carry a lot of weight, but I'm not willing to let it then finally really *be* everything. There are non-language-like processes of encounter. But there's nothing pre-relational, pre-encounter. So it is only in engagement that we, and everybody else, get our boundaries and our skins drawn. That's what I mean by saying everything is relational. (Bhavnani and Haraway 1994, p. 32)

If everything is relational, and people get their identity boundaries in engagements and encounters, but at the same time changes in narrative are significant to the extent that they stir up changes in how we live, the dialogical methodology I have used in the book is a valid way to try to modify those encounters that emplot the "others" in story lines in which the logic of either/or (inclusion/exclusion) is prevalent. Thus, what I tried to do in the process of reinterviewing people was to introduce my interviewees to the Derridian logic of the both/and. As Sampson (1989, p. 16) points out:

> . . . by thinking in terms of either/or, one creates the very conditions that oppose entities that are in fact members of the same system. In other words, only by thinking in terms of a logic of both/and can one see that the matter

is not one of opposition but only of difference: and as we know, differences do not inhere in the entity, but rather describe the relations among the parts of a system . . . This Western concept forces contrastive opposition where the mutual recognition of the other-in-self and the self-in-other is essential. The Derridian subject can never be set apart from the multiple others who are its very essence. Thus, the Derridian subject who would seek to oppose and enslave others can only suffer in kind, for those others are elements of the subject's own personhood.

My goal was to introduce my interviewees to this crucial idea that nobody can be set apart from the multiple others who are its very essence. Hence, I tried to show my Juarense interviewees how for many of them the Southern Mexicans were their *constitutive outside*. In the same way I tried to show some Mexican Americans how the Anglos and the Mexican nationals, some Juarense Catholics how the Southern Mexican and the Mexican American Catholics, some Juarense females how the American females, and so on, played the same role of being the supposed "outside" that, nevertheless, is the indispensable difference without which their identities do not make any sense.

Introduction

1. "Operation Blockade" is a metaphor that itself deserves to be analyzed. Its military references (you "blockade" an enemy, not a country you are going to engage in a process of free trade) did not escape the border patrol, which about a month after launching the operation changed its name to "Operation Hold the Line."

2. An *El Paso Times* poll conducted in October 1994 showed that 85 percent of El Pasoans favored the border blockade. Among them 78 percent of the Hispanics and 91 percent of the non-Hispanics favored the blockade (*El Paso Times*, October 30, 1994). Reading an early version of the book, Duncan Earle (personal communication, September 6, 1998) correctly noted that the blockade's popularity among Mexican Americans was largely due to the fact that stopping the illegal crossers at the border dramatically reduced border patrol harassment of Mexican American El Pasoans, who before were very often "confused" as being undocumented immigrants.

3. Nearly 70 percent of El Paso's population is of Mexican origin, and a significant number of these residents have arrived in the United States within the last twenty years.

4. I will discuss religion in two different chapters in my future book, *Border Identities: Narratives of Class, Gender, and Religion on the U.S.–Mexico Border*; see also Vila (1996).

5. For a full analysis about the relationship between photography, narrative, and the construction of identity, see Vila (1997a).

6. There is a small population of Korean Americans in El Paso that was not mentioned prominently in most of my interviews. It would be interesting to conduct research about social perceptions among them and regarding them in El Paso and Juárez.

7. Reading an early version of this manuscript, Dennis Bixler-Márquez noted that small rural crossings along the border (Palomas was his example) also have a very different dynamic than the large cities I mentioned (Bixler-Márquez, personal communication, July 18, 1997).

8. Initially, the chapters on religion, gender, and class were intended to appear at this point in the book, but finally had to be cut and transformed into a second volume, *Border Identities: Narratives of Class, Gender, and Religion on the U.S.–Mexico Border*. In the religion chapter I deal with the interesting way religious identities intertwine with region, nation, ethnicity, and race, in a process where a couple of thematic plots work as nodal points that "center" some narrative identities on the border. In this chapter I show how the "Juarenses are less Catholic than Southern Mexicans" and "Mexican Ameri-

cans are less Catholic than Mexican nationals" discourses on the border function as narrative plots around which many border inhabitants construct their "coherent" identities.

In the chapter on gender I address the particular ways gender identities overlap with region, nation, race, and ethnicity on the border. In the first part of the chapter I analyze how gender narratives are regionalized and nationalized on the Mexican side of the border, where many Southern Mexicans and Fronterizos believe that there are particular gender behaviors and attitudes that characterize Fronterizos as distinct from Southern Mexicans on the one hand, and Americans on the other. Those particular gender behaviors are thematized around several specific narratives well developed in the region. The two most important in my sample are (1) the figure of the libertine Fronterizo, which easily becomes the libertine prostitute (female or male) associated with the "city of vice" discourse I analyze in Chapter 1 of this book and (2) the figure of the bossy American woman.

In the American section of the chapter, analyzing two groups of Mexican immigrants that migrated to the United States in very similar circumstances, but that still show very different gender discourses, I point out the importance of the narrative plots those immigrants brought from Mexico and the subsequent modification of those plots due to their experience in the United States in the construction of their commonsense discourses about gender relations among Mexicans living on the U.S.–Mexico border.

In the chapter about class I show how class discourses are mostly absent from the area, proposing that this absence is linked to a metaphorical displacement through which to go up in the social scale is equated by many people with moving from one country (Mexico) to the other (the United States). In this kind of narrative the explanation of poverty (or its lack) is detached from any reference to class exploitation and is framed in regional and/or national terms. That is, regions and countries are poor or they are not; ergo, to leave poverty behind is to leave that region or country.

9. I concur with Bruner (1993, p. 1) in that the qualitative researcher is never an objective, politically neutral observer standing outside and above the text; he/she is historically positioned and locally situated as an all-too-human observer of the human condition; and in that the construction of meaning is radically plural, always open, and there is politics in every account. For that reason I attempted to include the Other in my research agenda. There are several ways of doing it. Some ethnographers do participatory or collaborative research. For other researchers, according to Lincoln and Denzin (1994, p. 577), including the Other

> means a form of liberatory investigation wherein Others are trained to engage in their own social and historical interrogative efforts, and then are assisted in devising answers to questions of historical and contemporary oppression that are rooted in the values and cultural artifacts that characterize their communities . . .

For yet other social scientists, including the Other means becoming coauthors in narrative adventures. And for still others, it means constructing what are called "experimental," or "messy," texts, where multiple voices speak . . . , often in conflict, and where the reader is left to sort out which experiences speak to his or her personal life. For still others, it means presenting to the inquiry and policy community a series of autohistories, personal narratives, lived experiences, poetic representations, and sometimes fictive and/or fictional texts . . . that allow the Other to speak for him- or herself. The inquirer or evaluator becomes merely the connection between the field text, the research text, and the consuming community in making certain that such voices are heard.

An additional problem linked to the crisis of representation embedded in any research project was to decide

the amount of the personal, subjective, poetic self that is in fact openly given in the text. Bruner (1993) phrases the problem this way: "The danger is putting the personal self so deeply back into the text that it completely dominates, so that the work becomes narcissistic and egotistical. No one is advocating ethnographic self-indulgence." The goal is to return the author to the text openly, in a way that does "not squeeze out the object of study." (Lincoln and Denzin 1994, p. 578)

Therefore, instead of writing a book in which (as some quite popular ethnographic works have done lately) the reader knows more about me than he/she knows about the subject of study, because most of the pages of the book are dedicated to the seemingly endless reflection of how my different subject positions (being from Argentina, in academia, a male, heterosexual, single parent of two children, of lower middle class origin, who worked for several years in working-class jobs, and lived in poverty for a while) biased the encounter with the social reality of the border, I decided to reinterview several of my subjects of study and offer my own "tale of the field" to their scrutiny and criticism. In that way I moved from monological reflection about my biases to a dialogical exposure of them to my interviewees — a strategy that is more in line with the political/academic project I am involved with.

10. I realize that I am not doing narrative analysis in this book, because I present very few complete narratives. Most of the testimonies are other forms of discourse — chronicles, arguments, question-and-answer exchanges — but not narratives. I do not perform complete narrative analysis of the stories I present, either. If I were to locate myself in the grid Catherine Riessman developed to "grade" narrative analysis, I would be below her worst category, because I do not pursue narrative analysis enough to merit the title! What I present in the following pages are some basic hegemonic discourses people use to construct key substantive narrative themes that cut across more than two hundred interviews. And there I stop my narrative endeavor. From then on, I do many things Riessman asks us to avoid in narrative analysis: I focus on summarizing the gist of what my interviewees said; I "clean up" disfluencies to render narratives eas-

ily readable (in this way I treat language as if it were a transparent medium, useful primarily to get at underlying content); the entire interview implicitly constitutes the narratives, and most of the excerpts are not narratives. In this way, I "used interview material much like traditional qualitative analysts, taking bits and pieces, snippets of a response, that supported [my] evolving theory" (Riessman 1993, p. 31). And, I display diversity by the contrasting themes different individuals chose to emphasize (as is the case in other forms of qualitative analysis) and not by the contrasting ways individuals chose to put their accounts together, that is, the form of telling (Riessman 1993, p. 33). I also did not avoid the tendency to read a narrative simply for content (Riessman 1993, p. 61). But if on the one hand I am totally aware of all these "mistakes," I made them because my chief purpose was not to analyze in detail the narratives I have found in the field, but to uncover those hidden narratives and to engage my interviewees in the discussion of stereotypes and prejudice those narratives entail.

11. I agree with several authors (Bourdieu 1984, 1990a; Elias 1991; Giddens 1984) about the importance of the nonlinguistic, largely unconscious aspects of identity construction. See also Vila (1985, 1987, 1989, 1995), in which I emphasize the role of social practices rather than narratives in the process of identity construction.

Chapter 1

1. When used by Juarenses the nickname "Juaritos" is always an affectionate way to talk about their city. When used by Paseños, its meaning depends on the context of the conversation, and in some instances can be a pejorative label, like "Juareños."

2. It is important to point out here that most people prefer to refer to themselves as "Juarenses" rather than as "Fronterizos." This preference is not by chance: it is related to a very strong orientation toward their city (a particular kind of regionalism, so to speak) that characterizes some parts of Mexico so strongly that it develops into a kind of microlocality-oriented identity. I thank Howard Campbell, an expert in Southern Mexico identity, for addressing this point to me. He prefers to talk about a microregional identity instead of a regional one. I prefer to talk about a regional identity that has flexible limits — it can be as big or as small as the speaker desires.

3. I have found that the label "Chilango" is used in the region in three different ways that nevertheless are connected. On the one hand, for some of my interviewees, it refers to everyone from Central and Southern Mexico. On the other hand it refers to all the inhabitants of Mexico City. Finally, due to the process of decentralization that the Mexican state has undergone in the last fifteen years (where many Mexico City inhabitants went to other Mexican states), for

some other people, Chilango refers only to *some* inhabitants of Mexico City. According to Elea Aguirre (personal communication, March 15, 1997), some people see a difference between *"gente del D.F."* [people from Mexico city] and *"ser Chilango"* [to be a Chilango]. In my experience even the same interviewee might use the label in those different senses. The polysemous character of the label and its use in a particular situation is not uncommon in a region (or a country, for that matter) where, for instance, when someone talks about "Mexico" you have to take into consideration the context to know whether he/she is referring to the country or Mexico City.

4. Regardless of local people's preference for *"los de Juárez"* or "Juarenses," I will use "Juarenses" for simplicity's sake.

5. Vizcaíno is quoted in Monsiváis (1981, p. 292).

6. Robustiano and Margarita came to Juárez from Parral, Chihuahua, more than twenty years ago. They live in an extremely poor colonia in East Juárez and both are self-employed. Margarita, who is illiterate, runs a small shop in the family house. Robustiano, who never finished primary school, raises chickens in a small plot of land near his house. He used to work in the United States illegally. Feliciano is Margarita's and Robustiano's son. He is fifteen years old and was born in Juárez. He has some high school education and works at all kinds of odd jobs.

7. *"Gabacho"* is one of many labels Mexicans use to name Anglos.

8. My assistant and colleague Angela Escajeda experienced a still more dramatic situation of extreme regionalism in Guadalajara: students coming from the state of Chihuahua had two different organizations, one representing those from the capital, Ciudad Chihuahua, and the other representing Juárez!

9. Maquiladoras (or maquilas) are foreign-owned (usually American and Japanese) assembly plants that take advantage of a commercial agreement established in the mid-1960s, through which they are allowed to import supplies from other countries (without paying duties), assemble the product in Mexico, and export it back without paying duties aside from the value added. The final product is formally an American product, but it was really produced in Mexico through the use of cheap and usually non-unionized labor (less than 50 cents per hour — or around 80 cents counting fringe benefits).

10. The use of this word—"to arrange" or "to fix"—in Juárez is striking. The object is always implicit; that is, exactly what is being *"arreglado"* is never made explicit. It is so culturally obvious that the main thing that needs to be arranged/fixed are the legal papers to cross to the "other side" that mentioning the object is unnecessary.

11. Here what "everyone knows" is wrong. According to the statistics available, Juárez immigrants come from the North (from the state of Chihuahua itself, or from the neighboring Northern states). Only a small portion of the total migration (less than 15 percent) comes from Southern or Central Mexico. This is also true in the case of the maquiladora workforce.

12. Here Alejandro is teasing his co-worker Francisco, who was born in Zacatecas.

13. *Operadores/as* [operators] is the euphemism the maquiladora industry uses to avoid talking about workers. The use of this euphemism, as well as that of *planta* [plant] instead of factory, is explained in the chapter on class of my forthcoming book, *Border Identities*.

14. These are sociology seniors at UACJ. Esteban is from Chihuahua, Josefina and Ernestina from Parral, Juan is from Delicias, and Analía and José are Juarenses.

15. Alejandra is in her late forties; she was born in Chihuahua City and moved to Juárez in 1974. Armida is sixty years old and is a native Juarense, and Rubisela is a 55-year-old native of Durango, who moved to Juárez when she was eighteen years old. All of them have completed high school and professional school.

16. All these students are in their twenties. Tomás and Rafa are native Juarenses. Agustín was born in Mexico city but has lived most of his life in Juárez. Chela and Lola (who are sisters) were born in Mexico City and migrated to Juárez only two years ago.

17. Actually the dialogue has still another layer of meaning that goes deeper into the sense of commonality Rafa wants to express to Chela and Lola. This other level is expressed in the use of the slur *fronteño* instead of the category Fronterizo; *fronteño* and *juareño* are the slurs many El Pasoans use to depict negatively the inhabitants of Juárez. This inversion of meaning in the use of a negative slur to talk about one's own group is very common, and it is present in the use of words like Chicanos, Niggers, and Meskins among Mexican Americans, blacks, and Muslims, respectively.

18. *Cholismo* is a working class youth subculture that is very important not only in Northern Mexico but also in the U.S. Southwest. A pathbreaking book about *cholos* is Valenzuela's *¡A la brava ése! Cholos, Punks, Chavos Banda* (1988).

19. Jalisco is not considered Central Mexico . . . from the point of view of those from Central Mexico! But for our Juarense interviewees Jalisco belongs to Central Mexico.

20. Elea Aguirre (personal communication, March 15, 1997), reading an early version of this chapter, pointed out the gender dimension of Tito's testimony. According to her, "to think they are Jorge Negrete" is to think they are "*muy machos*."

21. The quarrels between Chihuahuenses and Juarenses have a long history. According to Elea Aguirre (personal communication, March 15, 1997), Juarenses basically complain about Chihuahua's centralism, which discriminates against Juárez. Their complaints are different from those regarding Chilangos; many Juarenses criticize Chihuahuenses for their false moralism and exaggerated religiosity. According to some Juarenses, Chihuahuenses are as deceptive as Chilangos, but in different areas.

Chapter 2

1. Don Librado refers to the trains coming from Southern and Central Mexico.

2. The black bridge is an infamous place in the region. It divides both cities and was historically used to cross illegally from Mexico to the United States. Many people have died in the attempt, sometimes trying to escape from the Border Patrol, sometimes because they were assaulted by the black bridge gang.

3. Commonsense discourses among Fronterizos indicate that most of the poor colonias in Juárez are under the influence of the Comité de Defensa Popular (CDP), a leftist political party. One of the most prominent leaders of that party is Pedro Matus.

4. According to Victor Zúñiga (personal communication, December 15, 1992), the word "*droga*" originally referred to medicine. He hypothesizes the chain of meaning behind the word "*endrogarse*" as: illness, leading to economic problems trying to cope with the medical treatment, leading to loans to pay for the medicines, leading to impossible indebtedness. However, following Wittgenstein, I believe that words acquire their meanings in the language games in which they participate. Therefore, it seems to me that the "drug" in the word "*endrogarse*," at least for some people in Juárez, corresponds to illegal drugs.

5. Usually bridges unite, rather than divide. However, the experience of Mexican nationals living on the U.S.–Mexico border is that they have to wait forty-five minutes to "cross" the bridge to "enter" the United States, where the bridge represents the location of the border patrol, not the physical structure that bypasses a river.

6. Vicki L. Ruiz (1987, p. 73) found a very similar stance in her research on Mexican maids in El Paso.

7. Vicki L. Ruiz also reported this type of claim in her research on maids in El Paso (1987, p. 70):

> Life may not be any easier for maids employed by Mexican Americans. Some women assert that Hispanics treat them worse than Anglos. *Mexicanos: es lo peor*, one woman simply stated. Many prefer working for Anglos newly arrived in El Paso. Perhaps these newcomers (often first-time *patronas*) feel a bit guilty about hiring Mexicanas for such bargain rates. As a result, they may be more considerate and appreciative of their household workers.

8. Of course Don Librado's statement does not take into account that most El Pasoans of Mexican descent are not from Central or Southern Mexico, but from Northern Mexico.

9. I analyze extensively Edelmira's testimony in the chapter about class in my forthcoming book *Border Identities*; many testimonies collected during my fieldwork show how many Mexican nationals see that kind of Mexican Ameri-

can attitude as an impediment to their access to a better social status through immigration.

10. I examine in some detail in the chapter about class in *Border Identities* how this kind of discourse is linked to discussions about social mobility in the region, in which to go up in the social scale is equated by many interviewees with moving from one side of the border to the other.

Chapter 3

1. Demographically speaking, Mexican immigrants are Mexican nationals who have migrated to the United States. Mexican Americans, on the other hand, are people of Mexican descent who were born in the United States. Obviously, from the point of view of the narrative identities these people tell to themselves or others, the difference is much more complicated than that.

2. Reading a first draft of this chapter, Duncan Earle (personal communication, February 17, 1998) cited the necessity of addressing what he called the "phantasmatic" presence of the Anglo as the "unattainable other" in the process of identity construction among many Mexican Americans. According to Duncan,

> The process of Americanizing is inherently contradictory, because of racism against Latinos, and it is this other, the Anglo, that stands behind this scale of "we are more moral than them, but more modern than those others" that moves toward the ideal no Mexican American can attain: whiteness (in its U.S. cultural sense). The antagonisms that divide different sectors of El Paso–Juárez society cannot be fully understood without the context, the unspoken relation to the unattainable other. Such a contradiction between assimilation and racial/ethnic rejection places a burden of insecurity even on the most acculturated, and that has a profound role in the negative valuation of those less Americanized. In other words, part of the desperation in the narrative constructions of identity to denigrate the other from this side relates to the "white skin ceiling" that ultimately rejects Latinos from the top of the very things it promotes. Without taking that force into account, the other divisions cannot be fully accounted for.

However, Howard Campbell does not agree with Earle (personal communication, August 10, 1998). According to Campbell, "Highly assimilated wealthy West side Hispanics surely have attained cultural 'whiteness' in El Paso." He claims that Earle's "burden of insecurity even of the most acculturated" might apply to a person who leaves El Paso and goes inland in the United States, "but within El Paso an assimilated wealthy Hispanic is actually more secure than many whites because he/she has access to prestige, acceptance, and power in *both* cultures." I think that Howard's analysis is quite true in the case of wealthy Mexican nationals who are fluent in English. I have my doubts in the case of Mexican nationals who are not very fluent in English and, above all, in the case of Mexican Americans who do not speak Spanish.

3. I am fully aware of the usual difference made in anthropology and sociology between race and ethnicity. That is, race is considered as signifying rigidity and permanence of position based on what is understood to be the unalterable reality of innate biological differences, while ethnicity is understood to be conditional and temporal because it is based on cultural differences, not biological processes. I am also aware of the current debate in the literature about the "new racism" being constructed more in ethnic terms than in racial ones. However, in this book I am more concerned with showing the difference between a regional system of classification working on the Mexican side of the border versus a racial/ethnic one being important on the American side than in showing the differential use of ethnic and racial narratives on El Paso (an upcoming project).

Nevertheless, the regional system of classification used by many Juarenses shares some of the same elements that are present in the ethnic/racial one used by many El Pasoans. Both refer to characteristics that are either inborn or at least are so deeply ingrained that if changing them is not impossible, it is very difficult.

4. Reading an early version of this chapter, Howard Campbell (personal communication, August 10, 1998) noted that regional identities such as Texan, Southerner, or Northerner (or Yankee) are still important identities along the border. I agree with Campbell that those regional distinctions are downplayed by Hispanics but not "whites," who use them to mark their own identities and make distinctions.

5. On the Mexican side of the border, the opposite situation occurs: if a Juarense meets a black person from Veracruz, that person being from Veracruz is more important than her/his skin color.

6. Of course the picture is much more complex than that; Spanish was used for many years to "attract" tourism through the depiction of the city as the gateway to Mexico. This use of Spanish as something "refined" or "elegant" for commercial purposes is, according to Hill (1993), also part of the construction of the Mexican as a contemptible "other." For one thing, this practice entails the destruction of Spanish, as the name of one of the most important El Paso malls clearly shows: Cielo Vista Mall instead of the grammatically correct Vista del Cielo Mall.

7. In Mexico "colonia" is neighborhood; there are rich colonias (El Campestre in Juárez, for instance) and poor colonias (or *colonias populares*). That differentiation is blurred on the American side, where "colonia" means only "colonias populares."

8. As one Anglo patient said: "I can't read a lick of Spanish . . . but it seems to me that if the hospital is offering financial help to poor Spanish-speakers, it should do the same for those of us who only speak English. I know that a lot of Spanish-speakers can use the help, but it's rather silly to send a double message like that. There are poor Anglos, too" (*El Paso Times*, March 9, 1993).

9. I have not had the opportunity to interview many poor "whites" yet, and

the three interviews I have conducted were still being analyzed at the time of writing. They will be included in the chapter on class in *Border Identities*. Obviously, the process of identity construction in this group is tricky, because poor Anglos have to account for their poverty in the context of a hegemonic discourse asserting that whites are not poor. Nevertheless, we have some clues as to the kind of narratives this type of social actor constructs. Many times, in order to emplot their poverty, poor whites claim they are poor because they cannot get good jobs due to "reverse discrimination," usually linked to the necessity of being bilingual (something they are not) in order to get a good job in El Paso. Bilingualism is required by many retail employers, whose sales to Spanish-speaking customers account for almost 40 percent of their entire sales. In other cases poor whites who are fully aware of the real causes of their poverty do not have any problem recognizing that the hegemonic narrative plot of the region, "all poverty is Mexican," is actually false.

10. Robert is a maquiladora manager who works in Juárez but lives in El Paso. He is a thirty-six-year-old New Jersey native who has a high school diploma and identifies himself as Catholic. His company sent him to Juárez more than eight years ago.

11. The number of cars stolen in El Paso is very high. According to commonsense accounts of the situation, the cars are stolen in El Paso and sold in Mexico. After the implementation of Operation Blockade, the number of cars being stolen decreased for a while, but a couple of years later the number of cars stolen was gradually rising again.

12. These testimonies tend to ignore the fact that over half of the people living in El Paso's colonias are U.S. citizens or legal residents, and at least 5 percent are Anglos (Duncan Earle, personal communication, February 18, 1998).

13. Joe Williamson is in his late twenties. He owns a small business and has lived in El Paso since his early childhood (his parents, who were in the military, were stationed in Germany). He has completed two years of college. Theresa, his wife, is a housewife and native El Pasoan who holds a high school diploma. Their friend Jacob is in the military and was born in Kansas forty-one years ago. All of them are Christians.

14. It is important to stress here that the narrative identities of African Americans who are native El Pasoans are quite different from the narratives of those who are not natives, and some of them do not use the hegemonic plot asserting that all poverty is Mexican. In the past, black families of El Paso were confined to an area in the Segundo Barrio. Many spoke Spanish well, married Mexicans, and so on. Because of the Jim Crow discriminatory laws, they had to use segregated bathrooms and parts of buses, as did Mexicans. These people often view Mexicans and Mexican Americans as allies and the Anglos as the "others." Besides, they were really happy living near Juárez, a city and a country where they were treated as plain citizens, not as second-class citizens, as in El Paso. I want to thank Howard Campbell for bringing this information to my attention.

15. A Mexican American, Albert was born twenty-eight years ago in a poor neighborhood in El Paso. Today, he is a professional with a college degree working in a maquiladora in Juárez. He currently lives in an upper-middle-class neighborhood on the west side of town, and he identifies himself as being Catholic.

16. Albert's comments are similar to those produced by some Anglo interviewees:

Larry: . . . the Segundo Barrio [where supposedly Chicanos live] I think that's just, you know, boundary of themselves, you know? Everybody always complains, you know, "Segundo Barrio, help them get out" and everything. But the thing is why don't they do anything about themselves . . . ?

Ultimately, Albert is following the local hegemonic discourse of blaming Mexicans for their own poverty.

17. According to some preliminary figures from a National Science Foundation project directed by Kathy Staudt and Cheryl Howard, only 1 percent of their sample called themselves Chicanos (Staudt, personal communication, June 18, 1995).

18. This group was composed of the following: Alfredo is forty-nine years old, a native of El Paso, a third-generation Mexican American, and a lawyer. His wife Fanny is forty-five years old, a native El Pasoan, a fourth-generation Mexican American, and an elementary school teacher; she has recently returned to college. Oscar is fifty-two years old, a native of El Paso, a third-generation Mexican American, and a federal employee who holds a high school diploma. Rosa is forty-seven years old. Born in Ysleta, she is a third-generation Mexican American; she is a substitute teacher who is still in college. Susana is nineteen years old, a native El Pasoan, a fourth-generation Mexican American, and a bank employee. Finally, Francis is twenty-six years old, a native El Pasoan, and a third-generation Mexican American. He is employed and holds a high school diploma. All these interviewees are Catholics.

19. Thus, not only Anglos, but also some Mexican Americans in the Southwest "distort" Spanish. According to Hill (1993), Anglos distort the language in order to construct Mexicans as contemptible "others." Similarly, some "Spaniards" in New Mexico distort Spanish names in order to construct the Mexican and the Mexican American as the "others."

20. Of course, many of these New Mexicans really can track their ancestors directly to Spain. What I want to address here is the point that the New Mexicans use such a plot to differentiate themselves from Mexicans, some of whom, for that matter, might track their roots directly to Spain as well.

21. This group was composed of the following: Armando, a thirty-one-year-old native El Pasoan second-generation Mexican American, has a bachelor's degree in administration and works in sales at a very important company in El Paso. Serafín, a forty-one-year-old second-generation native of El Paso, holds a high school diploma and runs a small shop in El Paso. Sergio, a first-

generation Mexican American native of El Paso, has finished high school and works as a mechanic. Saúl, a forty-two-year-old teacher born in El Paso, is pursuing his master's in education. His wife, Irene, who is thirty-nine years old, has completed her secondary education and is a clerk working with Serafín in his shop. She was born in California but moved to El Paso when she was two years old. And Gabriela, Saúl's sister, is a forty-two-year-old native El Pasoan who is a second-generation Mexican American pursuing her college degree. All of them are Catholics.

Chapter 4

1. These interviewees are in their thirties and have only recently arrived in El Paso from Juárez. Moreover, some of them still have some of their children living in Juárez (they are not yet *arreglados*), and some others live for extended periods of time on the Mexican side. They work as maids, factory workers, and in other low-wage jobs. They speak no English at all, and live in one of the poorest neighborhoods in El Paso. Norma was born in Durango, but lived for more than eighteen years in Juárez before moving to El Paso ten years ago. She has not finished her elementary education. María is a housewife who was born in Juárez and, like Norma, has not finished her elementary education. She has lived in El Paso for only three years. Estela is a little bit older; she is in her fifties, arrived in El Paso two years ago, has not finished her elementary education, and was born in Delicias, Chihuahua. Anabel has some secondary education, is from Cuauhtémoc, and works as a seamstress, either in El Paso or Juárez. All of them are Catholics.

2. "La Malinche" was the Indian woman who married Cortés and, the story goes, helped him to conquer Tenochtitlán. In the chapter about gender in my forthcoming book *Border Identities*, I offer a more detailed explanation of the complex relationship between gender identity, La Malinche, and Mexican identity on the U.S.–Mexico border.

3. Nora and Pilar were born in different Northern Mexican states. They are housewives in their middle thirties. Nora has been in the United States for the last seven years and Pilar for more than fifteen years. Nora has completed more than one hundred college hours of education, while Pilar only went through three years of secondary education. Francisca is Rosalba's mother; she is sixty-five years old and was born in Durango. She is illiterate. Rosalba is in her forties and works as a janitor in a department store. She was born in Jalisco and has been living in El Paso for more than fifteen years. Quica was born in New Mexico in 1944, but moved to El Paso when she was seven years old. She is a housewife, first-generation Mexican American who has completed high school. All these interviewees are Catholics.

4. A specific expression is frequently used to address this particular issue of the "hundred percent" Mexican-looking guy who brags that he has class and money or who tries to avoid being identified as Mexican: "¡*Se le notaba el nopal*

en la frente! [The cactus on his forehead was very prominent!]." This expression is habitually used by some Fronterizos in relation to Chilangos with *sangrón* attitudes (full of themselves), or in relation to Mexican Americans who try to hide their ethnic origin (usually by refusing to speak in Spanish). Of course the expression wants to address the Indian character of the person at stake, because the *nopal* is one of the most important symbolic markers of Aztec heritage.

5. In these meetings with the López family, we interviewed Horacio, who is a fifty-two-year-old native of Parral, Chihuahua, and who moved to El Paso twenty-five years ago. He is a plumber and completed his elementary education in Mexico. Mónica is Horacio's wife. She is also in her fifties and was born in Aguascalientes, Mexico. She is a housewife who completed her elementary education in Mexico. Rosenda is their daughter. She is a twenty-two-year-old clerk who holds a high school diploma and was born in Juárez but moved to El Paso more than twenty years ago. Rick is one of López' sons. He is a twenty-three-year-old native El Pasoan who is a freshman at UTEP. Guillermo is the other son. He is also a native El Pasoan, fifteen years old and finishing his high school education. Finally, Laura is the other daughter. She is twenty-four years old, was born in El Paso and works as a clerk. All these interviewees are Catholics.

6. We will encounter the López family again in the chapter about religion in *Border Identities*. In that chapter it will be clearer that the pro-Mexican attitude of the male branch of the family finally constructs the "American" as the "other."

7. Alex is a twenty-six-year-old native El Pasoan, a third-generation Mexican American who works as a clerk in a small store. He holds a high school diploma. Alicia is a twenty-four-year-old Mexican immigrant born in Ciudad Chihuahua, with six years of residence in the United States. She also holds a high school diploma. In spite of her brief residence in El Paso, she is very Americanized and already uses a lot of code switching, among other reasons because Alex is not fluent in Spanish. They live in "America," one of the poorest neighborhoods in El Paso, which, at the time of the interviews, was without sewage or running water. They are both Catholics.

8. The same mechanism of separating people from culture was used by many interviewees to explain how dangerous it is to drive a car in Juárez. Here, however, the argument reverses itself—Mexican Americans, bearers of the American culture of good driving, are transformed into virtual "Mexican drivers" when they cross the border! But the explanation remains the same: "why not do it if everyone is doing it . . . ?" Again, it is the culture and not the people that explains behavior. Hence, a simple geographical move can transform a safe driver into an unsafe one or, more importantly for our purposes, a poor Mexican national without dignity into a Mexican immigrant or a Mexican American with dignity.

9. Leticia was born in Northern Mexico forty-two years ago. She has a high school diploma and has taken some classes at the El Paso Community Col-

lege. She has been a worker for many years, and at the time of the interview was the director of the grass-roots organization at "America." Rosario is a fifty-year-old native of Ciudad Chihuahua who completed only half of her elementary education in Mexico. Sukis was born in El Paso twenty years ago. She is a housewife and has lived in Juárez a great part of her life. She holds a high school diploma. While Leticia and Rosario identify themselves as Catholics, Sukis is a Jehovah's Witness.

10. Without denying the different levels of wealth that distinguish Mexico from the United States, I want to point out that the plot stressing that "all poverty is Mexican" produces a "surplus" of meaning in the sense that it structures the social perception even of people who, like Alex and Alicia, are not precisely enjoying the "American dream," and whose economic situation is much worse than that of many poor Mexican nationals.

11. Humberto and Marta Pérez were described in Chapter 1. The Antunes family has been living in El Paso for more than twenty years. Elena, who is thirty-nine years old, works taking care of old people at their homes. She was born in Torreón, Coahuila, and finished her primary education in Mexico. Beatriz, who is fifty-one years old, Elisa, who is forty-nine years old, and Catalina, who is forty-two years old, are housewives. All of them were born in Chihuahua and have completed some secondary education. Carlos is a warehouse employee who is forty years old and who also was born in Chihuahua. Adriana was my UTEP student who helped me to arrange this interview. She is in her late twenties, a first-generation Mexican American born in El Paso. All of them have lived part of their lives in Ciudad Juárez and define themselves as Catholics.

12. The members of the Armendariz family present at the interview were Encarnación, a forty-nine-year-old bar owner who migrated from Delicias, Chihuahua, with her high school diploma, in 1975, and her daughter Ivette, a twenty-seven-year-old accountant born in El Paso and currently working at a maquiladora in Juárez. Both are Catholics.

Chapter 5

1. It seems that what I have found in El Paso–Ciudad Juárez is not an isolated case. According to an Associated Press article, the relationships between many Chicanos and Mexican immigrants in Phoenix are problematic as well. The article quotes a third-generation Mexican American as saying: "They're [Mexican immigrants] taking over the neighborhood . . . It's disgusting. They kill their goats and pigs in the yard and dump everything in the alley. One family will rent a house, and next thing you know, there are ten or twelve people living there. Then, people think we live just like them. It's awful." Another Mexican American stressed that "'we've put everything we got into our homes and our neighborhoods . . . Now, all this is being ruined by the Mexicans . . . They don't care about our street. They're here to make money and send it back to

their families in Mexico,' she complained, noting that their yards have no grass, the screen doors are coming off the hinges and newspapers cover some of the windows. 'It almost feels like we're living in Mexico,' she said." According to the article, "Immigrants have their own share of complaints against their assimilated brothers. The newcomers chastise the Chicanos . . . for speaking broken Spanish. The immigrants also consider Mexican-Americans to be traitors to their heritage and mock them for having coddled childhoods compared with the upbringing in Latin countries, where children are put to work at very young ages. What's more, many Latin American immigrants say they are treated rudely by U.S.-born Mexican-Americans . . . 'If you are an immigrant, they treat you like dogs,' Ocheita said" (*The Prospector*, April 24, 1995, pp. 1, 9).

2. *El Paso Times*, March 20, 1994, p. 1A and October 30, 1994, pp. 1A, 4A, and 5A.

3. This is a joke: Unite El Paso is a community proposal to build a metroplex with Ciudad Juárez.

4. Reading an early version of this chapter, Duncan Earle (personal communication, September 6, 1998) aptly noted that until the blockade was launched,

. . . it was far more necessary for legitimately authorized Mexican Americans to carry identification to prove their citizenship, and that had led to some serious conflicts . . . [after the blockade] those kinds of altercations are . . . far more rare. Reyes himself states that the opportunities for INS Border Patrol abuses diminished significantly, both because there were far fewer of the chase-and-subdue incidents but also, less opportunity to harass and abuse legal residents. Without [taking into account] these factors, the popularity of Reyes' plan can be reduced unfairly to hostility toward Mexicans in Juárez, of which this is not a very "clean" and uncomplicated example . . . [for Mexican Americans] the Blockade resonated with their need to mark more clearly Otherness because the border had become blurred, too much so for the Americanized Mexicans. Blurred so that they could not draw the line of prejudice with precision, itself a threat to identity integrity . . . the condition before the Blockade was less "bordered"—and such obvious failure of mapped spatial experience to fit with the emplotting ideology of the group was a threat. Likewise having papers checked. It was not just the humiliation, it was the disbordering, the threat of being undone through some error in the way one was arreglado, or some unknown rule; it hit people in the place of vulnerability: acculturation anxiety. To be suspects in your own country is hard on esteem.

5. The border patrol rapidly discovered that the original name, "Operation Blockade," was not well suited to support the negotiations around NAFTA that the American and Mexican governments were doing: it is not very polite to "blockade" a friendly country. Therefore, after about a month they changed the name to "Operation Hold the Line."

6. Jay Armes (born Juan Armas) was a city representative who in a council meeting denounced vendors who cross from Juárez to work El Paso streets

and who told Armando Dominguez: "You better go back to where you come from." "I'm from the United States, and I served in the Vietnam War," Dominguez retorted. "Where did you serve?" Armes answered: "The Boy Scouts."

7. Cheryl Howard, who was involved in the design of the survey, later wrote a paper with Carrillo and Peregrino using, among other things, the results from the survey.

8. Quoted in Howard, Carrillo, and Peregrino (1994, p. 3).

9. Of course we cannot take these comments as representative of the Juarenses' feelings toward the undocumented workers. These reports appeared in the El Paso paper, and it is quite possible that the *El Paso Times* would report that their "sister city" understands the situation perfectly.

10. Of course, not all the people in Juárez depicted the undocumented workers in the way this journalist did. Others were really alarmed at the lack of support the undocumented got from their "*paisanos*" on the Mexican side of the border: "But what is not fair is that our own people oppose our undocumented brothers. Because they have, in this side of the border, the same kind of documentation that each of us has. The only shameful difference is that they do not have jobs available in this side of the border" (Rodolfo Elías Cruz, *El Fronterizo*, October 1, 1993).

11. I do not want to claim that the blockade did not produce any change in criminality in El Paso. Auto theft and the incidence of residential burglaries and purse snatching/pickpocketing declined somewhat, above all in downtown El Paso. My basic point is that crime clearly did not decline according to the expectations of most El Pasoans, expectations that I link to the narrative plots I have being discussing throughout the book, which provide the "surplus" of meaning that, in many cases, equated any criminality with the presence of the despised "illegal alien."

12. The hospital responded to Fisher in a letter published on October 14, pointing out that from January through August 1993, the hospital averaged 20.5 deliveries per day. Between September 19, when the blockade began, and October 11, the average was 22.3 deliveries per day (*El Paso Times*, October 14, 1993).

Chapter 6

1. I thank Sue Carter for addressing this point to me.

2. Cristóbal, the father, has a small key shop near his house. He is forty-nine years old and came to Juárez from Zacatecas when he was nine years old. He has completed only his elementary education. Araceli, the mother, who is forty-five, works as a clerk in a local school. She received some technical training at a vocational school in Juárez. She and Diana, her daughter, are native Juarenses. Diana, who is eighteen years old, attends the University of Juárez. The whole family is Catholic and their narratives are analyzed in full in the chapter on class in my forthcoming book, *Border Identities*.

3. Reading an early version of this chapter, Howard Campbell commented that this type of discourse totally ignores class: "Obviously there are many poor Anglos and wealthy Mexicans in a large community like El Paso–Juárez. For Chicanos or anyone else to claim that they are always the victims is disingenuous and anthropologically suspect" (personal communication, May 14, 1997).

4. In El Paso, this means a system that is racist and classist in particularly complex ways, because, for instance, not knowing Spanish in El Paso is often an economic liability, as several of my Anglo interviewees pointed out many times in our encounters. Those complaints can consist of a "mild" criticism like the one Arthur advanced:

> I know a dozen, a dozen people that have moved here in the last four years, friends of mine, and their wives, their wives have looked for jobs for weeks and weeks and they can't get them because they're not bilingual. And this is America! It shouldn't be a prerequisite to get a job!

Complaints also may include fierce racist grievances such as the one a letter writer expressed:

> *Preferential hiring.* When I see an employment ad requiring a "bilingual" applicant, it really means Hispanics are preferred. Some of them working in public offices understand what they are saying; many do not. As a result, they cannot make intelligent decisions or solve problems. When it comes to spelling, they murder the simplest words and think last names are first names . . . (Janice M. Westerholm, Las Cruces. *El Paso Times*, May 15, 1997)

5. We have to remember here that because many of El Paso's African Americans are in the military, they have more income and more education than many Mexican American El Pasoans. In early 1997 a fight at Austin High School between African Americans and Mexican Americans broke out between the "poor Mexican American native El Pasoans" and the "rich African American outsiders." Austin High School is the school where military children from Fort Bliss attend class.

Appendix

1. The way I am using the concept of interpellation has various sources. First, Althusser's original definition can be found in *Lenin and Philosophy and Other Essays* (1971, p. 174). Throughout the book, I have used the term as a general way to describe the process of "hailing into place" or "summoning into place" of the individual as the social subject of particular discourses. The basic idea behind Althusser's definition is that individuals, who are simple bearers of structures, are transformed by ideology into subjects, namely, that they believe they themselves were the autonomous principle of those structures (Laclau 1979, p. 100). The mechanism of this characteristic inversion is interpellation, a very precise operation of addressing or hailing.

The problem with Althusser's idea is that the constitution of subjectivity is indissolubly related to the ideological constitution of subjection. This is to say: the acquisition of subjectivity and subjection to authority are simultaneously achieved through ideological interpellation. To avoid this "reproductivist" aspect of Althusser's definition, Ernesto Laclau (1979), Emilio de Ipola (1982), and Goran Therborn (1980), among others, have tried to probe the possibility of alternative interpellations. As Laclau points out (1979, pp. 100–102):

> The mechanism of interpellation as constitutive of ideology operates in the same way in ideologies of dominant classes and in revolutionary ideologies. As de Ipola points out: "A juridical (and rhetorical) figure, interpellation may be detected both in a Christian religious discourse and in humanist discourse, and even in communist discourse such as that of the Communist Manifesto ('Workers of all countries unite!'). In some cases, interpellation of 'subjects' will be the concealed form of effectively ensuring a subjection; in others, by contrast, as in the Communist Manifesto, it will take the form of a political slogan which calls for the creation of conditions for the emancipation of the exploited."

However, I think that these authors have not solved the problem of the existence of a privileged subject in the source of discourses able to interpellate people. In this sense, if dominant ideology transforms individuals into subjects who live the relation with their real conditions of existence as if they themselves were the autonomous principle of determination of that relation, then revolutionary ideology necessarily also transforms individuals into subjects who live the relation with their real possibilities of change as if they themselves were the autonomous principle of determination of this relation, when they are not. I think that to solve this problem we have to move from the notion of interpellation toward the more intricate relationship between social categories, interpellations, metaphors, and narrative identities, which I will address below.

2. As noted in Chapter 4, the term "*malinchista*" comes from La Malinche, Cortés' mistress who, supposedly, helped the Spaniard to conquer Mexico. The relationship between La Malinche and treachery is discussed in the chapter about gender in my forthcoming book, *Border Identities*. The term "*pocho*" is usually used to refer to Mexican Americans who are highly Americanized. In *some* circumstances it can also mean treachery, but it can also be an affectionate nickname that, for instance, grandparents living in Mexico use to address their grandsons or granddaughters visiting them: "*mi pochita*."

Alegría Olazábal, Tito. 1992. *Desarrollo urbano en la frontera México–Estados Unidos*. Mexico City: Consejo Nacional para la Cultura y las Artes.

Alonso, Ana María. 1995. *Thread of Blood. Colonialism, Revolution, and Gender on Mexico's Northern Frontier*. Tucson: University of Arizona Press.

Althusser, Louis. 1971. *Lenin and Philosophy and Other Essays*. New York: Monthly Review Press.

Anderson, Benedict. 1983. *Imagined Communities. Reflections on the Origin and Spread of Nationalism*. London: Verso.

Anzaldúa, Gloria. 1987. *Borderlands/La Frontera: The New Mestiza*. San Francisco: Aunt Lute Books.

Barthes, Roland. 1991. *Camera Lucida: Reflections on Photography*. New York: Noonday Press.

Baudrillard, Jean. 1983. *In the Shadow of the Silent Majorities*. New York: Semiotext(e).

Bean, Frank D., Roland Chanove, Robert G. Cushing, Rodolfo de la Garza, Gary P. Freeman, Charles W. Haynes, and David Spener. 1994. "Illegal Mexican Migration and the United States/Mexico Border: The Effects of Operation Hold the Line on El Paso/Juárez." Research paper presented at the U.S. Commission on Immigration Reform, Population Research Center, University of Texas at Austin.

Berger, John. 1980. "Understanding a Photograph," pp. 291–294 in *Classic Essays on Photography*, edited by Alan Trachtenberg. New Haven, Conn.: Leete's Island Books.

Bhavnani, Kum-Kum, and Donna Haraway. 1994. "Shifting the Subject. A Conversation between Kum-Kum Bhavnani and Donna Haraway on 12 April 1993, Santa Cruz, California," pp. 19–39 in *Shifting Identities, Shifting Racisms: A Feminism and Psychology Reader*, edited by Kum-Kum Bhavnani and Ann Phoenix. London: Sage.

Bhavnani, Kum-Kum, and Ann Phoenix. 1994. "Shifting Identities. Shifting Racisms. An Introduction," pp. 5–18 in *Shifting Identities, Shifting Racisms. A Feminism and Psychology Reader*, edited by Kum-Kum Bhavnani and Ann Phoenix. London: Sage.

Bourdieu, Pierre. 1984. *Distinction: A Social Critique of the Judgment of Taste*. Cambridge, Mass.: Harvard University Press.

——. 1990a. *The Logic of Practice*. Stanford, Calif.: Stanford University Press.

——. 1990b. *Photography. A Middle-Brow Art*. Stanford, Calif.: Stanford University Press.

Brah, Avtar. 1992. "Difference, diversity and differentiation," pp. 126–145 in *Race, Culture and Difference*, edited by James Donald and Ali Rattansi. London: Sage.

BIBLIOGRAPHY

Bruner, Edward M. 1993. "Introduction: The Ethnographic Self and the Personal Self," pp. 1–26 in *Anthropology and Literature*, edited by Paul Benson. Urbana: University of Illinois Press.

Bruner, Jerome. 1987. "Life as Narrative." *Social Research* 54 (1): 11–32.

Bureau of Business and Economic Research, University of Texas at El Paso. 1992. *Preliminary Results*. El Paso: University of Texas at El Paso.

Burke, Kenneth. 1966. *Language as Symbolic Action*. Berkeley: University of California Press.

Bustamante, Jorge. 1983. *Tensiones sociales en la frontera norte y en la ciudad de México*. Tijuana: Centro de Estudios de la Frontera Norte de México.

Butler, Judith. 1990. *Gender Trouble*. New York: Routledge.

Calhoun, Craig. 1994. "Social Theory and the Politics of Identity," pp. 9–36 in *Social Theory and the Politics of Identity*, edited by Craig Calhoun. Cambridge, Mass.: Blackwell.

Campbell, Howard, et al. 1993. *Zapotec Struggles*. Washington, D.C.: Smithsonian Institution Press.

Clough, Patricia Ticineto. 1994. *Feminist Thought*. Cambridge, Mass.: Blackwell.

Crocker, J. Christopher. 1977. "My Brother the Parrot," pp. 164–192 in *The Social Use of Metaphor*, edited by J. Christopher Crocker and J. David Sapir. Philadelphia: University of Pennsylvania Press.

de Ipola, Emilio. 1982. *Ideología y discurso populista*. Mexico City: Folios Ediciones.

Derrida, Jacques. 1978. *Writing and Difference*. London: Routledge and Kegan Paul.

Elias, Norbert. 1991. *The Society of Individuals*. Oxford: Basil Blackwell.

Fernández, James W. 1986. *Persuasions and Performances: The Play of Tropes in Culture*. Bloomington: Indiana University Press.

———. 1991. "Introduction: Confluents of Inquiry," pp. 1–13 in *Beyond Metaphor. The Theory of Tropes in Anthropology*, edited by James W. Fernández. Stanford, Calif.: Stanford University Press.

Foley, Douglas E. 1990. *Learning Capitalist Culture. Deep in the Heart of Tejas*. Philadelphia: University of Pennsylvania Press.

Foucault, Michel. 1970. *The Order of Things: An Archaeology of the Human Sciences*. New York: Vintage.

Friedrich, Paul. 1991. "Polytropy," pp. 17–55 in *Beyond Metaphor. The Theory of Tropes in Anthropology*, edited by James W. Fernández. Stanford, Calif.: Stanford University Press.

García Canclini, Néstor. 1990. *Culturas híbridas*. Mexico City: Grijalbo.

Gergen, Kenneth J., and Mary M. Gergen. 1983. "Narratives of the Self," pp. 254–273 in *Studies in Social Identity*, edited by Theodore R. Sarbin and Karl E. Scheibe. New York: Praeger.

Giddens, Anthony. 1984. *The Constitution of Society: Outline of the Theory of Structuration*. Cambridge, Mass.: Polity Press.

Goodman, Nelson. 1978. *Ways of Worldmaking*. Indianapolis: Hackett.

Gramsci, Antonio. 1971. *Selections from the Prison Notebooks*. Translated and edited by Quintin Hoare and Geoffrey Nowell-Smith. London: Lawrence and Wishart.

——. 1975. *Quaderni del carcere*. Turin: Valentino Gerratana.

Hall, Stuart. 1996. "Introduction: Who Needs 'Identity'?" pp. 1–17 in *Questions of Cultural Identity*, edited by Stuart Hall and Paul du Gay. London: Sage.

Haraway, Donna. 1985. "A Manifesto for Cyborgs: Science, Technology, and Socialist Feminism in the 1980s." *Socialist Review* 15(2): 65–108.

Hawkesworth, Mary. 1989. "Knowers, Knowing, Known: Feminist Theory and Claims of Truth." *Signs* 14(3): 533–549.

Hidalgo, Margarita. 1995. "Language and Ethnicity in the 'Taboo' Region: The U.S.–Mexico Border." *International Journal of the Sociology of Language* 114: 29–45.

Hill, Jane H. 1993. "Hasta la Vista, Baby: Anglo Spanish in the American Southwest." *Critique of Anthropology* 13(2): 145–176.

Howard, Cheryl, Irma Carrillo, and Sylvia Peregrino. 1994. "Operation Blockade: A Tale of Two Cities." Paper presented at the Western Social Science Association, Albuquerque, N.M., April 22.

Institute of Manufacturing and Material Management. 1991. *Paso del Norte Regional Economy. Socioeconomic Profile*. El Paso: Institute for Manufacturing and Materials Management, University of Texas at El Paso.

Jakobson, Roman, and Morris Halle. 1956. *Fundamentals of Language*. The Hague: Mouton.

Johnson, Mark. 1987. *The Body in the Mind: The Bodily Basis of Meaning, Imagination, and Reason*. Chicago: University of Chicago Press.

Kearney, Michael. 1991. "Borders and Boundaries of State and Self at the End of Empire." *Journal of Historical Sociology* 4(1): 52–74.

Kerby, Anthony Paul. 1991. *Narrative and the Self*. Bloomington: Indiana University Press.

Labov, William. 1972. "The Transformation of Experience in Narrative Syntax," pp. 354–396 in *Language in the Inner City: Studies in the Black English Vernacular*, edited by William Labov. Philadelphia: University of Pennsylvania Press.

——. 1982. "Speech Actions and Reactions in Personal Narrative," pp. 219–247 in *Analyzing Discourse: Text and Talk*, edited by D. Tannen. Washington, D.C.: Georgetown University Press.

Laclau, Ernesto. 1979. *Politics and Ideology in Marxist Theory*. London: Verso.

——. 1991. *New Reflections on the Revolution of Our Time*. London: Verso.

Laclau, Ernesto, and Chantal Mouffe. 1985. *Hegemony and Socialist Strategy: Towards a Radical Democratic Politics*. London: Verso.

——. 1987. "Post-Marxism without Apologies." *New Left Review* 166: 79–106.

Lakoff, George. 1987. *Women, Fire, and Dangerous Things: What Categories Reveal about the Mind*. Chicago: University of Chicago Press.

Lakoff, George, and Mark Johnson. 1980a. "Conceptual Metaphor in Everyday Language." *The Journal of Philosophy* 77(8): 453–486.

——. 1980b. *Metaphors We Live By*. Chicago: University of Chicago Press.

Lau, Rubén. 1986. "Ciudad Juárez: Grupos de presión y fuerzas políticas," pp. 5–66 in *Sistema político y democracia en Chihuahua*. Ciudad Juárez: Instituto de

Investigaciones Sociales de la UNAM, Universidad Autónoma de Ciudad Juárez.

Lévi-Strauss, Claude. 1966. *The Savage Mind*. Translated by George Weidenfeld and Nicolson Ltd. Chicago: University of Chicago Press.

Lincoln, Yvonna S., and Norman K. Denzin. 1994. "The Fifth Moment," pp. 575–586 in *Handbook of Qualitative Research*, edited by Norman K. Denzin and Yvonna S. Lincoln. Thousand Oaks, Calif.: Sage.

Lorey, David E., ed. 1993. *United States–Mexico Border Statistics Since 1900–1990 Update*. Los Angeles: UCLA Latin American Center Publications, University of California.

Lozano, José Carlos. 1990. "Identidad nacional en la frontera norte." Paper presented at COLEF-1, Tijuana, El Colegio de la Frontera Norte.

Marcus, George E., and Dick Cushman. 1982. "Ethnographies as texts." *Annual Review of Anthropology* 2: 25–69.

Marcus, George E., and Michael M. J. Fisher. 1986. *Anthropology as Cultural Critique: An Experimental Moment in the Human Sciences*. Chicago: University of Chicago Press.

Martínez, Oscar J. 1986. "The Foreign Orientation of the Ciudad Juárez Economy," pp. 141–151 in *The Social Ecology and Economic Development of Ciudad Juárez*, edited by Young Gay. Boulder: Westview.

——. 1994. *Border People. Life and Society in the U.S.–Mexico Borderlands*. Tucson: The University of Arizona Press.

Mead, George H. 1934. *Mind, Self, and Society*. University of Chicago Press.

Minh-ha, Trinh T. 1990. *Framer Framed*. New York: Routledge.

Mishler, Elliot G. 1986. "The Analysis of Interviews-Narratives," pp. 233–255 in *Narrative Psychology: The Storied Nature of Human Conduct*, edited by Theodore R. Sarbin. New York: Praeger.

Monsiváis, Carlos. 1981. "La cultura de la frontera," pp. 289–310 in *Estudios fronterizos. Reunión de universidades de México y Estados Unidos (ponencias y comentarios)*. Mexico City: ANUIS.

Mouffe, Chantal. 1985. "Hegemony and Ideology in Gramsci," pp. 219–234 in *Culture, Ideology and Social Process: A Reader*, edited by Tony Bennett et al. London: Open University Press.

Novitz, David. 1989. "Art, Narrative, and Human Nature." *Philosophy and Literature* 13(1): 57–74.

Ortner, Sherry. 1973. "On Key Symbols." *American Anthropologist* 75(6): 1338–1346.

Parker, Ian. 1989. "Discourse and Power," pp. 56–69 in *Texts of Identity*, edited by John Shotter and Kenneth J. Gergen. London: Sage.

Polkinghorne, Donald E. 1988. *Narrative Knowing and the Human Sciences*. Albany: State University of New York Press.

Probyn, Elspeth. 1993. *Sexing the Self: Gendered Positions in Cultural Studies*. New York: Routledge.

Quinn, Naomi. 1991. "The Cultural Basis of Metaphor," pp. 56–93 in *Beyond*

Metaphor. The Theory of Tropes in Anthropology, edited by James W. Fernández. Stanford, Calif.: Stanford University Press.

Rabinow, Paul. 1985. "Discourse and Power: On the Limits of Ethnographic Texts." *Dialectical Anthropology* 10(1 & 2): 1–13.

Reagan, Charles E. 1993. "The Self as an Other." *Philosophy Today* 37(1): 3–22.

Ricoeur, Paul. 1984. *Time and Narrative.* Vol. 1. Translated by Kathleen McLaughlin and David Pellauer. Chicago: University of Chicago Press.

———. 1992. *Oneself as Another.* Translated by Kathleen Blamey. Chicago: University of Chicago Press.

Riessman, Catherine Kohler. 1993. *Narrative Analysis.* Newbury Park, Calif.: Sage.

Rorty, Richard. 1990. "Feminism and Pragmatism." *Michigan Quarterly Review* 30: 231–258.

Rosaldo, Michelle. 1972. "Metaphor and Folk Classification." *Southwestern Journal of Anthropology* 28(1): 83–99.

Rosaldo, Renato. 1989. *Culture and Truth: The Remaking of Social Analysis.* Boston: Beacon Press.

———. 1994. "Race and Other Inequalities: The Borderlands in Arturo Isla's *Migrant Souls*," pp. 213–225 in *Race*, edited by Steven Gregory and Roger Sanjek. New Brunswick, N.J.: Rutgers University Press.

Rosenau, Pauline Marie. 1992. *Post-Modernism and the Social Sciences.* Princeton, N.J.: Princeton University Press.

Rosenblum, Karen E., and Toni-Michelle C. Travis. 1996. *The Meaning of Difference. American Constructions of Race, Sex and Gender, Social Class, and Sexual Orientation.* New York: McGraw-Hill.

Rosenwald, George C. 1992. "Conclusion: Reflections on Narrative Self-Understanding," pp. 265–289 in *Storied Lives: The Cultural Politics of Self-Understanding*, edited by George C. Rosenwald and Richard L. Ochberg. New Haven, Conn.: Yale University Press.

Rosenwald, George C., and Richard L. Ochberg. 1992. "Introduction: Life Stories, Cultural Politics, and Self-Understanding," pp. 1–18 in *Storied Lives: The Cultural Politics of Self-Understanding*, edited by George C. Rosenwald and Richard L. Ochberg. New Haven, Conn.: Yale University Press.

Ruiz, Vicki L. 1987. "By the Day or the Week: Mexicana Domestic Workers in El Paso," pp. 61–76 in *Women on the U.S.–Mexico Border. Responses to Change*, edited by Vicki L. Ruiz and Susan Tiano. Boston: Allen and Unwin.

Said, Edward. 1979. *Orientalism.* New York: Vintage.

Sampson, Edward E. 1989. "The Deconstruction of the Self," pp. 1–19 in *Texts of Identity*, edited by John Shotter and Kenneth J. Gergen. London: Sage.

Sapir, J. David. 1977. "The Anatomy of Metaphor," pp. 3–32 in *The Social Use of Metaphor*, edited by J. Christopher Crocker and J. David Sapir. Philadelphia: University of Pennsylvania Press.

Sarbin, Theodore. 1986. "Introduction and Overview," pp. ix–xviii in *Narrative Psychology: The Storied Nature of Human Conduct*, edited by Theodore R. Sarbin. New York: Praeger.

Sewell, William H. 1992. "Introduction: Narratives and Social Identities." *Social Science History* 16(3): 479–488.

Somers, Margaret R. 1992. "Special Section: Narrative Analysis in Social Science, Part 2. Narrativity, Narrative Identity, and Social Action: Rethinking English Working-Class Formation." *Social Science History* 16(4): 591–630.

——. 1994. "The Narrative Constitution of Identity: A Relational and Network Approach." *Theory and Society* 23(5): 605–649.

Spivak, Gayatri Chakravorty. 1988. "Can the Subaltern Speak?" pp. 271–313 in *Marxism and the Interpretation of Culture*, edited by Gary Nelson and Lawrence Grossberg. Urbana: University of Illinois Press.

Stoddard, Ellwyn R., and John Hedderson. 1989. *Patterns of Poverty along the U.S.–Mexico Border*. Las Cruces: Joint Border Research Institute, New Mexico State University.

Taylor, Charles. 1989. *Sources of the Self. The Making of the Modern Identity*. Cambridge, Mass.: Harvard University Press.

Tedlock, Dennis. 1983. "The analogical tradition and the emergence of a dialogical anthropology," pp. 321–338 in *The Spoken Word and the Work of Interpretation*. Philadelphia: University of Pennsylvania Press.

Therborn, Goran. 1980. *The Ideology of Power and the Power of Ideology*. London: Verso.

Teschner, Richard V. 1995. "Beachheads, Islands, and Conduits: Spanish Monolingualism and Bilingualism in El Paso, Texas." *International Journal of the Sociology of Language* 114: 93–105.

Tobin, Joseph, and Dana Davidson. 1990. "The Ethics of Polyvocal Ethnography: Empowering vs. Textualizing Children and Teachers." *Qualitative Studies in Education* 3(3): 271–283.

Turner, Victor. 1974. *Dramas, Fields and Metaphors*. Ithaca, N.Y.: Cornell University Press.

Tyler, Stephen A. 1986. "Post-Modern Ethnography: From Document of the Occult to Occult Document," pp. 122–140 in *Writing Culture. The Poetics and Politics of Ethnography*, edited by James Clifford and George E. Marcus. Berkeley: University of California Press.

Valenzuela, José Manuel 1988. *¡A la brava ése! Cholos, Punks, Chavos Banda*. Tijuana, México: El Colegio de la Frontera Norte.

van Dijk, Teun A. 1993. "Stories and Racism," pp. 121–142 in *Narrative and Social Control: Critical Perspectives*, edited by Dennis K. Mumby. Newbury Park, Calif.: Sage.

Vélez-Ibáñez, Carlos G. 1996. *Border Visions. Mexican Cultures of the Southwest United States*. Tucson: The University of Arizona Press.

Vila, Pablo. 1985. "Rock Nacional. Crónicas de la resistencia juvenil," pp. 83–148 in *Los nuevos movimientos sociales/1. Mujeres. Rock Nacional*, edited by Elizabeth Jelín. Buenos Aires: Centro Editor de América Latina. Colección Biblioteca Política Argentina No. 124.

——. 1987. "Rock *Nacional* and dictatorship in Argentina." *Popular Music* 6(2): 129–148.

——. 1989. "Argentina's Rock *Nacional*: The Struggle for Meaning." *Latin American Music Review* 10(1): 1–28.

——. 1995. "Le tango et la formation des identités ethniques en Argentine," pp. 77–107 in *Tango Nomade. Études sur le tango transculturel*, edited by Ramón Pelinski. Montreal: Triptyque.

——. 1996. *Catholicism and Identity in the U.S.–México Border*. El Paso: University of Texas at El Paso. Chicano Studies, Occasional Papers in Chicano Studies no. 8.

——. 1997a. "Hacia una reconsideración de la antropología visual como metodología de investigación social." *Estudios sobre las Culturas Contemporáneas* 3(6): 125–167.

——. 1997b. "Narrative Identities: The Emplotment of the Mexican on the U.S.–Mexico Border." *The Sociological Quarterly* 38(1): 147–183.

Volosinov, V. N. 1973. *Marxism and the Philosophy of Language*. New York: Seminar Press.

Weedon, Chris. 1989. *Feminist Practice and Poststructuralist Theory*. Oxford: Basil Blackwell.

White, Hayden. 1981. "The Value of Narrativity in the Representation of Reality," pp. 1–24 in *On Narrative*, edited by W. J. T. Mitchell. Chicago: University of Chicago Press.

Wilson, Thomas M., and Hastings Donnan, eds. 1998. *Border Identities. Nation and State at International Frontiers*. Cambridge, U.K.: Cambridge University Press.

Zerubavel, Eviatar. 1991. *The Fine Line*. New York: Free Press.

Mexicans as *arregladas/os*, 33, 71,
77–78, 185, 255n.10, 262n.1,
265n.4
Mexicans as warm and wet, 62
"in Puebla people piss holy water,"
243
"*se le notaba el nopal en la frente*," 136,
262–263n.4
"sister cities," 10, 63–68, 80, 124,
127, 168, 233
methodology of the research, 2–4,
252–253n.9
Mexican Americans, 258n.1
as "brothers/sisters" with Fron-
terizas/os, 67–68, 127, 168,
182
ethnic loyalty among, 1, 106–107;
lack of, 131–134, 177
first and second generation: criticisms of, 111–124; portrayed as
the "others," 111–124
housewives as *fijadas* and worse
than Anglo housewives, 71
lack of common ethnic morals and
values of, 115
pride in U.S. military service, 123
as primarily "Americans," 123, 132,
136, 180
should help Mexicans but do not,
70–71, 135–137
third and fourth generation: and
"ideal" Mexico of the past, 112–
124; pride in Mexican heritage,
112, 115, 117–118
who claim that they "hate" Mexicans and they are not Mexicans
anymore, 121, 180–181
who do not want more Mexican
immigration, 75
who forget and/or reject their
Mexican heritage, 134, 136,
177, 180–181
Mexican Americans criticized as
"bastards" and egoist, 70, 74–75

changing identities and abandoning Spanish names, 73
lacking high morals of Mexican
immigrants, 132
lazy, alcoholics, drug addicts, drug
dealers, thieves, mentally disturbed, prone to crime, gang
members, 73, 100–101, 118–
119, 132, 134
living on welfare, 117–118, 130–
135, 177
mistreating and discriminating
against Mexican nationals and
immigrants, 69–72, 74–75,
135–137, 138, 177, 180–181,
264–265n.1
unwilling to speak Spanish, 136–
137, 146
Mexican Americans portrayed as
having an inferiority complex and
low self-esteem, 73
lacking identity and not being
either Mexicans or Americans,
73, 123, 177
not being "real" Mexicans, 72, 107
the "others," 11–12, 63–75,
130–135
pochos, 68–75, 106–107, 146, 147,
183, 268n.2
sangrones, 69, 262–263n.4
sharing some positive characteristics with Mexican nationals,
62–63
those to whom the "all poverty is
Mexican" thematic plot should
apply, 130–135
very similar to Fronterizas/os,
63–66, 127
Mexican ethnics and Mexican nationals, blurring of differences between, 86–101, 130–135, 142
Mexican immigrants, 258n.1
constantly mixing classification
systems, 129–130, 135, 147–148

material effects of, 192
and perception of photographs, 4, 97, 99, 154–155, 193–225
and perception of reality, 4, 15, 174, 188–190, 192–225, 234–235, 242–243, 245–248
providing "coherence" to portraying of self, 234, 247–248
re-articulation of, 215–217
and re-emplotment of previous experiences, 207–208, 215–217, 218–219
relation of, to social categories, interpellations, and tropes, 15, 80, 234–235, 239–243, 245–247, 267–268n.1
as stereotypes, 89
narrative plots, most important
"All Juárez' social problems and poverty are related to people from Southern Mexico," 19, 32–38, 43, 53, 135, 164–165, 195–206
"All poverty and social problems are Mexican," 11, 19, 52–53, 68, 83–84, 86–127, 130, 137–140, 155, 160–165, 169–177, 206–207, 215–222, 259–260n.9, 261n.16, 264n.10
"All poverty is Mexican due to the discriminatory character of American society," 105–109
"All poverty is Mexican national," 109–111, 148–153, 161–163, 200
"All poverty relates to undocumented Mexicans," 163
"American poverty is provisional due to governmental assistance," 156–157
"Americans are slaves of consumerism and their work attitudes," 56–61
in Ciudad Juárez, x, 15, 247

"The differences between Mexicans and Mexican Americans are due to the country of residence," 148–153
in El Paso, x, 15, 247
"If a Mexican is caught by the border patrol, it is better if the agent is an Anglo than if it is a Mexican American," 69–70
"If Mexicans have money it is due to their corruption and delinquent activities," 92
"Juarenses do not work at maquiladoras, only immigrants do," 37–38, 47, 198
"Mexican Americans are less Catholic than Mexican nationals," 251–252n.8
"Mexican immigrants do work and do not use welfare," 130–135
"Mexican nationals act differently in Mexico than they do in the U.S.," 149–150
"Mexicans are good people; the problem is Mexico and Mexican culture," 149–153, 263n.8
"Mexicans are poor because they are lazy and not work oriented," 89, 91–92, 101, 111
"Poverty in El Paso is the product of the presence of Mexicans in the U.S.," 92
"Poverty is everywhere, and not uniquely Mexican," 92–96, 137–138, 153–160
"Real Mexicans were those of the past," 111–124
"Southern Mexicans are drunks and lazy," 32–36
"Southern Mexicans are more Catholic than Fronterizos," 241–243, 251–252n.8
"Southern Mexicans are the real criminals in Juárez," 36–38

"There is no American poverty (or it is less extreme than Mexican poverty) because of governmental help," 156–157, 162–163
narratives
articulatory elements in, 243–244, 247–248, 251–252n.8
complete. *See* short stories
as cultural artifacts that bias vision, 13, 192–225
as "evidence," 239
and experience, 15, 191–192, 247–248
as plagued by categories, 238
as supporting connotations of categories and metaphors, 239, 242–243
truncated or unfinished, 236
narrative themes. *See* narrative plots
Negrete, Jorge, 42–43, 53, 256n.20
non-narrative descriptions as narrative-laden, 131, 240, 242–243
Norteñas/os, 9, 22–26, 43–45
Northerners. *See* Norteñas/os
Northern New Mexicans, 121–122
Novitz, David, 236, 239, 247

Ochberg, Richard L., 127, 224, 244, 247, 248
Operación Respeto, Operación Dignidad, 184
Operation Blockade, 1, 167–168
as anti-Mexican/anti-Hispanic, 174–175, 265nn.4–5
Catholic Church opposition to, 179–180
Ciudad Juárez reaction to, 12, 181–186
economic advantages of, 170, 172
El Paso's opposition to, 178–181
El Paso's support of, 1, 2, 8, 12, 85, 167–177, 265n.4
polls about, 1, 2, 181, 251n.2

as promoting intolerance in El Paso, 178–179
results of, 13, 186–189, 266nn.11–12
as solving all social problems of the city, 169–177, 187–188, 189–190, 260n.11, 266nn.11–12
Operation Hold the Line, 251n.1, 265n.5. *See also* Operation Blockade
Ortner, Sherry, 232
"otherness," 87–89, 91, 124–127, 223, 229, 231, 265n.4. *See also* Americans; Central Americans; Chicanas/os; Chilangas/os; Juarenses; Mexican Americans; Mexican immigrants; Mexican nationals; Mexicans; *pochas/os*; Sureñas/os

Parker, Ian, 230, 231
Peirce, Charles, 236
perceptual experience, structuring of, 4
Peregrino, Sylvia, 168, 181, 188, 266n.8
Phoenix, Ann, 14
photographs, common sense perception of, 3, 4, 97
photo-interviewing technique, 2–4
pochas/os, 10, 68, 106–107, 146, 147
Polkinghorne, Donald E., 197, 223, 235, 236, 243, 246, 247
poststructuralism, 227–228
poverty
as different from laziness, dirtiness, and messiness, 34, 94
with dignity, 34, 119, 133–134, 150–151
extreme, as Mexican, 110–111, 152–153, 161, 162–163
as foreign, 110, 151–153
interviewees differentiating degrees of, 110–111, 151–153

about Mexican Americans' desire
to be accepted by Whites, 216
about Mexican Americans' discriminatory attitudes toward
Mexican nationals, 71, 130,
136, 216
about Mexican immigrant children
and their demanding and disrespectful attitude toward America, 118
about Mexican immigrants and
first generation Mexican Americans taking advantage of welfare system, 119
about Mexican immigrants' difference from Mexican Americans,
142
about Mexican nationals avoiding
contact with Mexican immigrants, 144
about Mexican nationals being
dirty in Mexico but not in
El Paso, 149–150
about Mexican nationals complain-
ing naturalized Mexican immigrants will be disloyal to Mexico, 143–144
about Mexican nationals not having the high values and morals
of third and fourth generation
Mexican Americans, 113–114,
176
about New Mexicans discriminating against Mexican Americans,
122
about Tarahumaras not being
really Catholic, 241–242
about an ugly, shaggy, pockmarked
gentleman who was well educated, 207–208
sister cities, as a metaphor of connection and similarity, 10, 63–68,
80, 124, 127, 233
social categories, 5, 227–232

social identities. *See* identities
socioeconomic data of region, 16–19
Somers, Margaret R., 5, 238, 243, 244,
247
Southern Mexicans. *See* Sureñas/os
Spanish
identity in New Mexico, 122,
261n.19
as signifying Mexican in El Paso,
83, 259n.6
as signifying poverty in El Paso,
83, 259nn.6–7
Spivak, Gayatri Chakravorty, 19, 228,
229
Stoddard, Ellwyn R., 18, 19
stories. *See also* narrative plots; short
stories
construction of "better," 14, 223
function of, 3
structural conditions, and narratives,
15, 19, 100. *See also* socioeconomic data of region
structure of the book, 9–15
subjectivity, 228–229, 247
subject positions, vii
as cultural constructions, 230–231
overlapping of different, ix, 51, 62,
82–83, 85, 90, 114, 141–148,
164–165, 204, 222–223. *See also*
identities, overlapping of
process of negotiation of, 230
as spaces of struggle about meaning, 227–228
Sureñas/os
negative characteristics of, 32–39,
46–49, 53, 55–56, 135, 164–
165, 176–177, 199, 222
rejected by Juarenses, 46–48,
164–165
Sureñas/os portrayed as
ancestors of Mexican Americans,
72
"brown," 24–27
Chilangos, 29, 39

the despised "others," 9, 10, 13,
22–26, 32–38, 45–49, 51,
53, 55–56, 72–73, 164–165,
195–206
illegal aliens, 13, 185
Indians, 22, 24–27, 56
maquiladora workers, 37–38, 47,
164, 198
systems of classification. *See* categorical systems

Tarahumaras, 28, 241–243
taxonomies. *See* categorical systems
Taylor, Charles, 238, 239, 247
Tedlock, Dennis, 191
Teschner, Richard V., 17
theoretical approach, 14–15
Therborn, Goran, 267–268n.1
"Third World country versus First
World country," 11, 67, 88,
124–127, 233–234
time span of the research, 2
Tobin, Joseph, 191
Travis, Toni-Michelle C., 5
tropes
analogical, 233
of contiguity, 233–234
inventory, 233–234
as organizing experience, 232,
242–243
sister cities as, 10, 63–68, 80, 124
"Third World country versus First
World country," 11, 67, 88,
124–127, 233–234

use of, in identity construction, 15,
232–235
Turner, Victor, 232
Tyler, Stephen A., 191

underdevelopment. *See* "Third World
country versus First World
country"

Valenzuela, José Manuel, 256n.18
van Dijk, Teun A., 131, 240
Vélez-Ibáñez, Carlos, 6
Veracruzanos, 47–48
Vila, Pablo, 5, 7, 8, 9, 19, 20, 81, 82,
83, 84, 85, 86, 92, 97, 100, 101,
105, 109, 112, 113, 137, 138,
231, 232, 236, 239, 240, 242,
244, 246, 251n.4, 254n.11
Volosinov, V. N., 228

war against Apaches, 24, 26
Weedon, Chris, 227
welfare
Mexican Americans: abusing, 132;
living off, 117, 130–135
Mexican immigrants: abusing, 119;
living off, 92
wetbacks, 52, 70, 74, 79, 171
White, Hayden, 237–238
whites, poor, 259–260n.9
Wilson, Thomas M., viii, 9, 82

Zerubavel, Eviatar, 9